OUR PIONEERS *and* PATRIOTS

Architect of the Capitol

Columbus claims the New World for Spain on October 12, 1492. Christopher Columbus had landed on an island, which he named San Salvador—"Holy Saviour."

OUR PIONEERS *and* PATRIOTS

By

Most Rev. Philip J. Furlong
FORMERLY OF CATHEDRAL COLLEGE, NEW YORK

Educational Editor
Helen J. Ganey
DE PAUL UNIVERSITY, CHICAGO

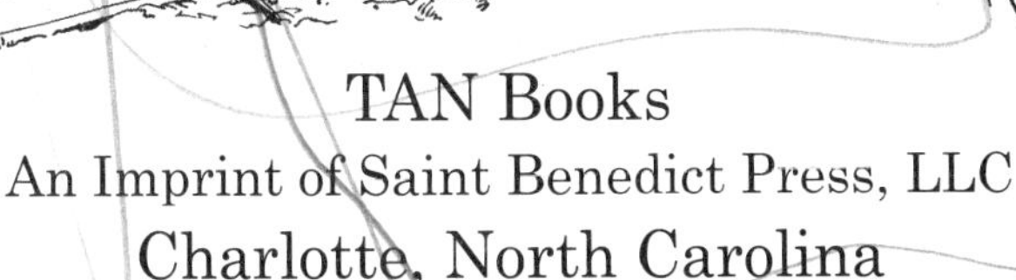

TAN Books
An Imprint of Saint Benedict Press, LLC
Charlotte, North Carolina

Nihil Obstat: Arthur J. Scanlan, S.T.D.
Censor Librorum

Imprimatur: ✠ Francis J. Spellman
Archbishop of New York
New York
January 1, 1940

Library of Congress Catalog Card No.: 96-61306

ISBN: 978-0-89555-592-2

Cover illustration: "Père Marquette and the Indians," by Wilhelm Lamprecht (1838-1906), by arrangement with Marquette University, Milwaukee.

Frontispiece from "Landing of Columbus," by John Vanderlyn. Photo courtesy of Architect of the Capitol, Washington, D.C.

Printed and bound in the United States of America

TAN Books
An Imprint of Saint Benedict Press, LLC
Charlotte, North Carolina
2012

Dedicated to
The Blessed Virgin Mary,
who, under the title of
THE IMMACULATE CONCEPTION,
was proclaimed by the Bishops of the United
States at the First Council of Baltimore in 1846
to be
THE PATRONESS
OF THE UNITED STATES OF AMERICA.

May she lead our Nation to
embrace the sweet yoke of her Son
Our Lord Jesus Christ.

—The Publishers, 1997

CONTENTS

UNIT I: DISCOVERY

UNIT II: EXPLORING THE NEW WORLD

UNIT III: THE ENGLISH COLONIES

UNIT IV: NEW FRANCE

UNIT V: THE GREAT STRUGGLE BETWEEN THE ENGLISH AND THE FRENCH

UNIT VI: THE BIRTH OF OUR NATION

UNIT VII: OUR NATION GROWS

UNIT VIII: INVENTIONS AND DISCOVERIES

UNIT IX: SLAVERY AND THE UNION

UNIT X: BUILDING THE WEST

UNIT XI: OUR NATION AT WORK

UNIT XII: GREAT LEADERS OF MODERN TIMES

To the Boys and Girls Using
OUR PIONEERS AND PATRIOTS

INTRODUCTION

We hope you enjoy reading and studying this text. The story of OUR PIONEERS AND PATRIOTS is told in a simple, yet in an interesting manner. Every new term is explained or defined. All the pictures and the maps in the text have been carefully selected. Study the pictures and the maps just as you study the text.

SUGGESTIONS

The *Study Summary* is a careful selection of the high spots of each chapter. *Terms to Know* will help you to have a wider vocabulary. *People to Know* will help you to become acquainted with the people about whom you have studied. *Places to Know* will widen your knowledge of Geography and make places of historic interest familiar to you. *Dates to Remember* are called to your attention because they are important.

The *Activities* are planned to make your study of history interesting and to help you to express your own ideas. These *Activities* will be fun as you learn.

Each *Study Test* has been planned to help you to

think, to learn, and to remember the most important facts of history.

Follow these simple rules as you do each *Study Test.*

1. Have nothing but this text, a sheet of paper and a pencil on your desk.
2. See that your pencil is well sharpened so that your work will be neat.
3. Read the instructions before you begin to write the answers.
4. Number your test paper for the same number of points as required in the *Study Test.*
5. Do not spend time copying the entire *Study Test.* Answers are all that you need.

Example: OUR PIONEERS AND PATRIOTS is a study of h_ _ _ _ _ _ _. You would not copy the sentence, but you would write the missing word: *history.*

OUR PIONEERS *and* PATRIOTS

UNIT I: DISCOVERY

BEFORE COLUMBUS CAME TO AMERICA

Read to learn

1. How the Norsemen came to America.
2. About the sea voyages of Leif Ericson.
3. How the crusades helped the people of Europe.
4. How Marco Polo helped the people of Europe know about the East.

AMERICA OUR HOME. We live in America. The Atlantic Ocean is to the east of America. Far across the Atlantic Ocean is the continent of Europe. There was a time when the people of Europe did not know about America. They did not dream that land could be reached by sailing to the west. Yet the first Mass said in America was probably said for men from Europe called the Norsemen.

Who were the Norsemen? What were they doing in America? The answer to these questions tells how America came to be known to Europeans.

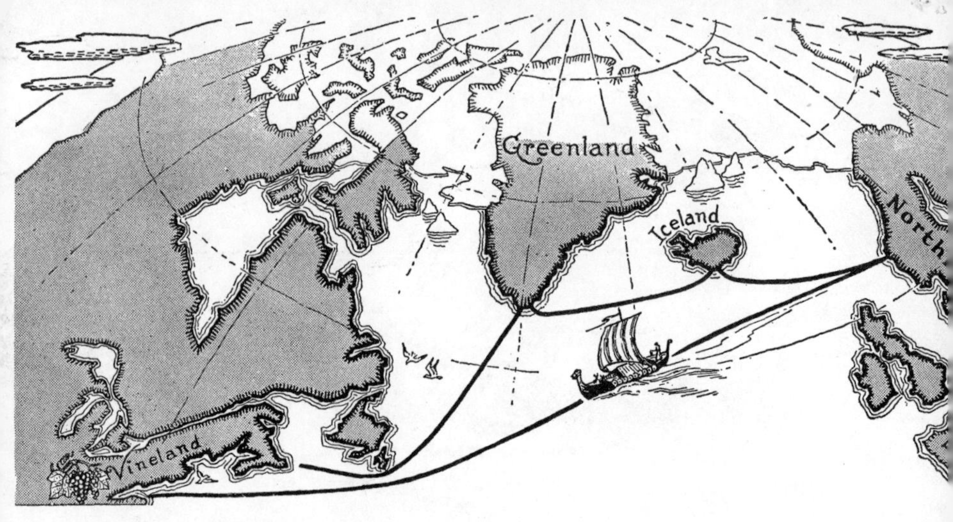

THE NORSEMEN

THE NORSEMEN. The Norsemen were a strong race of sea men. They lived long ago in the northern part of Europe. They were sometimes called Northmen. The Norsemen, or Northmen, lived in what is now known as Norway, Sweden, and Denmark. They were tall and strong. They had light colored hair and blue eyes and they loved adventure. The homes of the Norsemen were only log huts. Their villages were built close to the sea, often on a bay or, as the Norsemen called it, a vik. Sometimes you will hear the Norsemen called Vikings, which means "Men of the Bay." The Norsemen were pagans. They did not know about Our Lord.

NORSE VOYAGES. Their love of adventure led the Norsemen to travel far over the seas. In their light swift ships they even sailed far to the west to Iceland. There they made a settlement which has lasted to the present day. One of the leaders of the Norsemen in Iceland was named Eric the Red. He was a quarrelsome fellow. He did not get along with his neighbors. Eric decided that

he would sail even farther west. He went to Greenland, and took many followers with him. There he made a new settlement.

LEIF ERICSON. Eric the Red had a son called Leif. His full name was Leif Ericson, or Leif, son of Eric. He was often called Leif the Lucky. Leif Ericson went on a voyage to Norway to see the land where his father was born. In Norway Leif met King Olaf. There he learned about Christ and Leif became a Catholic. When it was time for Leif to return to Greenland, King Olaf gave him a fine new ship. Leif the Lucky sailed west from Norway. He was eager to tell his people in Greenland about the Catholic religion.

Just what took place on this voyage is not known. The ship did not reach Greenland. Leif and his party were blown far south of Greenland. It seems certain that his ship reached North America. Just where Leif and his men landed on the coast of North America is not known. Most likely it was some spot on the coast of the land we call New England. We do know that Leif and his party finally got back to Greenland.

LATER NORSE SETTLEMENTS. Leif told about the new land. He called it Wineland the Good, or Vinland, because of the grapes found there. Later, the people in Greenland became Catholic. Some Norsemen in Greenland decided to sail to Vinland. The first Mass in America may have been said for this party in Vinland. The settlement of the Norsemen did not succeed and was forgotten. The people in Europe knew little about the voyage of the Norsemen. What the Vikings did was forgotten. Many years later a little ship named the *Santa Maria* sailed from Spain. This ship was named in honor of the Mother of God. It was the ship of Christopher Columbus. The voyage of Columbus really did make America known to the people of Europe.

THE CRUSADES

GEOGRAPHY BEFORE COLUMBUS. Before Christopher could make his voyage the people of Europe had to learn something of the world beyond Europe. There was a time when they knew little about distant lands. There were two reasons for this. (1) Printing from type had not been invented. There were few books to tell of distant lands. (2) Few people traveled very far. The Holy Land and the East were the places most talked about.

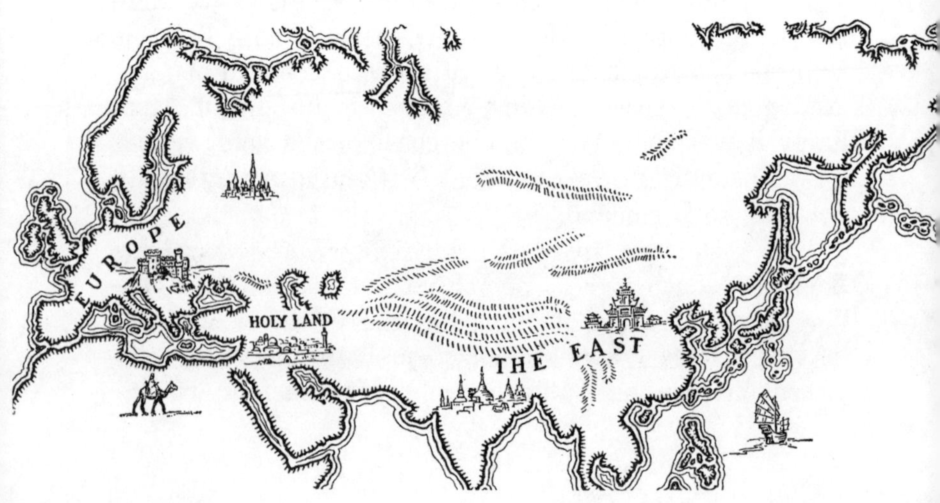

THE HOLY LAND. To the East of Europe is the land where Christ was born and where He died. It is called The Holy Land. Many people of Europe wished to see for themselves this wonderful land. They made a journey or pilgrimage to the Holy Land. They were called pilgrims. As time went on it became more and more difficult for pilgrims to reach the Holy Land. The Holy Land had been captured by the Turks, who were not Christians. The Turks were Mohammedans and did not believe in Christ. They disliked the Christians and made things difficult for them.

THE CRUSADES. The Pope became worried. He called upon the people of Europe to rescue the Holy Land from the Turks. Soldiers from all parts of Europe agreed to fight for the Holy Land. A war to rescue the Holy Land was called a crusade. Soldiers who took part in a crusade were called crusaders. The name crusade comes from a Latin word meaning cross. The soldiers often wore a cross made of cloth on their cloaks.

The Mohammedans were fierce fighters. They had large armies. Against such an enemy the crusaders were not very successful. The crusades did not succeed in rescuing the Holy Land from the Turks. The crusades did teach the people of Europe many things.

WHAT THE CRUSADES TAUGHT. Through the crusades the people of Europe learned about distant places. Many ships had to be built to carry crusaders to the Holy Land. Ship builders learned to build bigger and better ships. Many men living in seaports went to sea and became skilful sailors.

THE CRUSADES AND TRADE. Trade was greatly increased by the crusades. The returning crusaders often brought back strange products from the East. They also brought back rugs, silks, dyes, spices, and precious stones. Crusaders talked about other lovely things they had seen in the East. People in Europe began to want these fine things. A great trade between Europe and the East was the result.

MARCO POLO

MARCO POLO OF VENICE. As trade with the East grew, certain trading cities became important. One of these cities was Venice in Italy. The Polo family were rich traders who lived in Venice. Marco Polo belonged to this family. When he was only seventeen years old his father and his uncle took him on a trading trip to the far East. The party got on a little ship at Venice and set sail for Constantinople. This port is now named Istanbul. When there was no wind they used oars to move the ship. They traveled eastward from Constantinople on a land route across Persia. At length they arrived in China. China was then called Cathay. Here they met the ruler, Kublai Khan. He was very kind to his visitors and he liked young Marco. Marco Polo's father and uncle were able to collect many precious stones and to make plans for carrying on trade. Marco made notes of the wonderful things that he saw.

THE RETURN TO VENICE. After twenty-four years spent in the East the little party returned to Venice. Their looks had changed so much that nobody knew them. When they showed the treasures which they had brought back there was great excitement. Later, Marco Polo fought for Venice. A war was fought between Venice and Genoa. Marco Polo was taken prisoner during the war and put into a dungeon. There he spent his time telling a fellow prisoner about his travels. The fellow prisoner wrote the stories as Marco Polo told them. The stories were printed one hundred and fifty years later when printing was invented.

MARCO POLO'S STORIES. Marco Polo's book gives a wonderful account of his travels in the East. He told of rivers spanned by marble bridges. He told of a land where precious stones could be collected with little trouble. The rich people, in these wonderful lands wore clothes trimmed with glittering gems. Marco Polo's book described houses where gold and silver were used to beautify the walls.

Many people now began to have ideas about far off China and about the East. When Christopher Columbus was a young man, people were talking about the wonders of China and India. No doubt, Columbus enjoyed hearing about these strange lands.

STUDY SUMMARY

1. Terms to know. Be able to tell or to write one sentence which will explain the meaning of each term listed.

vik	open sea	crusade	crusaders
pagan	pilgrim	pilgrimage	dungeon

2. People to know. Tell one fact about each person named.

Leif Ericson	Olaf	Eric the Red
The Pope	Mohammedans	Turks
Marco Polo	Kublai Khan	

3. Places to know. Be able to show on a wall map where the following places are.

North America	Iceland	Norway
Atlantic Ocean	Greenland	Sweden
Europe	New England	Denmark
The East	Holy Land	China
Venice	Constantinople	Persia
Genoa	India	Cathay

Note: The name of Constantinople has been changed to Istanbul.

ACTIVITIES

1. Make a model of a Norse boat. Study pictures before you make the model. Be sure that the model shows: (1) a black hull; (2) a carved or painted dragon on the prow, and (3) a tall square sail.

2. A character study. Give one sentence to prove that each of the following statements is true. Re-read the text if you need ideas for your sentences.

1. The Norsemen loved adventure.
2. Norsemen were brave.
3. Eric the Red was quarrelsome.
4. Leif Ericson was generous. He was wise.
5. King Olaf showed that he was fond of Leif Ericson.

3. Make a list of five things which the crusaders brought back to Europe.

4. Tell three results of the crusades. Be sure to tell:
   1. How the crusades helped ship building.
   2. How the crusades helped trade.
   3. How the crusades helped the people of Europe to know about distant lands.

5. A play or drama. You can make a most interesting play about—THE STORY OF MARCO POLO. No scenery will be needed. Plan each scene to give a good picture of what happened.

Scene I.	The travelers leave Venice.
Scene II.	A day in the court of Kublai Khan.
Scene III.	The travelers return from Venice.
Scene IV.	Marco Polo in prison.
Scene V.	People of Europe talking about the of Marco Polo's travels.

STUDY TEST 1—SCORE 20

PART ONE—Fill in the missing letters.

1. The Norsemen called a bay a v – –.
2. The Vikings were N – – – – –men who lived in northern Europe a long time ago.
3. The Norsemen were often called N – – – – –men.
4. Eric the Red was a Norseman who moved to I – – land. Later he moved to G – – – – –land.
5. While in Norway Leif Ericson learned about Christ. Leif Ericson was baptized a C – – – – – – – –.

PART TWO—Answer each question with YES or NO.

1. Were books printed before the time of Columbus? ________
2. Did the crusaders fight to defend the Holy Land? ________
3. Did the Turks love the Christians? ________
4. Were the Turks Mohammedans? ________
5. Did the crusades help trade between Europe and the East? ________

PART THREE—Draw a line under the word which belongs with the first term on each line.

1. Marco Polo lived	Venice	Genoa
2. China once called	India	Cathay
3. Ruler of Cathay	Prince	Kublai Khan
4. Marco's father and uncle	seamen	traders
5. Polo party returned	Genoa	Venice
6. They brought back	books	treasures
7. Genoa and Venice were	rivals	friendly
8. Marco was made a	general	prisoner
9. Tales told by Marco printed	book	newspaper
10. Travels of Marco Polo helped people to know about	Italy	China

UNIT I: DISCOVERY

CHRISTOPHER COLUMBUS

Read to learn

1. How Columbus planned to reach the East.
2. How Father Perez helped Columbus.
3. How Columbus got ready for the great adventure.
4. When, where, and how the expedition landed.
5. Why the natives were called Indians.
6. How Columbus spent his last years.

THE BOYHOOD OF COLUMBUS. Genoa in Italy, like Venice, was a great trading city. In Genoa a boy was born who was called Christopher Columbus. Young Christopher must have liked to go to the docks to play. Many strange sights were to be seen there. Many tales were to be heard from the sailors. The boy Columbus listened to the stories. He dreamed of sailing far way to strange lands. As he grew older he went to school. There he learned more about distant lands. Geography was his favorite study.

THE GREAT PLAN. After leaving school Columbus became a sailor. He sailed away from Genoa to distant

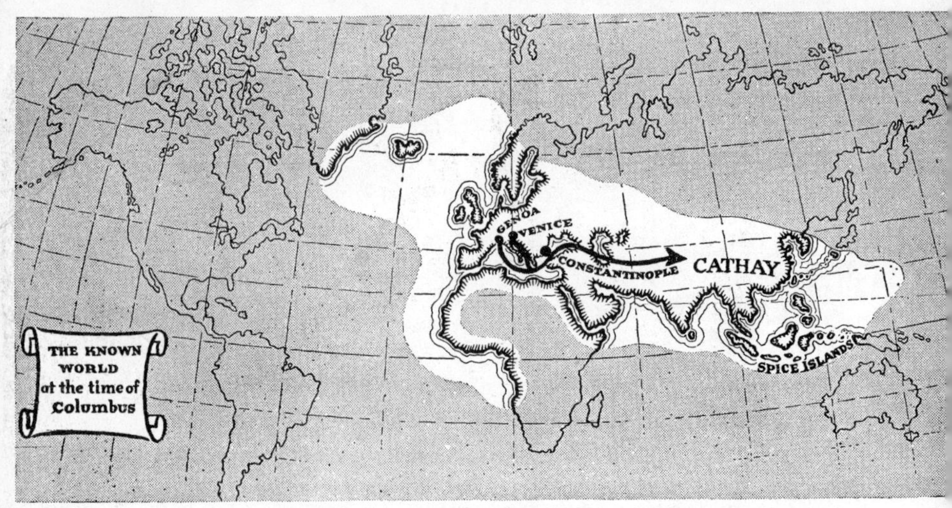

places. He dreamed of finding a new way to the East. He planned to reach India in the east by sailing to the west.

COLUMBUS AND THE KING OF PORTUGAL. Columbus knew that to make his dream come true he would need many things. He would need money, men, and ships. He must prove his plan to be good. He would have to find someone to help him.

Among the rulers of Europe, the King of Portugal was the most interested in trade with the East. His sailors for years had been searching for a new route to the East.

Columbus told the king of Portugal about his plan. The king at first seemed to think well of the plan. He promised to get ships and help for Columbus. The king did not keep his promise. Columbus was greatly disappointed but he would not give up. He left Portugal and with new hope he went to Spain to seek aid.

FATHER PEREZ. While travelling through Spain Columbus stayed at a Franciscan Monastery near the city of Palos. Father Perez was in charge of this monastery. This good priest was a friend of King Ferdinand and Queen Isabella of Spain. Father Perez thought Columbus's plan a good one. He succeeded in getting Queen Isabella to help Columbus.

PREPARATION FOR THE VOYAGE. The help given by Queen Isabella made Columbus very happy. He set to work at once to get ready for his great voyage. First it was necessary to get ships. Columbus got three ships. The largest was to be the leader, or flag-ship. It was named the *Santa Maria.* It was a small ship but its decks were covered and it had a little cabin. The other two ships were even smaller and their decks were not entirely covered. They were called the *Niña* and the *Pinta.* These two small ships had one good thing in their favor. They were in charge of two fine sailors, the Pinzon brothers. They were noted mariners. Often a sailor or a seaman is called a mariner. After some delay the Pinzon brothers were able to get crews for the *Niña* and the *Pinta.*

THE CREWS. Columbus was not a Spaniard. He was not well known. It was hard for him to get sailors for the *Santa Maria.* Not a man at the little seaport town of Palos would go with him. The sailors all thought that such a trip would be far too dangerous. The crew that Columbus finally got for the *Santa Maria* was a strange one. It was made up of men from many different places. There was an Englishman, an Irishman, an Arab, a Jew, and some Spanish sailors.

THE GREAT ADVENTURE

THE DAY OF SAILING. The day set for the ships to sail Columbus and his men went to Mass and Holy Communion. Father Perez blessed Columbus and asked God to watch over the men. Columbus was very happy. He believed three things. (1) He was sure he would find a new route to India. (2) He felt Spain would secure a rich trade with the East. (3) He believed there might be an opportunity to win souls for Christ.

THE BEGINNING OF THE ADVENTURE. Early on the morning of August 3, 1492, "In the Name of Christ," Columbus ordered the ships to sail. So began the most important voyage in history. They sailed onward for five days when the rudder of the *Pinta* began to give trouble. A ship is steered by the rudder so this was a serious matter. The ships were near the Canary Islands. They stopped at the Islands, repaired the rudder, and again put out to sea.

THE LONG DAYS AT SEA. Day after day, the ships sailed on. Each day they were farther from home. The

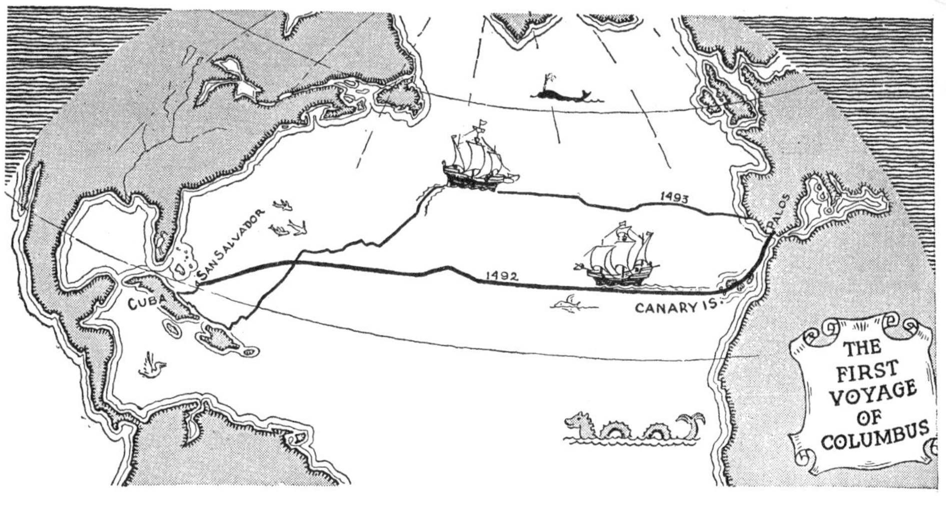

men began to be afraid. One day they saw a broken mast of a ship floating on the water. The sailors felt a ship had been wrecked. It made them more fearful. The needle on the compass began to do queer things. A compass is an instrument that tells direction. If the needle did not always point to the north the sailors would lose their way. Then the ships sailed into great patches of sea weed. The sailors thought that this meant shallow water and dangerous rocks. The wind became stronger. It blew away from home. The sailors felt they could never sail home against such a strong wind. Columbus never lost courage. He tried to cheer the men. Columbus pointed to flocks of birds. He called their attention to branches of trees floating in the water. They must be near land. The men began to have hope. Then the glad cry of "Land!" rang through the air. But it was a mistake. The sailors became greatly discouraged. Some of them were in such an ugly mood that it is said they planned to rise up against Columbus. The men were growing desperate. This was on October 10th. It was more than two months since they had left Palos. Columbus was calm and brave. No matter what was said to him his answer was, "Sail on!" He quieted his men and promised them that they would soon see land. Columbus was sure that land would be reached.

"LAND! LAND!" The sailors believed Columbus. They began to work more cheerfully. The next day the men would pause in their work and look ahead every little while. They strained their eyes for sight of land. Excitement increased as the sun set and darkness came.

Through the night Columbus kept watch. He searched far and wide and saw a light far ahead. The hours of the night wore on. At two o'clock the joyful cry of "Land! Land!" broke forth. It was October 12th, 1492. Christopher Columbus had reached America, the New World.

THE LANDING. At daybreak Columbus was ready to go ashore. He wore a suit of scarlet velvet. At his side hung a beautiful sword. Columbus was the first member of the party to step upon the shore of the New World. When all the men had landed the whole party knelt to offer thanks to God. Columbus bowed low and kissed the ground. Then he rose and took possession of the land in the name of the King and Queen of Spain. He ordered a

great cross built. In thanksgiving for the safe journey he called the place *San Salvador.* This means *Holy Savior.*

THE NEW LAND. The place where Columbus landed was an island. It may have been one of the Bahama Islands, which are near the eastern coast of North America. Columbus and his men began to explore the island and the waters nearby. He sighted a larger island. This made him happy as he was then sure he had reached the East. The island was really the island of Cuba.

THE INDIANS. Columbus was puzzled when he saw the natives of these islands. They were not light skinned like the Europeans. Neither were they dark skinned like Negroes. They had copper-colored skin and wore little clothing. Columbus was still certain he had reached India. That is why he called the natives Indians.

THE STAY IN THE NEW WORLD. The New World must have been something of a disappointment to Columbus. He thought the East was a place of riches. This land was not rich. Some gold and a few pearls were collected, but no great riches were found.

HOMEWARD BOUND. The trip home was started in the spring. It was not a pleasant trip. There were only two ships in the fleet. The *Santa Maria* had been wrecked. After a stormy voyage the remaining two ships arrived in the harbor of Palos. There was great excitement in the town. People rushed out of their houses and down to see the ships. The whole town gave "thanks to Our Lord for so great a favor and victory."

HOW COLUMBUS WAS RECEIVED. Columbus started for Barcelona where the king and queen were staying. The journey was a pleasant one for Columbus. People came out to greet him in every town through which he passed. The Indians he brought with him caused great comment. The chief men of Barcelona met Columbus at the gates of that city. They escorted Columbus and his party to the royal palace.

Seated under a great canopy of cloth of gold, King Ferdinand and Queen Isabella received Columbus. They asked him to sit before them and tell his story.

TREASURES FROM THE NEW WORLD. Columbus displayed the articles which he had brought back from the New World. There were no articles of great value to be shown. There were leaves and branches of certain trees. These were thought to be good as medicine. There were curious seeds, great gourds, cotton, and fruit. A number of beautiful birds had been stuffed for display. There were four live parrots that chattered and amused the people. Columbus was able to show a few gold ornaments and a few pearls. He had expected to bring back great treasures to the king and queen.

THE LATER VOYAGES. The Spanish rulers were eager to learn about the lands reached by Columbus. They wished to begin trading at once. A second voyage was planned. Columbus returned to the New World. He still thought he was trading in India. He set about exploring and trading with the Indians. He collected some gold but no great riches were found. After a stay of two years he returned home.

A SUPPOSED FAILURE. There was no royal welcome this time. The people could not understand why he did not bring back great riches. They were disappointed. His enemies began to make fun of Columbus. They called him the "Admiral of the Mosquito Land." Queen Isabella remained his friend. She firmly believed he would yet get the rich trade of India for Spain.

LAST YEARS OF COLUMBUS. Twice again Columbus returned to the land he had discovered. He made four voyages but no riches were found. Each time he met with disappointment. Then good Queen Isabella died. Columbus lost a good and loyal friend. He was neglected. Years later he died in a poor lodging house. Columbus had failed to reach India. He had found something greater. He discovered a New World. Looking for a land of gold and riches he had discovered a land of opportunity. His is one of the greatest names in OUR PIONEERS AND PATRIOTS.

STUDY SUMMARY

---

1. Terms to know. Be able to tell or to write one sentence which will explain the meaning of each term listed.

monastery	rudder	deck	cabin
flag-ship	crew	voyage	compass

2. People to know. Tell one fact about each person named.

   The King of Portugal　　Queen Isabella
   King Ferdinand　　Father Perez
   Pinzon brothers

3. Places to know. On a wall map be able to locate and tell one fact about each place listed.

Palos	Canary Islands	Palos
Spain	Portugal	Barcelona
San Salvador	Cuba	

ACTIVITIES

1. Make a list of four products from the East which the people of Europe desired.
2. Name three things Columbus needed before he could start on the great journey.
3. Plan and give a play or drama about Columbus. No scenery or costumes will be necessary. Plan each scene to tell one part of the story. This can be great fun.

PART ONE—The Great Plan.

Scene I. The boy Christopher playing on the docks at Genoa.
Scene II. Columbus as a visitor at the court of the King of Portugal.
Scene III. Father Perez listens to Columbus explain his great plan.
Scene IV. Columbus a visitor at the court of Spain.

PART TWO–The Great Voyage.

Scene I. On board the Santa Maria.
Scene II. Land is sighted.
Scene III. The landing.
Scene IV. The return voyage.
Scene V. Columbus is received by the King and Queen.

3. Make a set of panel posters to show the story of THE LITTLE FLEET. Each panel is to show one event.
    1. The three ships ready in the harbor at Palos.
    2. Getting the crews together.
    3. Father Perez giving his blessing.
    4. Columbus commanding the ships to sail.

STUDY TEST 2—SCORE 15

PART ONE—Draw a line under the word or words which answers the question.

1. Was Columbus born in Venice or in Genoa?
2. Did Christopher Columbus dream of being a map maker or a sailor?
3. Did Columbus plan to sail westward or eastward to India?
4. Did Queen Isabella help or refuse to help Columbus?
5. Did Columbus remember to be grateful to God or did he forget to be grateful?

PART TWO—Select and fill in the term which fits the description. Use only terms listed.

1. ———— Port in Spain from which Columbus sailed.
2. ———— Instrument used to tell directions.
3. ———— Never lost courage.
4. ———— A long journey on the sea.
5. ———— Name which Columbus gave to the island where they landed.
6. ———— The large island reached by Columbus and his party.
7. ———— Name given to natives by Columbus.
8. ———— Thought to be a land of great wealth.
9. ———— City where King and Queen received Columbus.
10. ———— Remained a loyal friend to Columbus.

Indians	Palos	San Salvador
compass	voyage	Barcelona
Cuba	Queen Isabella	Columbus
	The Indies	

THE PEOPLE COLUMBUS FOUND

Read to learn

1. How Indian life was changed when white men came to the New World.
2. The four chief types of houses made by the Indians.
3. The name of some of the foods which the Indians had to eat.
4. Why an Indian man was called a brave.
5. Work done by the Indian squaw.
6. Some of the tools which the Indians made.

THE INDIANS

THE NATIVES. Columbus, as you know, met strange people when he landed. He thought he had really reached India. That is why he called the natives Indians.

Later, other European people came to the New World. They met Indians in different places in North America and in South America. The Indians of one region were different from those of another region. Yet they were alike in some ways.

The Indians who lived in what is now the United States are of most interest to us. They were of medium height. Their skin was the color of copper. Their eyes were dark and piercing. They had very high cheek bones. They had stiff straight black hair. They held their bodies erect when they walked.

INDIAN DIVISIONS. The Indians were separated into many groups. These groups were called tribes. Each tribe had its own language and its own customs. Indians of one group had a language so different from that of

another group that they could not understand each other. That is why they used signs to express their thoughts to one another. Each group had its own way of making war. They had different ways of burying their dead.

There were great differences in the types of houses which the Indians made. The pueblo, the long house, the round house, and the tepee were some of the types of houses which the Indians made.

THE PUEBLO. The land which is now the southwestern part of our country is a hot, dry land. Here lived the Pueblo Indians. They lived in homes called pueblos.

A pueblo was really an Indian apartment house. Many families lived in a pueblo like the one pictured on this page. Ladders were used to climb up to the different stories of the pueblo. The pueblo was really a house made of clay. The clay was made into bricks. These were dried in the sun until they became very hard. These sun dried bricks were called adobe.

The Pueblo Indians were intelligent. They raised vegetables for food. They dug ditches to drain water into their gardens. They were wise because they knew how to bring water to the dry land.

The Indians were skillful weavers. They made water-tight jars. These were made from clay. The clay jars were baked in the hot sun.

LONG HOUSES. Some of the Indians who lived in what is now the eastern part of our country made long houses. These dwellings were narrow but long. They were built by first setting up a frame of saplings. This frame was then covered with bark or mud. The long house was often large enough to shelter twenty or thirty families.

ROUND HOUSES. The round house was built much like the long house. It was different in shape and in size. A round frame was made from saplings. This was covered with bark, dry grasses, or mud. Usually only one family lived in a round house like those in the picture.

THE TEPEE. The Indians who lived on the plains of the West usually lived in wigwams. A wigwam is often called a tepee. It was really a tent. The frame was made with a number of poles. Deer skin or buffalo hide was stretched over the frame. There was a hole at the top to let out the smoke. An opening at the bottom of the tepee served as a door. There was no floor covering. A number of tepees are shown in the picture on page 26.

The tepee was easily made and it was quickly moved. It was not much protection against heavy rain or very cold winter winds.

INDIAN FOOD. The Indians used simple foods. Meat and fish were important foods. Much food was obtained in the forest where hunting was good. Deer, rabbits, squirrels, and fowl were hunted. The Indians used bows and arrows, spears, or slings. Fish were caught in the streams and lakes. The fish were caught by spears or on hooks made of bone.

The Indians who lived near the Atlantic Ocean gathered clams and oysters. These they ate with great relish. Even today we find the remains of great piles of clam shells left from Indian feasts.

Some of the Indians did not move about very much. They depended upon their gardens and cornfields more than they depended upon game or fish. They raised potatoes, corn, tomatoes, melons, pumpkins, squash, peas, and beans. Nuts, wild berries, roots, and wild rice were also used as food. They sweetened food with maple sugar. The Indians taught the white men how to use some of these new foods.

THE INDIAN FAMILY. The Indian father was the head of the family. The most important thing he did was to fight. That is why an Indian man was called a brave. He was fond of hunting. He hunted and gathered nuts and wild berries for his family.

The Indian wife was called a squaw. The housework was simple. Corn was ground by the women to make meal. Skins of animals were tanned and used to make clothing. An Indian baby was called a papoose. The squaw cared for the garden or farm. She had to do all the farm work with very poor tools.

INDIAN TOOLS. The Indians did not use iron. They made a crude hoe. A flat shell or stone was fastened to a pole. This served as a hoe. They made hatchets from flint. Flint is a hard stone. A piece of flint was tied to a short stick. A strip of deer skin was used to tie the flint

to the stick. This made a good hatchet. Flint was also used for knives. The edges were skillfully sharpened by chipping the flint.

THE INDIANS AND THE WHITE MEN. The coming of white men brought a great change in the lives of the Indians. The natives were driven from their best lands and their best hunting places. The Indians fought to defend their lands. There were many bitter wars between the Indians and the white men. The white men had firearms. White men fought in a manner that the Indians did not understand. The white men won. The sad Indians moved westward. Now many Indians live on government land. Government lands where the Indians live are called reservations.

INDIAN CHILDREN. Indian children had few advantages. Yet they knew how to enjoy life. They knew how to model animals from clay. The clay was obtained near the river bank. Indian girls made dolls. Grass was used to make the body of a doll. Skins were used to make clothes. Boys used the bones of big animals to make sleds. Boys also made stilts. Then enjoyed walking on the stilts. Indian boys made tops. Some Indian boys were able to spin a top on ice. This requires great skill.

Indian boys and girls liked to play games. They enjoyed running races. One game the Indian children liked very much was rolling a hoop. The hoop was made by bending a branch from a young tree. As the hoop was rolled a stone was thrown through the rolling hoop. This was training in speed and in accuracy.

STUDY SUMMARY

1. Terms to know. Be able to tell the meaning of each term listed.

native	tribe	squaw	reservation
papoose	tepee	flint	irrigation
pueblo	adobe	brave	wigwam

2. People to know. Be able to give three facts about the life of each person listed.

   Indian brave   Indian squaw   Indian children

3. Places to know. On a wall map of North America be able to show:
   a. Eastern North America where the Indians made long houses.
   b. The south-western dry lands where Indians made pueblos.
   c. The plains where tepees were used as homes.

ACTIVITIES

1. Make a set of models of some of the type homes made by the Indians. Be sure to make a tepee, a pueblo, a round house, and a long house.
2. Make a set of posters to show some of the games which Indian children enjoyed.
3. Write three sentences telling how the coming of the white men changed the lives of the Indians.

STUDY TEST 3—SCORE 50

Fill in the missing letters in each term. Re-read your outline.

1. How the Indians looked:

   a. They were of medium h——————.

   b. Their s——— was the color of copper.

   c. Their cheek-bones were very h———.

   d. They had straight black h———.

2. Types of houses built by the Indians:

   a. The pueblo was made of sun-dried b——————.
   Some pueblos were several stories h———.
   Many families lived in a p——————.

   b. There were Indians who used s———————— to build their houses.
   These houses were called l——— houses.
   The f————— of the house was made of saplings.
   Mud or b——— was used to cover the frame.
   Twenty or thirty families lived in a l——— house.

   c. Some Indian tribes made r————— houses.
   Only one family lived in each r————— house.
   Saplings were used to make the f————— of a round house.
   Dry grass, b———, or m—— was used to cover the frame.

   d. Indians who lived on the plains made w———————.
   A wigwam was called a t—————.
   A tepee was a kind of a t———.
   Poles were used to make the f—————.
   Buffalo h——— or deer s——— was stretched on the frame.

3. Indian foods:

   a. Most Indians like to eat m———.

   b. Squirrels, rabbits, d———, and f——— were hunted.

   c. Indians also liked to eat f———, oysters, and c————.

   d. Some of the vegetables the Indians ate were:
      w———— potatoes c———
      s———— potatoes m—————
      tomatoes, p———, and b————

   e. Maple s———— was used to sweeten foods.

4. The Indian family:

   a. The Indian man was called a b————.

   b. The Indian b———— was a fighter.

   c. An Indian woman was called a s————.

   d. The squaw took care of the f————. She ground the g————. She prepared the s———— for use. She cooked the m————.

   e. An Indian b——— was called a papoose.

5. Indian weapons and tools:

   a. Indians used the b—— and arrow. This was a good weapon for hunting or for fighting.

   b. They made hatchets from f————.

   c. A crude h—— was made to loosen the soil.
      A flat s———— was fastened to a pole to make a hoe.

   d. Knives were made by chipping f————.

UNIT II: EXPLORING THE NEW WORLD

SEAMEN OF PORTUGAL AND SPAIN

Read to learn

1. About the work of Prince Henry the Navigator.
2. How Bartholomew Diaz reached the tip of Africa.
3. How Vasco Da Gama rounded Africa.
4. How America got its name.
5. How Florida was discovered.
6. How the Pacific Ocean was discovered.
7. Why the voyage of Ferdinand Magellan was important.

PRINCE HENRY THE NAVIGATOR

PRINCE HENRY THE NAVIGATOR. Before Columbus started on his voyages other countries were searching for a new route to India. Even when Columbus was a young man there was great interest in such a route. There lived in Portugal a prince named Henry. Prince Henry was interested in the trade with the East. He was anxious to have Portugal profit by such trade. He believed a

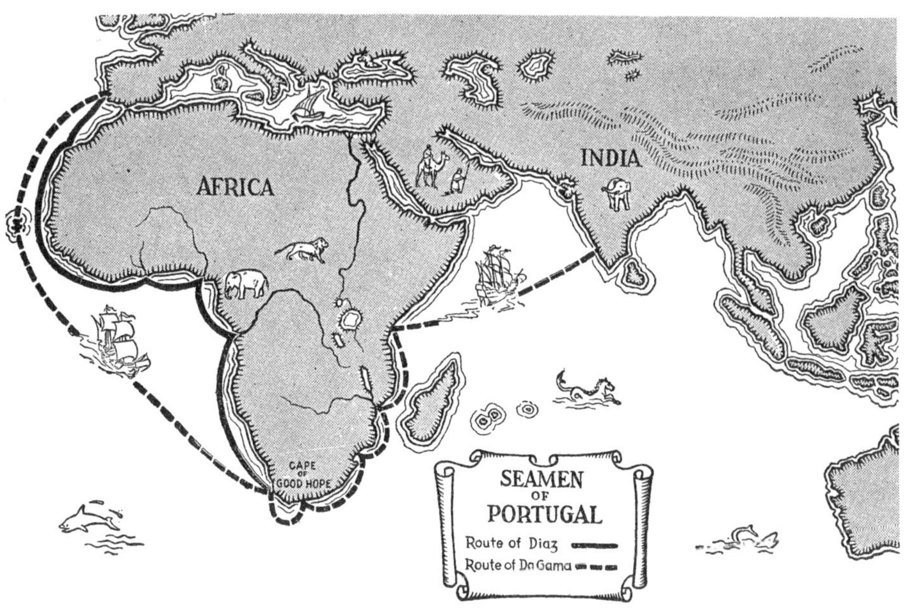

route to India could be found by sailing around Africa. He also hoped to spread the Catholic religion. In order to insure the success of this plan he started a school for seamen. This school trained the seamen in the use of maps and sailing instruments. They were taught how to use the compass. It helped the sailors to know exact directions. The use of the astrolabe was also taught. It helped the seamen know their location at sea. Before Prince Henry died his men had learned much about the west coast of Africa. Because Prince Henry was interested in sailing or navigation he was called Prince Henry the Navigator.

THE CAPE OF GOOD HOPE. After his death the Portuguese continued sailing south along the coast of Africa. A daring Portuguese finally reached the southern cape of Africa. His name was Bartholomew Diaz. This was in 1486. Diaz named it the "Cape of Storms." The King of Portugal was happy. He ordered the name changed to the "Cape of Good Hope." Notice on the map that the Cape of Good Hope is at the very southern tip of Africa.

THE VOYAGE OF VASCO DA GAMA. The Portuguese were not satisfied just to reach the Cape of Good Hope. They still hoped to reach India by sailing around Africa. In 1497 Vasco Da Gama began such a voyage. He steered his little ship along the west coast of Africa until he reached the Cape of Good Hope. The map on page 31 shows the route of Da Gama's voyage. He did not stay there. He sailed on until he reached Calicut in India. After this voyage the merchants of Portugal began trading with the merchants of India.

AMERICUS VESPUCIUS

AMERICUS VESPUCIUS. Although the Portuguese had found a route to India by sailing east, they did not give up hope of reaching India by sailing west. It was from one of their voyages to the west that America received its name.

Among the seamen attracted to Portugal was an Italian by the name of Americus Vespucius. He took part in a Portuguese voyage to the New World. After his return he drew maps of the lands he had seen. About this time a German scholar was writing a geography. He used the map Americus Vespucius had made. He gave the name *America* to the land Americus Vespucius had visited. This map was copied so often that the name America came into general use.

JUAN PONCE DE LEON

AN ADVENTUROUS SPANIARD. Explorers from Europe were learning many things about the New World. Many strange tales were told. Men who liked adventure were anxious to go to the New World. Among these were

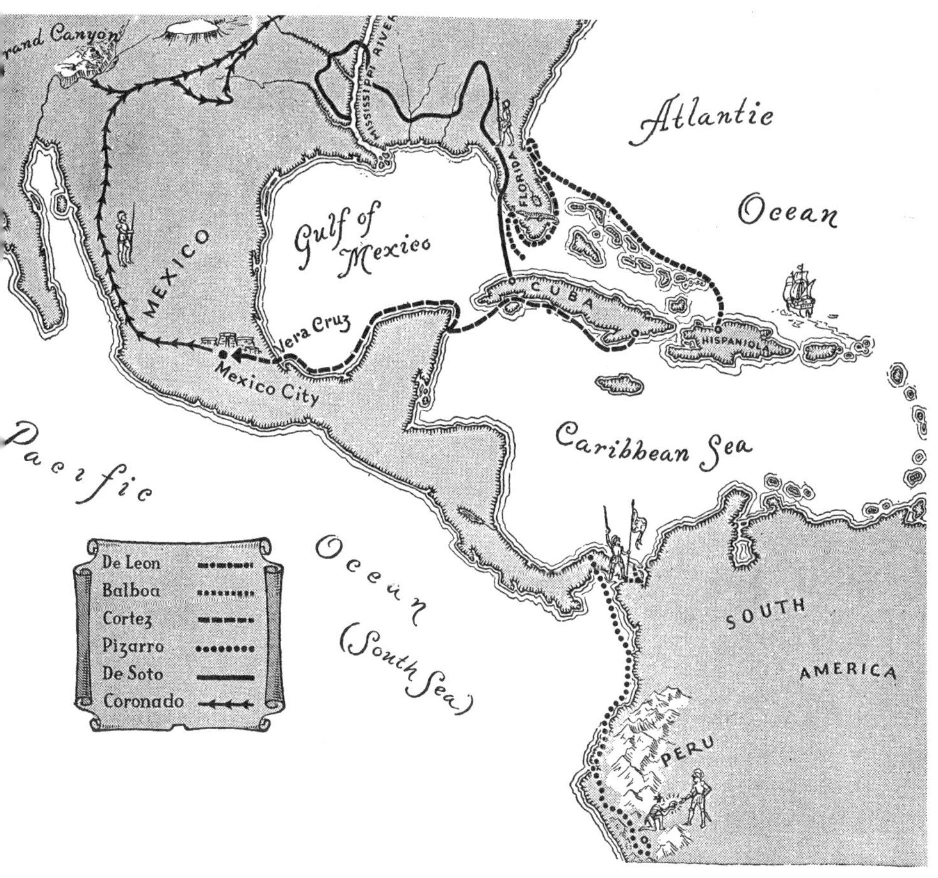

many good priests who wanted to work with the Indians of the New World.

Juan Ponce de Leon was a Spaniard. He listened to tales about the New World. He liked the stories about the great wealth to be found. Ponce de Leon liked adventure. So he left Spain on an expedition going to America.

It is said that on the trip Ponce de Leon was searching for the fountain of youth. This was supposed to be a magic spring that made old men young again. This was a silly idea. Ponce de Leon did not find the fountain of youth for there is no such thing. His search had one good result. He did discover land.

DISCOVERY OF FLORIDA. It was in the spring of 1513 that Ponce de Leon landed. It was Easter time. The

Spanish term for Easter is Florida. That is why he called the new land Florida. The map on page 33 shows that Florida is near the West Indies. Some Spanish people had already settled on the smaller islands of the West Indies and in Cuba.

VASCO DE BALBOA

ANOTHER ADVENTUROUS SPANIARD. Vasco de Balboa came to the New World to make a fortune. He tried farming on one of the islands of the West Indies. Balboa was not a successful farmer. He went into debt. It was not pleasant to owe bills. Balboa was worried.

A party of Spaniards had gone to the mainland. They were in search of gold. Their supplies gave out. They sent back to the islands for help. An expedition was made ready to go to their aid. Balboa saw a chance to escape from his debts. This was not an honest thing to do.

HOW BALBOA ESCAPED. Balboa hid in a barrel. A workman put the lid on the barrel. No one knew that a man had hidden in the barrel. Then the barrel was placed on the ship. The ship was going to the aid of the party on the mainland. Before the ship reached land a strange thing happened. The barrel began to move. Everyone was surprised. Some of the men were frightened. Soon Balboa stepped out of the barrel.

The commander of the expedition was very angry. There was no way of sending Balboa back. The commander decided that Balboa might be helpful. He would be able to fight the Indians. The commander feared that the Indians might prove unfriendly. The party landed on the mainland. They went in search of the Spaniards who were in distress. The part of the mainland where they landed is called the Isthmus of Panama. This isthmus is a

narrow strip of land which connects North America with South America. Find the isthmus on the map on page 33.

BALBOA BECAME THE LEADER. Balboa was a man of great force. Soon he became the leader of the party. One day his men heard great news. An old Indian told them about a land of great wealth. It was a land where there was plenty of gold.

The Spaniards were eager to get gold. Gold meant wealth to them. Balboa led a party of about two hundred men. They went in search of the rich land. They spent eighteen weary days in the search. It was hard work. They had to cut their way through the thick growth of plants. There was no path to follow.

One day Balboa climbed to the top of a high hill. He looked in every direction. Off to the south he saw a great body of water. Balboa was excited. He made his way down the hillside. His men were excited as they followed Balboa down to the sea. Here Balboa stepped into the ocean. He waved his sword over his head. Then he showed his love for Spain. In the name of the King of Spain Balboa took possession of all the lands touched by the sea.

THE PACIFIC OCEAN. It was the year 1513 when Balboa discovered the sea. He called it the "Great South Sea." Later another explorer named it the Pacific Ocean. Notice these interesting facts.

1. We think of the Pacific Ocean as to the west. But where Balboa crossed the Isthmus of Panama the ocean is to the south.

2. The whole west side of the New World is touched by the waters of the Pacific Ocean. Spain based her claim to these lands on the discovery by Balboa.

3. During the twentieth century the United States built the Panama Canal across the Isthmus of Panama. This gives a direct waterway between the Atlantic and the Pacific Oceans.

FERDINAND MAGELLAN

AN ADVENTUROUS NOBLEMAN. Ferdinand Magellan was a member of a noble family. He lived in Portugal. As a young man Ferdinand liked excitement. He entered the service of the King of Portugal. Young Magellan was sent to India. Later he visited the Spice Islands. He gathered many ideas about the value of the trade with the East. The voyage from Portugal around Africa to India was a long one and it was tiresome.

A NEW PLAN. Magellan began to wonder how a shorter way to the East could be found. He knew that a shorter way would mean a cheaper way. Magellan thought that the westward direction was the right one. He believed that Columbus had the correct idea. Magellan formed a plan to reach the East by a westward route.

Magellan asked the King of Portugal to aid him. The King refused to help him. Magellan believed that his plan was a good one. He left Portugal and went to Spain.

MAGELLAN WELCOMED TO SPAIN. Portugal and Spain were rivals. The King of Spain was interested when Magellan told of his plan to reach the East by sailing westward.

The King knew that great wealth could be gained if a short route could be found. The King of Spain promised to aid Magellan. A fleet of five ships was outfitted for the voyage.

Magellan believed in the value of prayer. He visited a monastery. The men who live a religious life in a monastery are called monks. Magellan begged the monks to pray for the success of his voyage.

MAGELLAN REACHES SOUTH AMERICA. The fleet set sail from Spain in August 1519. Magellan planned to sail westward and to the south. The vessels sailed on and on. The weeks passed by. The coast of South America was sighted. Magellan sailed as close to shore as was safe. He was looking for a water-way through the continent. He did not find one because there was none.

Magellan saw some of the natives. They were very large men. They looked like giants. Magellan called them "the men with big feet." This land is now called Patagonia. The name Patagonia means "the land of men with big feet." This land is in southern South America.

TRIALS. The weather grew very, very cold. Magellan had sailed far south along the coast of South America. He decided to anchor the ships. The crew did not like this. They wanted to return to Spain. The men began to grumble. They begged Magellan to return to Spain. Magellan had no thought of returning until he had reached the East. Some of the men plotted against Magellan. The leaders were punished with terrible harshness. Magellan was determined to sail onward in an attempt to reach the East.

THE CHANNEL OF THE SAINTS. After some time Magellan decided to sail on. The little fleet sailed until it reached the strait which connects the Atlantic and the Pacific Oceans. A strait is a narrow body of water which connects two larger bodies of water. Magellan called it the Channel of All Saints. A channel is another name for a strait. This strait is now called the Strait of Magellan. The fleet sailed through the strait. They had reached a new sea. They wondered if they dared to sail onward on this unknown sea.

MEETING OF THE CAPTAINS. Magellan called a meeting of his captains. All but one captain agreed to sail until they reached the East. The captain who refused said that he feared that the food supply might not last. Magellan answered, "If I have to eat the leather on the yards I will still go on and discover what I have promised to the King, and I trust that God will aid us and give us good fortune." This brave little speech shows us three things about the character of Magellan.

1. He was a determined man. He would not turn back. He intended to go on until the East was reached.

2. He valued a promise. He intended to keep his promise to the King of Spain.

3. He placed his trust in God.

MEETING GREAT TRIALS. Magellan planned that the fleet would sail onward. There were only four ships now in the fleet. Misfortune awaited them. One of the vessels ran aground. This means that the bottom, or keel of the boat, became stuck in the bottom of the sea. The water was too shallow for the ship to float. This ship was destroyed. The fleet now numbered three. The courageous fleet which sailed from Spain was dwindling.

The largest ship was loaded with most of the supplies. This vessel deserted the fleet. That is it left the fleet without permission. The fleet now numbered two ships. Magellan gave orders to sail on.

ON THE PACIFIC OCEAN. The two little ships sailed out on a great ocean. The wind was favorable and the sea was calm. Magellan called the ocean the Pacific, it was so peaceful and calm.

The little vessels were sailing on a broad unknown sea. No European seamen had ever sailed on its water before. Week after week passed. No land was sighted. The supplies were nearly gone. There was no good drinking water left. Many of the sailors were sick. Some of the men died. Magellan was very much worried.

THE ROBBER ISLANDS. The vessels sailed for three months. They kept a westward direction. Land was sighted at last. Magellan ordered the ships to sail close to the land. The natives tried to steal everything from the ships. That is why Magellan called this group of islands the Robber Islands.

PHILIPPINE ISLANDS. The two little ships sailed on. Ten days later they came to some more islands. Magellan named this group of islands the Philippines in honor of King Philip of Spain. At last the sailors were able to get plenty to eat.

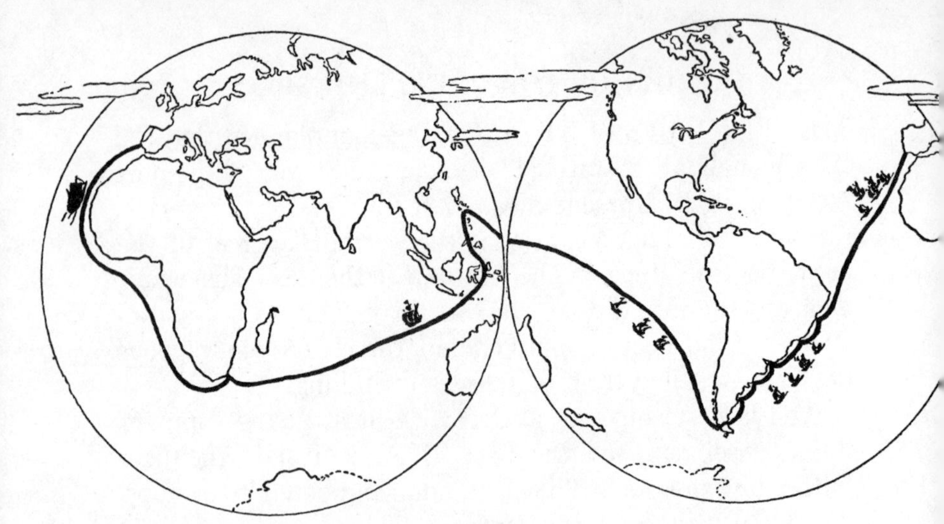

Then a very sad event happened. A war was going on between two native chiefs. Magellan took part in the war. He was killed in the fighting. The little fleet had lost its leader. The weary crew set sail once again.

REACHING THE MOLUCCAS. At last the Molucca Islands were reached. The crew began trading with the natives. The Spaniards had red caps, glass beads, little bells, mirrors, and gayly colored cloth. These things were traded for spices. These spices were worth a very great sum of money in Europe. The two ships were filled with cargoes of spices.

THE RETURN TO SPAIN. The two ships decided to take different routes to return to Spain. Only one ship, the *Victoria*, reached Spain in 1522. This ship carried a cargo of twenty-six tons of spices. The sale of these spices paid all the expenses of the voyage. This voyage was important because it proved three things.

1. The world is round. A ship can sail around the world.
2. The land discovered by Columbus was not a part of Asia. It really was a New World.
3. The East could be reached by sailing westward.

STUDY SUMMARY

1. Terms to know. Be able to give the meaning of each term listed.

   fleet, aground, channel, monastery, monk, strait, grounded, deserted

2. People to know. Be able to tell at least two facts about each person or group of persons listed.

   Vasco Da Gama, Bartholomew Diaz, Vasco de Balboa, Prince Henry, the Navigator, Americus Vespucius, Juan Ponce de Leon, Ferdinand Magellan

3. Places to know. Be able to locate each place named. Give one fact as you locate each place.

   Portugal, Philippine Islands, India, Isthmus of Panama, Atlantic Ocean, Mediterranean Sea, Pacific Ocean, Cape of Good Hope, West Indies, Florida, Strait of Magellan, South Sea, Patagonia, Spain

ACTIVITIES

1. Make a table by filling in the names and the dates.

GREAT SEAMEN OF PORTUGAL		DATE
1. He was a great hero	Prince H– – – –	——
2. He discovered the Cape of Good Hope	Bartholomew D– – –	——
3. He found an all water route to the East	Vasco Da G– – –	——

GREAT SEAMEN OF SPAIN		Date
1. He discovered Florida	Ponce de L---	—
2. He discovered the Pacific Ocean	Vasco de B------	—
3. His voyage proved that the world is round	Ferdinand M--------	—

2. Write three sentences telling how our land came to be called America.

3. A THINKING GAME. Make a list of the persons and places you have learned about in this chapter. The leader begins—"I have discovered Florida. Who am I?" The pupil who correctly answers—"You are Ponce de Leon" is the winner and becomes the leader. The new leader may say—"I claimed the lands touched by the waters of the South Sea for the King of Spain. Who am I?" This can be a lively game if the pupils think fast. It is a game that will help you to remember the deeds of some of the men who explored for Spain.

4. Make a drawing to show a strait.

5. Imagine you were one of the crew who sailed with Magellan. You were one of the lucky men who returned to Spain. Tell some of the adventures you had while on the voyage. Try to make your story as interesting as possible.

6. Write one sentence about each person whose name is listed. Try to tell the most important thing each of these men did.

   Vasco de Balboa
   Juan Ponce de Leon
   Ferdinand Magellan

7. Make a list of five articles which Magellan's men traded for spices.

STUDY TEST 4—SCORE 15

PART ONE—After each sentence write the matching term. Use only terms listed below the Study Lesson. Cross out each term as you use it.

1. He founded a school for navigators. ____________
2. Portuguese seaman who discovered the Cape of Good Hope. ____________
3. Portuguese seaman who found the all water route to India. ____________
4. Spaniard who discovered Florida. ____________
5. An Italian navigator who sailed under the flag of Portugal. ____________

Prince Henry	Bartholomew Diaz
Vasco Da Gama	Ponce de Leon
Americus Vespucius	

PART TWO—Draw a line under the word which gives the correct ending.

Put a period after the word chosen as the correct ending.

1. Ponce de Leon liked study adventure
2. Florida was discovered by Ponce de Leon Balboa
3. Ferdinand Magellan was born in Spain Portugal
4. Portugal and Spain were friends rivals
5. Magellan placed his trust in God himself
6. Magellan thought that the natives of Patagonia were dwarfs giants
7. A narrow body of water connecting two larger bodies of water is called a strait sea
8. The voyage of Magellan proved that the world is flat round
9. The South Sea was discovered by Magellan Balboa
10. Later the South Sea was called the Atlantic Pacific

UNIT II: EXPLORING THE NEW WORLD

NEW SPAIN IN AMERICA

Read to learn

1. How DeSoto was rewarded by the king.
2. How the Mississippi River was discovered.
3. The lands claimed by Spain.
4. How the Spanish Missionaries spread the Gospel.
5. Why Father Las Casas is called the Protector of the Indians.

FERDINAND DESOTO

A DARING LEADER. Ferdinand DeSoto was a Spanish soldier. He served under Pizarro when Peru was conquered. DeSoto had some thrilling experiences. He was a good soldier and he fought bravely. After Peru was conquered the King of Spain wished to reward DeSoto. So the King of Spain made DeSoto governor of Cuba. This was a good position. DeSoto found the life as governor of Cuba too quiet. He liked excitement. He dreamed of cities filled with treasures like those he had seen in Peru.

The King of Spain wanted to control the land north of Mexico. He gave DeSoto orders to conquer this land and to settle it. DeSoto was pleased to be active again.

DeSoto had a party of over six-hundred men under his command. They were well armed. They carried a good supply of food. The party set sail from Cuba. Before long they reached Florida. The map on page 33 shows that Cuba is only a short distance from Florida.

THE DISCOVERY OF THE MISSISSIPPI RIVER. DeSoto and his men landed in Florida. They started to march overland. The journey was very unpleasant. The Spanish army had to cross many swamps. A swamp is a lowland where the water does not drain away. The journey across the swamps was slow and tiresome. DeSoto led the party westward beyond the swamp lands. The men marched overland for weeks. At length they reached a mighty river. Here they had to halt.

DeSoto and his men had not yet seen any rich cities. They still hoped to find cities of wealth like those DeSoto had seen in Peru. He was determined that the river should not stop the march overland. Some way must be found to cross this mighty river.

The men cut trees and made logs. These they fastened together to make rafts. It took months to build the needed rafts to carry the party across the wide river. Neither DeSoto nor his men realized their trip across the river would later have great influence.

THE DEATH OF DE SOTO. The men were beginning to show the hardships of the journey. DeSoto was losing strength. He became very weak. He died before his men realized how very sick he was. The leader was dead! The men wrapped his body in a blanket. Then they weighted it with sand. At night DeSoto's body was lowered into the mighty river. The men did not want the Indians to know that the Spanish leader was dead.

The expedition under DeSoto had not found rich cities. It had discovered the Mississippi River. This event was not thought of as very important at this time. The followers of DeSoto were disappointed. Many of them were discouraged. Only half of the men ever got back to Cuba. Some time later Spain realized the importance of the discovery of the mouth of the Mississippi River.

FRANCISCO CORONADO

ANOTHER SEARCHER FOR GOLD. Francisco Coronado undertook an expedition in search of rich cities. He had heard tales about the "Seven Cities." These "Seven Cities" were said to be filled with gold and silver. These cities were supposed to be to the north of Mexico. Coronado had heard about these cities from Father Marcos. This good priest had gone far into the country. He wanted to tell the Indians there about God. Coronado led an army of about three-hundred Spaniards. Many hundreds of Mexican Indians had also joined this expedition. Coronado led his army as far north as the present state of Kansas. The map on page 33 shows the route taken by Coronado.

They saw many buffalo feeding on the prairies. They failed to find any sign of the "Seven Cities." Coronado sent out scouting parties. One of these parties discovered the Grand Canyon of the Colorado River.

The expeditions of DeSoto and Coronado failed to add to the wealth of Spain. The Spanish began to give greater

attention to settlement than to searching for gold. Most of the Spanish settlements were made in South America and in Mexico. Some Spanish settlements were made in what is now the state of California.

EARLY SPANISH MISSIONARIES

SPREADING THE GOSPEL OF CHRIST. It is true that some Spaniards were attracted to America by the desire to find gold. They wished to be wealthy men. This was a selfish motive. Other Spaniards came to America for conquest. They wished to add to the power and glory of Spain. The lands they conquered came under the rule of Spain and the natives became Spanish subjects.

There were other Spaniards who came to America. They were not interested in gold. They had no desire to conquer lands. They were earnest men who were eager to convert the Indians. They were prompted by a high spiritual motive to win souls for Christ.

The Spanish priests who came to America were good men. They left the comforts of Spain and came to a wilderness. They were not interested in finding gold, or in becoming famous. These priests only wanted to work for

God and for His Church. They hoped to make the Indians good Catholics. They wanted to show the poor savages how to lead useful lives. Some of the priests were Franciscans; some were Jesuits. There were also Dominicans and Carmelites.

TASKS OF THE MISSIONARIES. The missionaries who came to America had many things to learn. They had to get used to living in a strange land. The climate was somewhat different and this was often quite trying. The missionaries had to learn to prepare and to eat many strange foods.

The missionaries met people of a strange race. So it was necessary to learn the language of the Indians. This was no easy task. Each tribe had its own language. The Indian languages are difficult for the white man to learn.

These priests were zealous men. They were able to accomplish many difficult tasks and to suffer many hardships. Their labor was all for the honor and glory of God so their reward in heaven will be very great.

FATHER LAS CASAS. Bartholomew Las Casas came to America in 1502. He came here in search of wealth. Las Casas was not a man to be satisfied with mere wealth. God blessed him with a religious vocation. So Las Casas studied to become a priest. He may have been the first priest ordained in America. Sometime later Father La Casas entered the Dominican Order.

This good priest tried to impress upon the Indians the ideal of peace. He defended the Indians wherever he could justly do so. It was Father Las Casas who persuaded the rulers of Spain to put an end to Indian slavery.

Father Las Casas labored sixty years for the welfare of the Indians. That is why he is often called the Protector of the Indians.

FATHER CANCER. Father Louis Cancer was a Dominican priest. He was a friend of Father Las Casas. Father Cancer came to America in 1549. He visited Florida in an attempt to convert the Indians. The Indians living in Florida were very savage. Father Cancer was scalped by the Indians. He died a martyr. A person who sacrifices his life for the Faith is a martyr.

TRUE MARTYRS. Many of the good missionaries who labored along the Atlantic coast met death for the Faith. The Indians along the southern coast were most unfriendly. They killed many missionary priests. No doubt the martyrdom of these good priests brought many blessings to our country.

STUDY SUMMARY

---

1. Terms to know. Be able to explain the meaning of each of the following terms.

   swamp martyr conqueror

2. People to know. Be able to give at least two facts about each person listed.

Father Cancer	Francisco Pizarro
Francisco Coronado	Ferdinand DeSoto
Father Las Casas	

3. Places to know. Be able to locate the following places on a wall map. Tell one important fact about each place as it is located.

California	Cuba	Isthmus of Panama
Mississippi River	Peru	South America
Grand Canyon of the Colorado River	Florida	California
	Mexico	

ACTIVITIES

1. A DIALOG. Select four pupils. Each pupil is to represent one of the Spanish explorers. Each speaker tells of the deeds he accomplished for the glory of Spain. After the four speakers have finished other pupils are permitted to ask questions and to add facts about the Spanish explorers.
2. A GAME. Write the names of the Spanish explorers on cards. On matching cards write the name of the place in the New World where these men explored. Play the game like any matching card game. It can be fun if you try to make it so.
3. Character Study. Write one sentence to prove that each character trait fitted the Spanish missionaries.
   a. They were unselfish.
   b. They were zealous.
   c. They were good planners.
   d. They were hard working men.
   e. They were peace loving men.
4. Write a paragraph about early Spanish missionaries. Be sure to tell:
   a. Why they came to the New World.
   b. The tasks they had to learn.
   c. Their work.

STUDY TEST 5—SCORE 20

PART ONE—Answer each question with YES or NO.

1. Was DeSoto contented in Cuba? ______
2. Did DeSoto and his men have a pleasant journey across Florida? ______
3. Was the mouth of the Mississippi River discovered by DeSoto? ______
4. Did Coronado find the "Seven Cities"? ______
5. Were the "Seven Cities" ever found? ______
6. Did the expeditions of DeSoto and Coronado add to the wealth of Spain? ______
7. Did the Spanish give more attention to the establishment of settlements or to search for gold? ______
8. Were most of the Spanish settlements made to the south of our country? ______
9. Were any Spanish settlements made in what is now California? ______
10. Did DeSoto discover Florida? ______

PART TWO—Put T after each true statement. Put F after each statement which is false.

1. All Spaniards who came to America were seeking gold. —
2. The Spanish missionaries were noble men. —
3. The missionaries wished to convert the Indians.
4. It was difficult to learn the Indian language. —
5. Bartholomew Las Casas came to America in search of wealth. —
6. Father Las Casas tried to teach the Indians to live in peace. —
7. The rulers of Spain ended Indian slavery. —
8. Father Las Casas served sixty years as a missionary. —
9. The Indians of Florida were friendly toward the white man. —
10. A martyr is a person who gives up his life for his Faith. —

THE ENGLISH EXPLORERS

Read to learn

1. How John Cabot, a Venetian trader, served England.
2. How Cabot took possession of North America.
3. About England's claim to the continent.
4. How Francis Drake served England.
5. Why Drake did not return to England by the Atlantic.
6. How Queen Elizabeth honored Francis Drake.

JOHN CABOT

A VENETIAN TRADER. It seems certain that John Cabot was born in Genoa, Italy. He was born about the same time as Columbus. He may have left Genoa as a little boy. Later, he became a citizen of Venice.

John Cabot was a successful trader. He made money by selling foreign goods. Goods from another land are called foreign goods. Cabot traded in products from the East. He became a wealthy man. It is not known just why John Cabot left Venice. It may be that he realized that the fall of Constantinople meant the end of the trade cities of Italy. Genoa and Venice were wealthy trade cities. The Turks captured Constantinople in 1453. This shut off, to some extent, the trade routes to the East.

AN ITALIAN MERCHANT IN ENGLAND. John Cabot left Venice and went to live in Bristol, England. This was an important seaport in those days. Many seamen and traders lived in Bristol.

The story of the voyage of Christopher Columbus caused great excitement in this lively seaport. Among the traders who were interested in the voyage of Columbus, was the Venetian trader, John Cabot.

JOHN CABOT MAKES A PLAN. Probably the report of the voyage of Columbus gave Cabot ambition to plan a voyage to the New World.

The English King, Henry VII, gave John Cabot permission to undertake a voyage of discovery. The king gave permission but did not give Cabot much help. A little ship called the *Matthew* was given to Cabot to command. The ship had a crew of eighteen men.

THE VOYAGE OF DISCOVERY. John Cabot and his brave little crew left Bristol in May 1497. They sailed for weeks across the stormy Atlantic Ocean. They finally reached the coast of the land now called Labrador. John Cabot thought he had reached a part of China.

He took possession of this land in the name of King Henry VII of England. Cabot set up a cross. As a sign of English possession he placed the English flag on one side of the cross. Then he placed the flag of Venice at the other side of the cross. This was done in honor of the city where he had been a citizen. The picture on page 53 shows Cabot taking possession of the land. Then Cabot and his men set sail for England.

ENGLAND'S DEBT TO JOHN CABOT. King Henry VII did not seem to realize how great a thing Cabot had done. The king showed but little appreciation. Many people realized that Cabot had made a real discovery. These people honored Cabot and gave him great praise.

The merchants of Bristol were delighted with the voyage of Cabot. They were sure that if he were given the chance John Cabot could find new markets for trading.

The merchants fitted out a fleet of five vessels. It was easy now to get crews to man the boats. John Cabot took his son, Sebastian, on this voyage.

Very little is known about this second voyage of Cabot. John Cabot seems to have been forgotten. His discoveries were not forgotten. England based her claims to the North American continent on its discovery by John Cabot.

FRANCIS DRAKE

A BOLD SEAMAN. Other seamen went on voyages of discovery for England. One of these was a bold seaman named Francis Drake. Like other mariners of his time Drake wanted to reach the East. He sailed across the Atlantic Ocean and turned southward. He sailed through the Strait of Magellan in 1577.

Francis Drake was an able seaman but he was not an honest man. He robbed the Spanish settlements along the west coast of South America. A sea-robber is called a pirate. The Spanish considered Francis Drake a pirate. He stopped at many Spanish settlements. Wherever Drake stopped he engaged in plunder. This means that he took

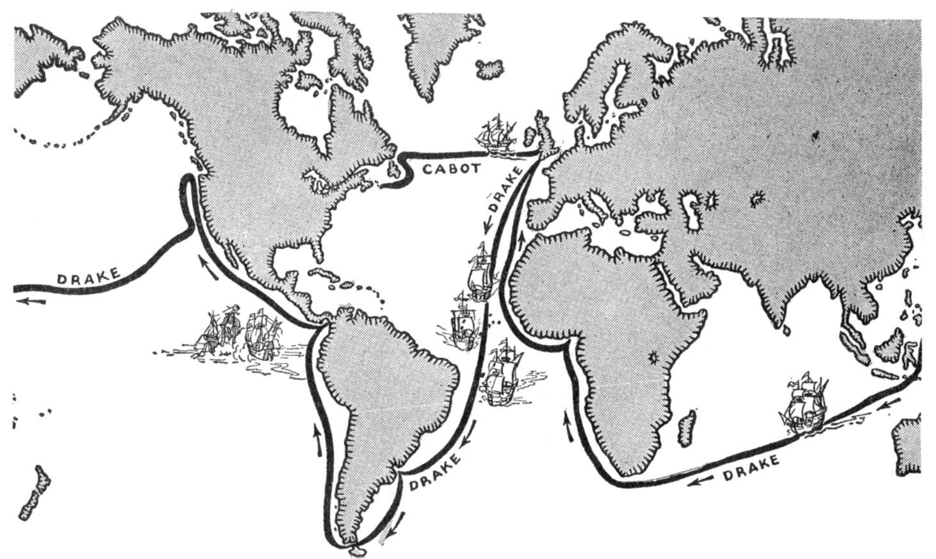

by force any treasures, or things of value, that he wished to take from the Spanish.

Then he sailed north as far as what is now our state of California. Here he spent the winter. He dared not return to England by the same route he had taken. He knew that Spanish ships would be waiting for him to return with his booty. Things taken from an enemy are called booty.

Francis Drake did a very daring thing. He steered his ship westward across the Pacific Ocean. He returned to

England by way of the Cape of Good Hope. The ship commanded by Francis Drake was the second ship to sail around the world.

The Queen of England was very proud of Francis Drake. She thought that he had done a most wonderful thing. She was proud too, of the booty Drake brought back from the Spanish. Queen Elizabeth was so pleased with Drake that she made him a knight. A knight is a noble of low rank. Francis Drake was given the title of Sir Francis Drake. He was a hero in England.

The Spanish never forgot how Francis Drake plundered their villages and their ships. The Spanish always considered Francis Drake to be a pirate.

STUDY SUMMARY

1. Terms to know. Be able to give the meaning of each term listed.

foreign	booty	pirate
citizen	knight	plunder

2. People to know. Be able to give one fact about each person whose name is listed.

John Cabot	Queen Elizabeth
King Henry VII	Francis Drake

3. Places to know. Be able to locate on a wall map each place listed. Tell one fact about the place as it is located.

Labrador	Strait of Magellan
Bristol, England	Cape of Good Hope
Genoa	Pacific Ocean
Venice	California

4. Dates to remember. Tell one important event that happened on each date listed.

   1453 1497 1577

ACTIVITIES

1. Discuss the question—Which man, John Cabot or Francis Drake, served England in the better way?
2. Trace the journey of Sir Francis Drake on a wall map.
3. Make pencil sketches to show:
    1. John Cabot taking possession of North America.
    2. Queen Elizabeth making Francis Drake a knight.
4. Explain why Francis Drake was called a pirate by the Spanish yet he was honored by the English queen.

STUDY TEST 6—SCORE 15

Identify the persons described. Put *C* after each sentence which refers to John Cabot. Put *D* after each sentence which refers to Francis Drake.

1. Once he was a Venetian trader. . . .
2. He moved to Bristol, England. . . .
3. He was a citizen of Venice. . . .
4. He was a very bold seaman. . . .
5. He was a pirate. . . .
6. He commanded the *Matthew*. . . .
7. King Henry VII gave him permission to go on a voyage of discovery. . . .
8. He reached the coast of Labrador. . . .
9. He was honored by Queen Elizabeth. . . .
10. He plundered Spanish settlements. . . .
11. He claimed North America for England. . . .
12. He took booty from the Spanish. . . .
13. He made the Spanish very angry. . . .
14. He was made a knight. . . .
15. He erected a cross when he landed in America. . . .

THE FRENCH EXPLORERS

Read to learn

1. About the coast explored by John Verrazano.
2. The desire to find a passage across North America.
3. How Jacques Cartier prepared for his journey.
4. The discoveries made by Jacques Cartier.
5. Why Cartier was disappointed.
6. How France profited by the explorations of Cartier.

FRENCH INTEREST IN THE NEW WORLD. The explorers for Spain and for England had made successful voyages to the New World. French sailing vessels came to the North Atlantic banks to fish. A shallow place in the water where fish live is often spoken of as a fishing bank. The cool shallow waters of the Atlantic Ocean near the coast of North America are excellent fishing banks.

The French people became interested in the land across the Atlantic Ocean. The King of France was anxious to add to the glory of France. Spain, France, and England, at this time, were great rivals. Each nation wished to be more powerful than her neighbors. France was eager to send explorers to the New World. She did not want her rivals, Spain and England, to have all the glory.

JOHN VERRAZANO

AN ITALIAN UNDER THE FLAG OF FRANCE. The King of France fitted out a ship for a voyage to the New World. John Verrazano was made captain of the ship. He was an experienced Italian seaman.

The ship commanded by Verrazano reached the coast of North America. Verrazano and his men explored along the coast. They travelled from what is now North Carolina to Newfoundland. Notice on the map on page 62 that this was a long journey along the coast. Some people think that this may have been the first ship to sail into New York harbor. Later France based her claim to part of North America on the explorations of John Verrazano.

JACQUES CARTIER

A SEARCH FOR A WESTWARD PASSAGE. Many people in Europe believed that a pasage across America could be found. This is often spoken of as the search for the westward passage. The nation which could find a route across America to the East would become wealthy. There was a profitable market in Europe for the rich products of the East.

The King of France ordered Jacques Cartier to go in search of a passage across North America. Jacques Cartier was an experienced seaman. Some time he may have sailed to the East by the route around Africa. He may have sailed to the fishing banks off the coast of Newfoundland.

Jacques Cartier was ambitious. He was anxious to find a westward passage to the East. He was thrilled when the King commanded him to make the voyage to America.

PREPARING FOR THE JOURNEY. Jacques Cartier was a good Catholic. He knew how to prepare for a journey. He received the Sacrament of Penance. Then he attended Holy Mass and received Holy Communion. He was well prepared before he sailed from France.

The soul of Jacques Cartier was filled with zeal as he faced westward. He was eager to have the knowledge of

God spread to the New World. That is why Cartier is said to have been a zealous man.

THE EXPEDITION. Jacques Cartier steered his ship due west. He reached the shores of Newfoundland. Then he and his men explored along the coast. They discovered a great gulf. A large body of sea water extending into the land is called a gulf. A gulf is sometimes spoken of as an arm of the sea. Cartier named the gulf he discovered the Gulf of St. Lawrence. He made the discovery on the feast of St. Lawrence.

Cartier took possession of the land bordering the Gulf of St. Lawrence in the name of the King of France. Then Cartier and his men sailed back to France. They were anxious to tell the King what they had accomplished.

THE SECOND VOYAGE. The next year Jacques Cartier made another voyage to the New World. Cartier discovered a great river flowing into the Gulf of St. Lawrence. He named it the St. Lawrence River. Cartier thought that at last he had discovered a westward passage. He sailed up the St. Lawrence River on an exploring trip.

The trip up the St. Lawrence River was an interesting one. Cartier and his men saw a small Indian village where the city of Quebec is now located. They sailed on up the

river. Farther up the river they saw another Indian village. It was on an island. This village was well protected because it was surrounded by water. Behind this village there was a high hill. Cartier climbed this hill. He called the place Montreal which means Royal Mountain. Study the map on page 62. Trace Cartier's journey up the St. Lawrence River. Note the locations of the two Indian villages which Jacques Cartier discovered.

DISAPPOINTMENT. Jacques Cartier wished to make a settlement somewhere along the St. Lawrence River. Cartier knew that a settlement would strenghen the claim of France to this land. The weather was very cold. Some of the men died. This was a very sad experience. Cartier was so disappointed that he planned to return to France. Jacques Cartier felt that he had made three failures:

1. He failed to find a westward passage to the East.
2. He failed to establish a French settlement in America.
3. He had failed to spread the Catholic religion.

FRENCH CLAIMS IN AMERICA. Jacques Cartier felt a personal disappointment about his voyages. France profited by his journeys. The explorations by Cartier gave

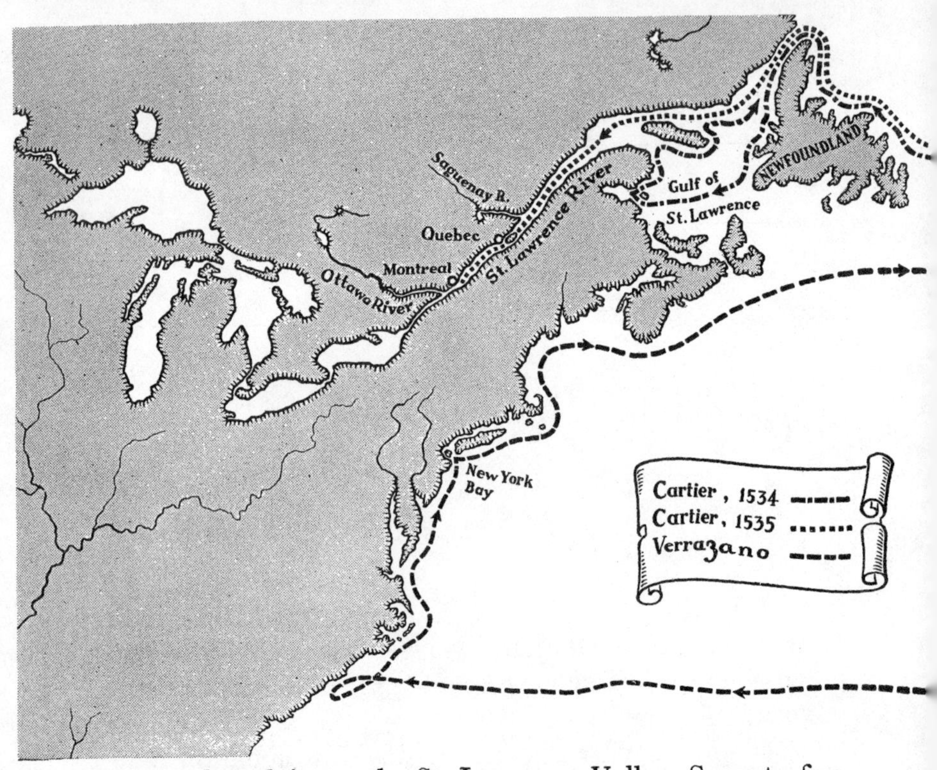

France her claim to the St. Lawrence Valley. Seventy-five years later France began settlements in New France.

Land is claimed by the men who discover it. They claim it in the name of the country for which they are laboring. When land is explored it strengthens the claim. When settlements are made the claim is more or less final. It is well to remember these steps:

1. Discovery. 2. Exploration. 3. Settlement.

STUDY SUMMARY

---

1. Terms to know. Be able to explain the meaning of each term listed.
   - rivals
   - westward passage
   - gulf
   - fishing bank
2. People to know. Be able to tell about the explorations of
   - John Verrazano
   - Jacques Cartier

ACTIVITIES

1. Make a table and fill in the facts.

JACQUES CARTIER
He succeeded: 1. 2. 3. He failed: 1. 2. 3.

2. A character study. Prove that Jacques Cartier had the following character traits:

   daring　　zealous
   ambitious　　religious

3. Places to know. Be able to locate on a wall map each place listed. Give one fact about the place as it is located.

   Montreal　　Quebec
   Gulf of St. Lawrence　　Newfoundland
   Valley of the St. Lawrence River

STUDY TEST 7—SCORE 15

Draw a line under the term which gives the correct ending.

1. John Verrazano was an
   Italian　　Frenchman　　Spaniard
2. Verrazano sailed under the flag of
   England　　Italy　　France

3. Spain, France, and England at this time were

   great friends   bitter rivals   good neighbors

4. Verrazano explored the coast of

   Africa   North America   Spain

5. The King of France ordered Cartier to search for

   a westward passage   gold   a settlement

6. Jacques Cartier was a very good

   ruler   Catholic   soldier

7. Cartier discovered the

   Gulf of Mexico   Gulf of St. Lawrence

8. A body of sea water extending into the land is called

   a pond   a river   a gulf

9. Cartier named the island which he discovered

   Quebec   Montreal   Newfoundland

10. Cartier was unable to make

    a settlement   money   a voyage

11. The land drained by the St. Lawrence River was claimed by Cartier for

    England   France   Spain

12. The French did not make settlements for

    ten years   fifty years   seventy-five years

13. France based her claims to the St. Lawrence Valley on the explorations made by

    John Verrazano   Jacques Cartier

14. Shallow water where fish live is called

    a bay   a bank   a gulf

15. The last of the three European rivals to make their settlements in America was

    Spain   England   France

VIRGINIA

Read to learn

1. What is a colony? Who are colonists?
2. Why England desired to have colonies in America.
3. What Sir Walter Raleigh attempted to do.
4. Why King James I. liked the plan of the London Company.
5. How Jamestown was settled.
6. How John Smith helped the Jamestown colony.
7. The beginning of slavery in America.
8. What Bacon's Rebellion proved.
9. The religious ideas of the Virginia colonists.

STARTING COLONIES IN AMERICA. There were some patriotic Englishmen who believed that England should establish colonies in America. A colony is a settlement. When a group of people leave their own country and settle in another land they establish a colony. Persons who live in a colony are called colonists. The colonists remain citizens of their native land. The native land is the land where a person is born. English people coming to America to establish a colony were still Englishmen. They were still subjects of the British ruler. English people are often called British because they live in Great Britain.

SIR WALTER RALEIGH. Wise Englishmen knew that colonies would strengthen the land claims of England in America. These Englishmen wanted colonies for another reason. They believed that colonies would be profitable for those who would establish them. Sir Walter Raleigh was an Englishman who wanted to found a colony in America.

This gentleman was well liked by Queen Elizabeth. Elizabeth gave Raleigh as much land in America as he wanted. Twice Raleigh sent ships with settlers to Virginia. The first time the colonists soon returned to England. The second colony just disappeared. No one ever found out what became of it. It is called the Lost Colony. Raleigh could do no more. He did not have enough money to try once again to establish a colony.

THE LONDON COMPANY. It seemed sure that one man alone could not found a colony. So a group of nobles, merchants, and seamen formed a company. They called it the London Company. It was really a trading company.

The members of the London Company went to see King James I, who was then King of England. They explained their plan and asked permission to establish a colony in America. The King claimed that he alone had the power to grant permission for a colony. King James liked the ideas of the London Company. He realized that a colony in America would have two advantages. 1. It would strengthen the English land claims along the Atlantic coast. 2. It would encourage trading.

There was another reason why Englishmen wanted colonies in America. Patriotic Englishmen looked upon

colonies as one way of checking the power of Spain.

The King was generous to the London Company. He gave them plenty of land in Virginia. The London Company paid no money for the land. One-fifth of all the gold and silver that the colonists might find, and one-fifteenth of all the copper found was to be given to the King.

FIRST ENGLISH COLONISTS. Many men were willing to leave England to go to Virginia. Most people believed that there was a great deal of gold in the New World. They thought that America was a place where they could get rich without doing work. They learned the sad lesson that this was a wrong idea. There is no place where people get rich without some kind of work.

JAMESTOWN, 1607. A little fleet of three ships carried the colonists to America. The *Sarah Constant*, the *Goodspeed*, and the *Discovery* were the ships. One-hundred-four men left England on the three vessels. The voyage was a long, weary one. The men quarreled. This made the voyage more unpleasant.

At last the fleet arrived at the entrance of Chesapeake Bay, and sailed into the bay. Here they entered a broad river which flowed into the bay. They named it the James River in honor of King James I. Next the colonists chose a place for their settlement. They decided to settle on a lower bank of the river. The lower banks of a river are near its outlet. The men thought this looked like a good place for a settlement so they landed. They named the settlement Jamestown. It was the first permanent English settlement in America. A permanent settlement is one that lasts a long time. The settlement at Jamestown was founded in 1607.

NEW HOMES IN A NEW LAND. The Jamestown settlement did not get a good start. The colonists began their settlement with some wrong ideas. There were plenty of trees. These could be cut to make logs and lumber. Comfortable houses could have been made with logs and lumber. Many of the settlers seem to have been lazy men. They were satisfied with the poorest kind of a shelter. They were content to hang a piece of sail-cloth on a pole to make a tent-like shelter. They did not even bother to get the soil ready for planting. So food became scarce.

Some of the settlers had made the Indians angry. This made matters worse in the settlement. A few of the settlers began a useless search for gold. Largely because of these stupid mistakes the Jamestown colony was facing failure. John Smith, a man of very strong character, took over the direction of the Jamestown settlement. His strong leadership helped it to become a permanent settlement.

THE GROWTH OF VIRGINIA

THE STARVING TIME. There were five hundred colonists in Jamestown when John Smith sailed back to England. No man seemed able to act as a leader to take

John Smith's place. The winter was very severe. Only sixty colonists were alive in the spring. Three things had caused the many deaths. 1. Hunger caused many of the colonists to die of starvation. 2. Sickness due to improper foods caused many deaths. 3. Unfriendly Indians had killed some of the colonists.

BETTER TIMES. The little colony at Jamestown was determined not to give up. Wise rules were made. During the early days of the colony all the colonists used a common storeroom. All the food that was raised was stored there. This was not a wise policy. A man who worked hard and raised much food put it all into the common storehouse. A man who was lazy and raised only a little food also put his supply in the common storehouse. When supplies were given out all men received an equal share of food. It was not just that the hard working man and the lazy man should receive the same share of food.

Governor Thomas Dale changed this unjust rule. Each man was given a plot of land to cultivate. Thus he became a land owner. He could keep all the products he raised except a small amount of corn. At harvest time each farmer put some corn into the common storehouse. This corn was stored to prevent another starving time. The Jamestown colony got along very well under this more just plan. The colonists learned that honest toil meant a sure food supply.

It was discovered that tobacco would grow very well in Virginia. The climate and soil were just right for the tobacco plant. There was a good market for tobacco in Europe. Farmers turned their earnest attention to the growing of tobacco. This became the most important crop in Virginia. Later, it influenced the history of America.

SLAVERY BEGINS IN VIRGINIA. One day in 1619 a Dutch ship sailed up the James River. There were twenty negroes on the vessel. They had been captured in

Africa. The negroes were sold as slaves. The planters thought their problem of field laborers was partly solved. The large farms were called plantations. Many workers were needed on a plantation. A planter bought a slave as he might buy a horse or a plow. The negro slave became the property of the planter just as the horse or the plow which he bought was his property. The bringing of slaves to Virginia was a great evil. Later, this evil caused great sorrow not only to slaves and planters but to the nation.

The picture shows negro slaves working on a plantation. Oxen were often used to haul the products to the wharf. A wharf is a platform where ships are loaded or unloaded.

HOW VIRGINIA WAS GOVERNED. Virginia was a charter colony. The London Company had been granted a charter by the King of England. A charter was a written agreement. It gave to the London Company a certain area of land. It also gave to the London Company the right to appoint governors to rule the colony.

Trouble arose between the Virginia colonists and the Indians. The King of England blamed the London Company for the trouble with the Indians. The King punished the London Company by taking their charter from them. Virginia then became a royal colony. The word royal refers to the ruler who wears the crown. A royal colony belonged directly to the ruler. That is why a royal colony is sometimes called a crown colony.

After Virginia became a royal colony the King appointed the governor. Virginia had some wise and good royal governors. There was one very bad royal governor. He was William Berkeley. He ruled Virginia for nearly forty years. Governor Berkeley became a tryrant. A cruel or unjust ruler is called a tyrant. The unwise and unjust rule of Berkeley caused very bad times in Virginia. Conditions became so bad that the people rose in rebellion. A fight against the lawful government is called a rebellion. The people who take part in a rebellion are spoken of as rebels. The cause for which rebels fight may be just.

BACON'S REBELLION. The rebellion in Virginia was led by Nathaniel Bacon. That is why it is sometimes called Bacon's Rebellion. Nathaniel Bacon was a young planter. He thought something had to be done to get rid of the tyrant Berkeley. The rebellion failed. It had one good result. The King of England learned of the rebellion. He also learned what a tyrant Berkeley was. The King ordered Berkeley to return to England. A wiser governor was appointed to rule the Virginia colony.

Bacon's Rebellion was a failure but it proved certain truths.

1. It showed that the people of Virginia loved liberty.

2. It proved that the Virginians hated to be ruled by a tyrant.

3. The rebellion showed that the people were willing to fight for their rights.

4. The rebellion awakened the King to the fact that the colonists could not be neglected by the ruler.

STUDY SUMMARY

1. Terms to know. Be able to give the meaning of each term listed.

colony	council	native land
pirate	charter	plantation
colonist	tyrant	royal colony
wharf	rebel	rebellion

2. People to know. Be able to give one fact about each person whose name is listed.

   Sir Walter Raleigh — William Berkeley

   Nathaniel Bacon

3. Places to know. Be able to locate on a wall map each place listed. As the place is located tell one fact about each place.

   Chesapeake Bay — Jamestown

   James River — Virginia

4. Dates to remember. Be able to tell one important event that took place on each of the following dates

   1607 — 1619

ACTIVITIES

1. Make a sketch map of the Atlantic Coast of North America. Locate and put in the name of each place term listed.

   a. Virginia. b. James River c. Jamestown

2. Character studies:

   a. Prove that Governor Berkeley was a tyrant.
   b. Prove that Nathaniel Bacon did much good.

STUDY TEST 8—SCORE 20

Fill in the letters to complete the missing words.

1. A colony is a ———————————.
2. Persons who live in a colony are called ——————————.
3. The lower bank of a river is near the———————.
4. A settlement which lasts a long time is said to be ——————————.
5. Trouble arose between the Virginians and the ————————.
6. The Jamestown settlers put the food in a common ———————————.
7. The climate and soil of Virginia were well suited to the growing of————————.
8. Large farms came to be called ————————————.
9. A platform where ships are loaded and unloaded is a—————.
10. The most important crop raised in Virginia was ————————.
11. Negro slavery was started in —————————— in 1619.
12. A written agreement was called a ————————.
13. Royal refers to the ruler who wears the——————.
14. A royal colony was the same as a ——————colony.
15. The governor of a royal colony was appointed by the ————.
16. A cruel or unjust ruler is a———————.
17. A fight against the government is a ——————————.
18. Persons who take part in a rebellion are———————.

OTHER SOUTHERN COLONIES

Read to learn

1. Who Lord Baltimore was.
2. Where Lord Baltimore established a colony for Catholics.
3. What famous law was passed in the Maryland colony.
4. How the Carolinas came to be settled.
5. What happened, in England, to poor people who owed money.
6. How the settlement of Georgia helped poor debtors.

MARYLAND

RELIGIOUS TROUBLE IN ENGLAND. When America was discovered all the people of Europe, except the Jews and the Turks, were Catholics. Religious troubles began not long after America was discovered. The religious difficulties were very serious. Many Catholics were weak and they gave up their Faith. These people were no longer willing to be guided by the Pope. They were called Protestants.

A great number of the English people became Protestant. These people caused laws to be passed that were very severe for Catholics. One of the unjust laws considered it a crime for a person to be a faithful Catholic. Under these laws the faithful Catholics suffered greatly. Often Catholics were forced to give up their property. Frequently Catholics were fined or put in prison just because they were Catholics. Some Catholics were killed.

They died rather than give up their Faith. Only people of great courage were able to remain true Catholics and remain loyal to the Pope.

GEORGE CALVERT, LORD BALTIMORE. George Calvert lived in England when Charles I was king. The King and George Calvert were great friends. George Calvert was a Protestant gentleman. He began to do some real thinking and some real study about religion. He discovered that the Protestant church was built on false ideas. George Calvert realized that the only true religion was the Catholic religion.

George Calvert was a brave man to become a Catholic at this time. He ran the risk of losing everything he owned. He was willing to make this sacrifice if necessary. His religion meant more to him than all the riches and the honors that could be given to him.

George Calvert lost nothing by becoming a Catholic. The King still liked him and still considered him as a friend. Indeed, the King gave him a great tract of land and made him a noble. George Calvert was given the title, Lord Baltimore.

A PLAN TO HELP CATHOLICS. Lord Baltimore was a very earnest man. He desired to help the Catholics living in England. Many English Catholics had to suffer for the Faith.

Lord Baltimore planned to secure a place in America for English Catholics. He wished them to be able to live in a land where they could practice the Catholic religion in peace.

A place in Newfoundland was selected for the settlement. Newfoundland is an island off the northeastern shore of Canada. The brave little group of men tried to settle there. The attempt was a failure. The very cold climate was too severe for the Englishmen.

REPORTS FROM VIRGINIA. The reports sent to England from Virginia told of the sunny climate and the very fertile soil. These reports made Lord Baltimore eager to secure land near the Jamestown settlement.

He asked his friend, the king, for a grant of land. The king, Charles I, promised Lord Baltimore a large piece of land just to the north of the Jamestown settlement. Lord Baltimore was to pay rent for the use of the land. The rent was to be two Indian arrow heads each year. The new colony was to be called Maryland. Just when almost everything was ready Lord Baltimore died.

CECIL CALVERT. The death of Lord Baltimore was a sad blow. Yet his plans for a settlement for Catholics did not fail. Cecil Calvert was the oldest son of Lord Baltimore. This noble son was eager to carry out the plans made by his father.

Charles I was generous to Cecil Calvert. All that the king had promised to Lord Baltimore was given to Cecil Calvert. The king even gave Cecil Calvert the title of Lord Baltimore. The new Lord Baltimore set to work earnestly to carry out the plans prepared by his father. It happened that Cecil Calvert had to remain in England. He appointed his brother, Leonard Calvert, as leader of the expedition. Leonard Calvert was to be the governor of the new colony.

It was not hard to get men to go to America. Before long twenty gentlemen were ready to go. These gentlemen were rather wealthy men. They planned to take their servants with them. Workmen also joined the group going to America. Over two hundred persons were willing to brave the hardships of founding a colony in America.

THE JOURNEY. *The Ark* and *The Dove* were the two sail boats that set out to carry the settlers across the Atlantic. It was a long, long trip from England to the mouth of the Potomac River. While crossing the Atlantic

the ships met a hurricane. A hurricane is a very severe wind storm. The two ships became separated during the storm. After three months the weary travellers reached the mouth of the Potomac River. It had taken them three months, or ninety days, to make the journey in sailing vessels. Steamers now make this journey of three thousand miles in four or five days.

THE LANDING. The settlers landed on a lovely spring day in 1634. It was "Our Lady's Day In Lent." The settlers took possession of the country for Our Savior, and for the King of England. A great cross was raised. Father Andrew White, a Jesuit father, offered a Mass of Thanksgiving.

ST. MARY'S SETTLEMENT. Governor Calvert selected a place for a settlement. There was an Indian settlement at the place where he wished to settle his colony. The Indians liked these Englishmen. That is why the Indians were willing to sell their land. The Indians gave up their land, part of the growing crops, and even their wigwams. The Englishmen gave the Indians cloth, axes, and hoes in exchange for the gifts they gave the white men.

The best wigwam in the village was given to Father White to be used as a chapel. Here he offered Mass for the settlers and for the friendly Indians. These settlers got along very well with the Indians.

The first settlement was called St. Mary's. It was a small settlement on the coast of Maryland. The people were hard working.

One of the most famous laws ever passed in America was made by the people of Maryland. This law was known as the Toleration Act. It said that every Christian would be allowed to worship God in his own way.

The Toleration Act did not last very long. The Protestants gained control of Maryland. They made life very difficult for Catholics.

THE CAROLINAS AND GEORGIA

THE CAROLINAS. South of Virginia there was very fertile land. Like Virginia, the land was well suited for the growing of tobacco. Some of the land was marsh. A marsh is a wet lowland. It is a good place for the growing of rice.

Men from Virginia began to move south. They settled on these fertile lands. The King of England, Charles II, learned of these rich lands. He made a grant of land to eight noblemen in 1663. Settlements at Albemarle and at Charleston were made. Later, these settlements came to be called North Carolina and South Carolina.

GEORGIA. There were some very strict laws in England at this time. There was one law that was very hard on people who owed money. If a man owed money, he was in debt, so he was called a debtor. When a man could not pay his debt he was put in prison. This was a very foolish thing to do. A man in prison could not earn money to pay the debt he owed. The prisons were horrible places.

Many of the prisoners became sick and died as a result of the terrible prison conditions. There were earnest Englishmen who realized this great evil. They were anxious to help the prisoners but could think of no good plan.

James Oglethorpe was a brave and sensible man. He had a wise plan to save debtors from prison. He explained his plan to King George. It was a very simple plan. King George was to give James Oglethorpe a grant of land in America. Men who owed debts would be allowed to settle on the land. The crops the debtors raised were to be sold in England to pay the debts owed. King George realized that this was a sensible plan. A strip of land south of the Savannah River was given to James Oglethorpe for a colony for debtors. The colony was called Georgia in honor of King George. James Oglethorpe lived to see the colony of Georgia become prosperous. Tobacco and rice were the chief crops raised.

STUDY SUMMARY

---

1. Terms to know. Be able to give the meaning of each term listed.

hurricane	settlement
toleration	debtor

2. Persons to know. Be able to give one fact about each person whose name is listed.
   George Calvert, Lord Baltimore
   Cecil Calvert, second Lord Baltimore
   Leonard Calvert
   Father Andrew White, S. J.
   James Oglethorpe
3. Places to know. Be able to locate on a wall map each place listed. Tell one fact about each place as it is located.
   Maryland — South Carolina
   Georgia — Potomac River
4. Dates to remember. Be able to tell one important event that took place on each of the following dates.
   1634 — 1663

ACTIVITIES

1. Try to imagine yourself to have been on *The Ark* or *The Dove*. Write a story telling:
   1. Why you were coming to America.
   2. The journey.
   3. Landing.
   4. The settlement of St. Mary's.
2. Make a sketch map of the Atlantic Coast of North America. Put in the name of each place listed:
   Maryland — North and South Carolina — Georgia — Virginia
3. Have a play about the settlement of Maryland.
   Scene 1. Lord Baltimore explaining his idea of a colony to the King.
   Scene 2. Leaving England.
   Scene 3. Landing.
   Scene 4. Trading with the Indians for their land.

4. CHARACTER STUDIES. Prove that:
   a. Lord Baltimore was a brave man.
   b. Cecil Calvert was a faithful son.
   c. James Oglethorpe was a sensible man.

STUDY TEST 9—SCORE 15

Fill in the letters to complete the words.

1. Maryland was a colony established for _ _ _ _ _ _ _ _ _ _ _.
2. A severe wind storm is called a _ _ _ _ _ _ _ _ _ _ _.
3. The King made George Calvert a _ _ _ _ _ _.
4. Governor Calvert's little settlement was called _ _ _ _ _ _ _ _.
5. A Mass of Thanksgiving was offered by Father _ _ _ _ _ _ _ _ _ _ _ _ _.
6. The King gave Lord Baltimore land just _ _ _ _ _ of the Jamestown settlement.
7. One of the most famous laws was the Law of _ _ _ _ _ _ _ _ _ _ _ _ _ _ _ _.
8. A wet lowland is a _ _ _ _ _ _.
9. Georgia was established as a colony for _ _ _ _ _ _ _ _ _ _.
10. The marsh lands of the Carolinas were good places to raise _ _ _ _.
11. People of great courage remained loyal to the _ _ _ _ _.
12. A hurricane is a severe wind _ _ _ _ _ _.
13. The Indians gave up their land and some of their _ _ _ _ _ _ _.
14. The best wigwam was used as a _ _ _ _ _ _ _ _.
15. Rice and tobacco were the chief crops raised in _ _ _ _ _ _ _ _ _.

UNIT III: THE ENGLISH COLONIES

HOW THE SOUTHERN COLONISTS LIVED

Read to learn

1. About the homes of the southern colonists.
2. How farming was carried on in the South.
3. Three staple crops grown on plantations.
4. How children were educated.
5. How people travelled from place to place in the South.

EARLY HOMES. The first settlers who came to America built very crude homes. The simplest houses were made on the side of the clay hills. The clay hill was used as one side of the house. Logs were used for the other sides of the house. The logs were just set on the ground. The hard ground served as a floor. The roof was also made of logs. Strong logs called rafters supported the roof.

Better homes were built when the settlers had more time. The four walls of these homes were built with logs. The roofs were made of thatch. Straw or reed used to cover a roof is called thatch. The custom of using thatch for roofs in America was natural for the English colonists. Homes in England often had thatch roofs.

After saw mills were put up homes were often built of planks. Thick sawed pieces of timber are called planks. Sometimes these plank houses are spoken of as frame houses. The roofs were often covered with shingles. The thin pieces of wood used to cover roofs are called shingles. Most of the houses were small. There was one large room on the ground. A loft, a small room under the roof, was used for a place to sleep. The family climbed a ladder to get to the loft.

HOW FURS AND SKINS WERE USED. The skins of the raccoon, the opossum, and the deer were used for clothing. The skin of a raccoon made a fine cap. Deer skin was very useful. It made a strong, soft leather, which was often called buckskin. Clothing for men was often made from buckskin. Deer skin had many uses in the home. A deer skin made a good rug for the bare floor. A deer skin made a soft, warm blanket for the bed. A seat for a chair could be made from a buckskin.

FARMING IN THE SOUTH. The chief occupation of the settlers in the South was farming. Before planting could begin the ground had to be cleared. This means that trees and bushes were removed to clear the ground for the planting of crops.

The southern farmers early turned their attention to the growing of staple crops. A staple crop is an important or a principal crop. A staple crop is grown to sell, that is why it is sometimes called a money crop. Tobacco was the most important staple crop grown in the South. It was the money crop of the South for many, many years. The planters became wealthy selling tobacco to the people of the countries in Europe. This was one of the reasons why southern planters were able to buy furniture, clothing, and many other things from England.

Rice and the indigo plant were also grown. The indigo

plant was valuable because it yielded a blue dye. Tobacco, rice, and indigo were the three chief staple crops of the South in the early days. Later cotton became the most important staple crop. These crops were raised on large farms called plantations. Slaves were used to do the work in the field. This form of farming came to be called the plantation system. There are three facts to remember about the plantation system of farming. 1. The plantations were very, very large. 2. A staple crop was usually grown on the plantation. 3. The work was largely done by slaves.

Each planter set aside a garden patch. Here wheat, corn, and vegetables were raised for the planters and the slaves. These were not money crops because they were raised to use rather than to sell. The vegetables most commonly grown were potatoes, carrots, turnips, and parsnips.

Young pear trees and apple trees were brought to America from England. These fruit trees grew well on the fertile soil of Virginia.

THE MEAT SUPPLY. The early settlers had plenty of meat. Cattle and hogs were brought over from Europe to America. Cattle were raised on the farms. Hogs were allowed to run about in the nearby woods. Here the hogs fed upon acorns and grew fat.

There was plenty of game. Birds and wild animals which

are hunted for their flesh are often called game. It was good sport to hunt for ducks, wild turkeys, rabbits, squirrels, raccoons, opossums, and deer. The flesh of the duck, turkeys, and rabbits was used as food. The early settlers liked the deer meat. It is called venison.

The hunter shown in the picture on page 84 has just shot a very, very large wild fowl.

LATER HOMES. As time went on better houses were built. Some houses had six or more rooms. Wealthy settlers were able to build large houses of brick, stone, and timber like the one shown on this page. The woodwork inside these homes was of the finest woods. The wealthy planters could afford to have furniture sent over from England.

The houses of the poorer settlers remained very simple. These poor people made their own furniture. It was crude but strong. A tree stump was sometimes used as a chair. A split log, with the flat side up, was held up by log legs, and served as a table. Benches and stools were often made in the same fashion.

EDUCATION IN THE SOUTH. The plantation system of farming made it neecssary for people to live far apart. This made it difficult to have schools for the children. That is chiefly why most of the children were taught in the home.

Wealthy planters were able to hire private teachers for their children. These private teachers were known as tutors. Ministers were often willing to earn money as tutors. The sons of very wealthy planters were sometimes sent to England or to other countries in Europe to be educated. The daughters were taught fancy sewing and good manners. It was not thought very necessary for girls to be sent away to school. As early as 1693 the William and Mary College was established in Virginia. This was the second college to be established in the colonies. It was named in honor of the two rulers of England, King William and his wife, Queen Mary.

RELIGION IN THE SOUTH. The Church of England was the established church in the southern colonies. The Church of England came to be known as the Episcopalian Church. Every settler was compelled to attend the services held in the Church of England. If a person failed to attend the religious services he was fined. There was little money in the colonies. So the fine was paid in tobacco. It took twenty pounds of tobacco to pay a fine for not attending church. This was a heavy fine because tobacco was a valuable product.

There were other severe laws in the Virginia colony. Catholics and Quakers were not allowed to enter the

Virginia colony. The people of Virginia did not practice toleration toward people who did not belong to the Church of England. Maryland was the only colony where Catholics were ever able to live in peace.

TRAVEL IN THE SOUTH. Travel in the South was not easy. Many of the plantations were located on rivers. These could be reached by sailboats. Travel by sailboat was a common means of going from place to place. There were no good roads. Indian trails and paths made by the planters were used by horseback riders. It was many years before the South gave any attention to the making of roads. Then travel by horse and carriage or by stagecoach became possible. A stagecoach was a coach or a carriage drawn by horses. The stagecoach travelled over a regular route. The distance between two places on a journey was called a stage. The carriage or coach which travelled between places came to be called the stagecoach.

People lived so far apart in the South in those days that a visit was a real adventure. Southern families took great pride in caring for their visitors. Southerners came to be known for their hospitality. The friendly welcome given to visitors is called hospitality.

AMUSEMENT IN THE OLD SOUTH. Horse racing was the favorite amusement. Good race horses were brought over from England. Every man wanted to own a fast running horse. The horse-race was a real social event. The Southerners were very fond of horses. Horse-back riding was a pleasant kind of recreation. Men, women, boys, and girls all delighted in riding horseback.

Hunting was another pastime. Hunting for fowl was a very popular sport. Any bird of the air or any water bird is a fowl. Plenty of fowl lived in the woods and in the lowland marshes. There was an abundance of wild life in the woods. Wild animals are called game. Game hunting was real sport. Often the game was hunted just for the fun of the hunt, not because the animal was needed for its flesh or fur. This was unwise because animals were needlessly killed. Later game became very scarce in certain parts of the South.

Dancing was a very popular amusement in the South. The violin or the flute was played to supply the music for the dancers. The violin was sometimes called the fiddle. That is why the man who played the violin for the dancers was called the fiddler. Card playing was another favorite amusement among the southern colonists.

STUDY SUMMARY

---

1. Terms to know. Be able to tell the meaning of each term listed.

fowl	plantation system
planks	stage coach
thatch	buckskin
staple	hospitality
tutors	shingles
game	venison

2. Word study. Be able to use correctly each word listed:

hunt	hunted	hunter
fiddle	fiddler	

ACTIVITIES

1. Make a set of posters to show the four types of houses:
   a. The house made on the clay hill.
   b. The log house with a thatch roof.
   c. The plank or frame house with a shingle roof.
   d. The plantation home built with brick, stone, and timber.

   Use the posters for a class discussion.

STUDY TEST 10—SCORE 15

Draw a line under the word or the term which answers the question.

1. Did the early settlers in the South build their homes of bricks or of logs?
2. Were the early homes built by the colonists crude or were they furnished?
3. Is thatch made from wood or from straw?
4. Are planks thin or thick pieces of timber?
5. Were shingles used for roofs or for furniture?
6. Are shingles thick or thin pieces of wood?
7. Was the loft of an early colonial home reached by a stairway or by a ladder?
8. Did poor or wealthy colonists use brick and stone to build homes?
9. Was hunting or farming the chief occupation of the southern settlers?
10. Is a staple crop grown to sell in the market or to use by the family?
11. Was rice or tobacco the chief staple crop of the South at this time?
12. Did the southern planter market tobacco in Europe or in Asia?
13. Was the indigo plant valuable for dye or for fiber?
14. Was game plentiful or was it scarce in the South?
15. Was travel in the South difficult or easy?

UNIT III: THE ENGLISH COLONIES

NEW ENGLAND COLONIES

Read to learn

1. Who the Puritans were. Who the Pilgrims were.
2. Why the Pilgrims were unhappy in Holland.
3. About the journey of the *Mayflower*.
4. When and where the Pilgrims landed.
5. What the Mayflower Compact was.
6. How the Indians helped the Pilgrims.
7. About the First Thanksgiving.
8. How John Winthrop helped the Puritans.

RELIGIOUS DISORDER IN ENGLAND. There was much religious disorder in England during the time America was being settled. The people who had left the Catholic Church became Protestants. The people who left the Catholic Church denied two important beliefs. 1. They denied the authority of the Pope. 2. They denied that the Catholic Church was the supreme, or highest authority, in spiritual matters. Before long these Protestants began to disagree among themselves. There were many things which did not please the Protestants. They were unhappy. They missed the spiritual peace of the Catholic religion.

The Protestant Church in England was called the Church of England. The king was made the head of the Church of England. The Church of England would have nothing further to do with the Pope. Its members denied the authority of the Vicar of Christ, as the Pope is often called.

THE PURITANS. There were some members of the Church of England who were not satisfied with the new form of worship. These people had some very decided notions. 1. They disliked most ceremonies. 2. They wished a very simple form of worship. 3. They believed in very strict rules of conduct. These Protestants said that by getting far from the Catholic Church they would make their religion more pure. That is why they came to be called Puritans.

THE PILGRIMS. There were some Protestants in England who desired even greater changes in the form of worship. They were not willing to belong to the Church of England. They wanted to make up a form of worship to please themselves.

A law was passed commanding all people to attend the Church of England. Many Protestants would not obey this law. They separated themselves from the Church of England. That is why they were called Separatists or Independents. The Separatists were in a very bad fix. The law forbade them to have their own form of religion while they lived in England. There seemed only one way out of the difficulty. They left England and went to Holland in search of religious freedom. Persons who go on religious journeys are often called pilgrims. So the English Protestants who had journeyed to Holland were called Pilgrims.

THE PILGRIMS

HOW THE PILGRIMS LIVED IN HOLLAND. The people of Holland were very kind to the Pilgrims. Yet the Pilgrims were not happy. They were troubled about many things. The Pilgrims did not feel at home in Holland. They longed for their native land, England. It was not easy to change their manner of living. England and Holland were different in so many ways.

The language was strange and so were the customs of the people. Customs are the ways or manners of doing things. The customs of the Hollanders were quite different from those of the English in many ways. The picture shows some Pilgrims in Holland.

The Pilgrims had a very serious worry. They began to be afraid that their children would grow up just like the little boys and girls of Holland. The Pilgrims wished their children to keep the language and the customs of England.

Pilgrim leaders began to dream of going to America. This seemed a good plan.

PREPARING TO GO TO AMERICA. Permission had to be obtained from the King of England before the Pilgrims could go to America. The king was very slow in granting his permission. At last he gave his consent. Most of the Pilgrims were poor folk. They were badly in need of money. They were able to borrow enough money to buy supplies and ships.

The Pilgrims were brave folk. It took great courage to start for America with their families. These people were earnest. They were willing to face many hardships. They only desired to reach a place where they could practice their own religion. They knew that in America they would be free to worship as they believed they should.

LEAVING HOLLAND. The Pilgrims left Holland in a little ship called the *Speedwell.* This was not a good name for the boat for it was a very slow moving vessel. At last the *Speedwell* reached the port of Southampton in England.

The *MAYFLOWER*. The *Speedwell* was joined by another ship called the *Mayflower*. The two ships set sail from England on the journey to America. Before the *Speedwell* had sailed very far the captain decided that the vessel was unsafe. He ordered the *Speedwell* to return to port. Some of the passengers in the *Speedwell* were transferred to the *Mayflower*. The sturdy little *Mayflower* spread its sails and set off for America.

THE VOYAGE. It was a very stormy voyage. The *Mayflower* was tossed about on the waves. The great waves battered against the vessel. The vessel was damaged. One of the Pilgrims had a large bolt among his possessions. The damage to the vessel was repaired by using the bolt to hold the broken pieces together. It took the *Mayflower* sixty-three days to reach America. Fast steamers now cross the Atlantic between England and America in four or five days.

THE MAYFLOWER COMPACT. The Pilgrims held a meeting before they landed. All the Pilgrims signed an agreement. An agreement is sometimes called a compact. The agreement signed by the Pilgrims was called the Mayflower Compact.

Under the terms of the Mayflower Compact all of the Pilgrims promised to obey the laws. They also promised to work for the good of the colony. John Carver was elected governor of the colony. Miles Standish was made the military leader. The Pilgrims felt that Miles Standish would be a strong leader although he was not a Pilgrim.

THE LANDING. The *Mayflower* first dropped its anchor where the shores were rocky and barren. Where land is barren no crops can be grown. This was not a good place for a settlement. John Carver and Miles Standish, with a few of the men, set out in a small boat. They explored along the shore. They searched for a safe place to begin the settlement.

PLYMOUTH ROCK. The little exploring party had many exciting adventures. They had one unpleasant experience with unfriendly Indians. At last they reached a fine little harbor. They returned to the *Mayflower* to make their report. They then led the *Mayflower* into the harbor which they called Plymouth. Here the Pilgrims landed on December 10, 1620. They knelt and thanked God for a safe landing. They were indeed grateful for a safe landing after the long sea voyage.

THE FIRST DAYS IN AMERICA. It was very, very cold when the Pilgrims landed. The weather was ever so much colder than winter weather in England or in Holland.

The bad weather at sea, the cold weather after they landed, and the poor food caused much sickness. Those who were able began to work. First they decided to build

a fort. A fort is any strong building or enclosed place that can be used as a defense against an enemy. It was wise to build a fort because of the Indians.

Captain Miles Standish decided that the fort should be built on top of a hill as shown in the picture. This fort was strong but it was simply made. A space was enclosed by strong logs. A platform was built. The men placed several cannons on the platform. Cannons are big guns mounted on a frame. The Pilgrims had brought the cannons from England. They felt safe once the fort was made and the cannons were in place. Then they began to build a house to serve as a shelter.

THE FIRST HOUSE. The first building was a large log cabin. It had a roof of thatch. Some of the settlers moved into this house. The other settlers decided to remain on the *Mayflower*. One day a sad thing happened. A spark from the fire blew into the roof. The thatch caught fire and the house burned to the ground.

Very little work could be done while the winter lasted. The snow was very deep and the cold was very bitter. This was very hard on the Pilgrims who were used to mild winters. Many of the Pilgrims who were sick died. Fifty-one persons died during that first winter. Even the death of Governor Carver did not discourage the Pilgrims.

Later the Pilgrims were able to build a saw mill. Then they built better homes. Chests of drawers and cabinets were also made at a later date.

The large room of the log cabin was used not only as a living room but also as a kitchen and as a workshop. All meals were cooked in the open fireplace. Logs were used as fuel. The kettles, pots, dippers, pans, and large ladle were hung near the fireplace. Dried apples, ears of corn, smoked hams, and sides of bacon were hung from the large timbers which supported the roof.

This living room was indeed a great workshop. Here the candles were made. Tallow was melted over the fire. Wicks were dipped into the melted tallow. Sometimes the melted tallow was poured into wooden molds. This process made better candles. The women and girls had their spinning wheels in this room. Here they spun flax fiber to make linen thread or they spun wool to make woolen yarn. The loom stood in a corner of the room. Cloth was woven on the loom. Boots, shoes, and harness were made by the men. Brooms were made by tying twigs into bundles. The women and girls knitted scarves and mittens. Games, too, were played in this room. The living room was indeed a most useful and a pleasant place.

THE NEW TOWN. It was slow work building the little town as shown in the picture on page 95. Even when it

was finished it was not a very pleasant looking town. There was only one street. It ran from the shore to the top of the hill where the fort had been built. The street was not paved. At first there were no sidewalks or street lights. It was more like a path than a street.

THE FIRST THANKSGIVING. Conditions in the little settlement were very good by the end of the summer. The Pilgrims had raised a good crop of corn. There was plenty of game, and fish had been salted and stored for the coming winter.

The Pilgrims were a religious people. They were ready to forget their sufferings. They were already counting their blessings. The Pilgrims decided to spend some time in thanksgiving. They decided to have a feast. They invited their Indian friends to help them to celebrate.

The Thanksgiving lasted three days. Captain Miles Standish led the little army on a parade. Then they had a drill. Games were played. After that came the feast.

Four hunters had been sent into the forest to kill wild turkeys and other game. The Indian guests brought five deer. Corn bread was baked for the feast. Cranberries were cooked. Plenty of nuts were gathered. There was a supply of cooked vegetables and a little fruit. It was indeed a great feast. The Pilgrims and the Indians were better friends at the end of the three days of thanksgiving.

A GOOD EXAMPLE. The Pilgrims set two very good examples.

1. Their plan of a thanksgiving at the end of the harvest season has been followed by our nation. Each year our President orders the people to set aside a day for thanksgiving. Thanksgiving day usually is the last Thursday in November.

2. The great courage of the Pilgrims was their second good example.

The Puritans decided to follow the example of the Pilgrims and establish a settlement in America.

THE PURITANS COME TO AMERICA

WHY THE PURITANS LEFT ENGLAND. The Protestants in England were having a great deal of trouble. The King looked upon the Puritans as his enemies. He had two reasons for considering the Puritans to be his enemies. 1. The Puritans disagreed with the Church of England on matters of the form of worship. The King was the head of the Church of England. 2. The Puritans disagreed with the King on questions of government.

The Puritans realized that to remain in England meant unhappiness. They decided to follow the brave example of the Pilgrims. The Puritans planned to go to America. They knew that life in the New World would be hard. They were willing to endure hardships. They wanted to be able to worship God as they thought right.

The success of the Puritan colony owes a great deal to a wise leader. John Winthrop deserves much credit for planning, directing, and governing the colonists.

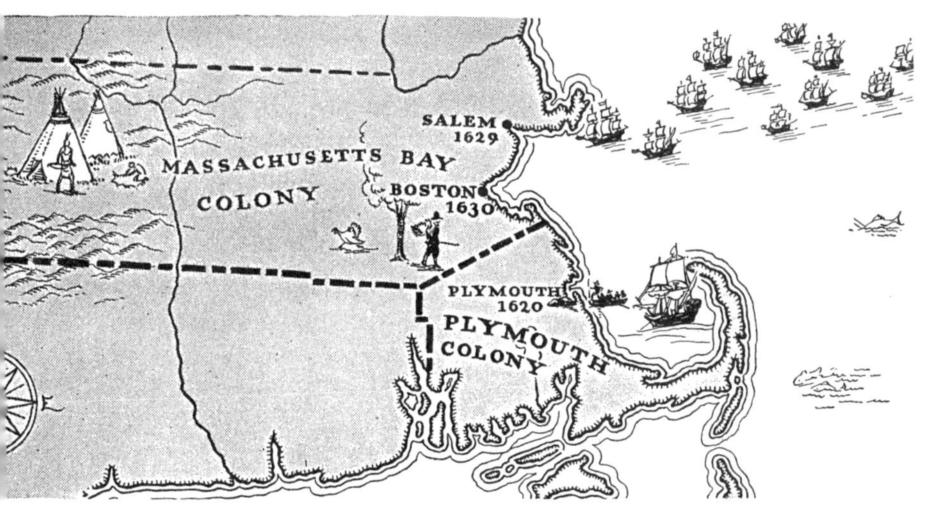

LEAVING ENGLAND. Eleven ships set sail from England in the spring of 1630. The ships carried about seven hundred people. The journey was far more pleasant than was the voyage of the Pilgrims. The Puritans landed at a place which they called Salem. This colony later was called the Massachusetts Bay Colony.

THE MASSACHUSETTS BAY COLONY. The Puritan Colony made a better beginning than did the Pilgrim Colony. The Puritans were wiser. They came to America in the spring. This group of settlers were not all poor people. Some of them were quite wealthy. They were able to bring horses, cows, goats, and hogs to America. They also were able to bring good farming tools, seeds, and cuttings of fruit trees. These thoughtful Puritans did not neglect to bring fishing tackle. Rods, lines, and hooks used to catch fish are often called fishing tackle. The supplies which the Puritans brought were much better and more plentiful than those the poor Pilgrims were able to bring.

The Puritans knew they would have to face long cold winters. They would need good warm houses. It would take too long for each settler to build his own home. So whenever a new house was to be built, all the people of the town helped. The work was done quickly and easily. Soon Massachusetts Bay Colony had many towns and villages, with Boston as the capital.

PURITAN PENALTIES. The Puritans came to America to be able to worship God as they thought right. Those who belonged to other religions were not allowed in the Puritan settlement. Only members of the Puritan Church could come into the colony. Only members of the Puritan Church had the right to vote. Severe penalties were inflicted on persons who were not members of the Puritan Church. It was partly because of this that some of the Puritans left Massachusetts and started other colonies.

STUDY SUMMARY

1. Terms to know. Be able to tell the meaning of each term listed.

cannon	tackle	Protestant
fort	charter	compact

2. People to know. Be able to tell at least one important fact about each person or group of persons listed.

Pilgrims	John Carver	John Winthrop
Puritans	Miles Standish	Protestants

3. Places to know. Be able to locate on a wall map each place listed. Give one fact about the place as it is located.

   Holland Salem Plymouth English Channel

4. A date to remember. Give the important event that took place on December 10, 1620.

ACTIVITIES

1. Make a set of posters about the Pilgrims to show:
   a. The Pilgrims living in Holland.
   b. On the *Mayflower*.
   c. Landing at Plymouth.
   d. The first town.
   e. Learning from the Indians.
   f. The First Thanksgiving.
2. Make a list of the four animals which the Puritans brought to America.
3. Discuss the living room of a Pilgrim home as to:
   a. A place where meals were cooked.
   b. A great workshop.
   c. A pleasant room.
   d. A useful room.
4. A Character Study. Give one fact to prove that the Pilgrims had each of the following character traits.

brave	willing workers
earnest	grateful

STUDY TEST 11—SCORE 20

This is a test to identify facts in each group.

Group I. Put *C* after each fact that refers to Catholics. Put *P* after each fact that refers to Protestants.

1. They remained loyal to the Pope. ____
2. They left the Catholic Church. ____
3. They denied the authority of the Pope. ____
4. They did not believe in the teaching of the Catholic Church. ____
5. They made up their own form of worship. ____
6. They remained true to the one true Church. ____
7. They disagreed among themselves. ____
8. They quarreled about the form of worship. ____

Group II. Write *Pilgrims* after each fact that refers to the Pilgrims. Write *Puritans* after each fact about the Puritans.

1. They went to Holland to practice their own form of religion. ____________
2. Most of them were poor people. ____________
3. They had a very stormy voyage. ____________
4. They had a very pleasant voyage. ____________
5. Many of them were wealthy people. ____________
6. They signed a compact before they landed. ____________
7. John Winthrop was their first governor. ____________
8. They landed at Plymouth, Dec. 10, 1620. ____________
9. Miles Standish was their military leader. ____________
10. They came to America in the spring. ____________
11. They made their settlement at Salem, Massachusetts. ____________
12. They brought horses, cows, hogs, and goats to America. ____________

OTHER FOUNDERS OF COLONIES

Read to learn

1. Why Roger Williams left the Massachusetts Colony.
2. Why Roger Williams could not return to England.
3. How the colony of Rhode Island was founded.
4. Why Thomas Hooker left the Massachusetts Bay Colony.
5. What the Fundamental Orders of Connecticut were.
6. How New Hampshire was opened up to settlement.

ROGER WILLIAMS

A NEW PASTOR. About ten years after the Pilgrims settled at Plymouth, Roger Williams joined the colony. He was a well educated young man. He was made pastor of the church at Plymouth. After two years Roger Williams left Plymouth. He became the pastor of the Puritan church at Salem. Roger Williams was a forceful speaker. He became well known as a preacher. Very soon he found himself in trouble.

THE RIGHTS OF THE INDIANS. Roger Williams found himself in trouble for two reasons. 1. The Puritans did not like his ideas about religion. 2. The officers of the King did not like Roger Williams' idea that land in America belonged to the Indians.

Roger Williams decided to flee from Massachusetts. He escaped in the middle of winter. The snow was very deep and it was bitterly cold. The paths through the forest

were covered with snow so that it was hard to follow them. Bravely Roger Williams pushed along as shown in the picture. He suffered many hardships. At last he reached the wigwam of an Indian friend. Chief Massasoit had been the friend of Roger Williams for a long time. The chief made his friend welcome. Roger Williams remained with his Indian friends through the winter. He tried to give the Indians some ideas about Christianity. Roger Williams went into the country near Narragansett Bay.

THE FOUNDING OF PROVIDENCE. The Indians gave their friend, Roger Williams, a piece of land for a settlement. A settlement was founded in 1636 by a number of friends who joined Roger Williams. They called their settlement Providence. The settlement was the beginning of the colony of Rhode Island.

RHODE ISLAND. There were many people who liked the ideas of Roger Williams. They believed that his ideas were good. Many followers moved into Rhode Island. A number of towns were settled on the territory granted to Roger Williams. Later, the towns were united under one government. Rhode Island became a prosperous colony.

THOMAS HOOKER

ANOTHER EARNEST PREACHER. The example of Roger Williams was followed by Thomas Hooker. He, too, was a preacher. Roger Williams left Massachusetts for religious reasons. Thomas Hooker left Massachusetts because of the harsh government in the colony. This earnest preacher believed that all the people should have a voice in the government.

THE JOURNEY INTO CONNECTICUT. All the people who attended the church where Thomas Hooker preached believed in his ideas. They believed in his ideas of government just as they believed in his religious ideas. These people were willing to follow Thomas Hooker into the new lands. More than one hundred people made up the group ready to go where Thomas Hooker led them. The men drove all their cattle ahead of them. They drove about one hundred sixty head of cattle out of Massachusetts. It was June 1636 when the journey was begun. There were no roads. The party followed an old

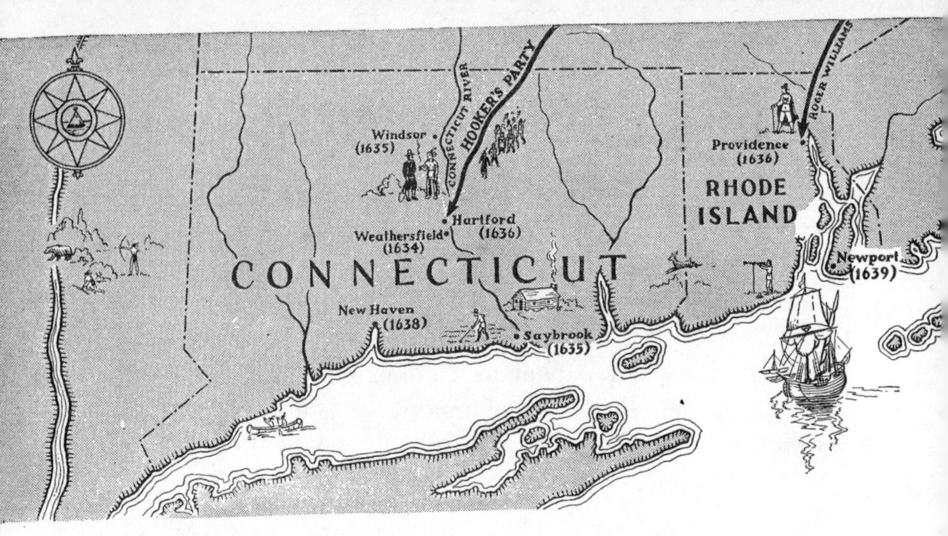

Indian trail. A path across a wild or unsettled region is called a trail. They carried all their possessions with them as shown in the picture on page 105.

THE NEW SETTLEMENT. The new settlement in Connecticut was a success. Eight hundred settlers moved into Connecticut by the end of spring. They built homes in the towns of Hartford, Windsor, and Wethersfield. They chose the sites carefully and the towns grew to be cities.

These people wanted to have a good government. They drew up a set of rules to protect their freedom. This set of rules was called The Fundamental Orders of Connecticut. Fundamental means necessary, and orders are laws. So we may think of the Fundamental Orders of Connecticut as necessary laws or rules for the people of Connecticut. This set of laws protected the rights of the people and gave them a voice in the government. It was a simple step in self-government.

NEW HAMPSHIRE. Between Maine and Massachusetts there was a strip of sea coast. Some fishermen had made a few little settlements along the coast. A few fur traders had cabins in this region. Some farmers from Massachusetts had moved into this land. This part of the country became the New Hampshire Colony.

STUDY SUMMARY

1. Terms to know. Be able to give the meaning of each term listed.

   trail — orders — fundamental

2. People to know. Be able to give two facts about each person whose name is listed.

   Roger Williams — Thomas Hooker

3. Places to know. Be able to locate on a wall map each place listed. Tell one fact about each place.

   Providence — Hartford — Connecticut Valley — Rhode Island — Plymouth — Massachusetts — Connecticut — New Hampshire

ACTIVITIES

1. A debate. Have a debate on the rights of the Indians.
2. Make a table about the New England Colonies.
   Copy and fill in this form.

THE NEW ENGLAND COLONIES			
Name of Colony 1. 2. 3. 4.	When Founded	Leader	Date

3. Character Study. Prove these facts:
   1. Roger Williams was an earnest man.
   2. Thomas Hooker was an earnest man.
   3. The followers of Thomas Hooker had ideals about good government.

STUDY TEST 12—SCORE 15

Draw a line under the word or term which answers the question.

1. Was Roger Williams a poor or a powerful speaker?
2. Did Roger Williams never or always say what he thought?
3. Were the Puritans easy or strict rulers?
4. Did the Puritans like or dislike Roger Williams' ideas about religion?
5. Did the officers of the King believe that the Indians or the King owned the land in America?
6. Was it spring or winter when Roger Williams escaped from Massachusetts?
7. Did Roger Williams think of Chief Massasoit as an enemy or as a friend?
8. Was Providence or Salem the place where Roger Williams made a settlement?
9. Were there few or many people who followed Roger Williams into Rhode Island?
10. Did Rhode Island become a poor or a prosperous colony?
11. Is a trail a road or a path across an unsettled region?
12. Does fundamental mean necessary or unnecessary?
13. Did the Fundamental Orders of Connecticut deny or did they protect the rights of the people?
14. Did Thomas Hooker begin a settlement in Connecticut or New Hampshire?
15. Did the land between Maine and Massachusetts become Connecticut or New Hampshire?

UNIT III: THE ENGLISH COLONIES

LIFE AND WORK IN NEW ENGLAND

Read to learn

1. How the early New England homes were made.
2. How sawmills changed the kind of homes built.
3. The chief occupations of the New England settlers.
4. The importance of the church in the life of the settlers.
5. About the early schools in New England.
6. The amusements and sports which the early settlers enjoyed.

HOMES AND HOME LIFE. The houses of New England were made of wood. Logs were used at first. Later, sawmills were set up on the banks of the swift flowing streams. Now logs could be sawed to make planks. Heavy timbers for house frames, boards for siding, and shingles for roofs were also cut from logs. The settlers were now able to build fine frame houses.

Most of the colonial frame houses built in New England were almost square. A large fireplace was built so that the house could be heated. Wood was the fuel burned in the

fireplace. A large chimney carried off the smoke from the burning wood. Most of the houses built in the early days were one-story high. Later colonial homes two-stories high were commonly built. The roof of the New England colonial house was built steep. This was done so that rain and snow would easily run off. Windows were small to keep out the cold. Glass was very scarce because it had to be brought from England. Oiled paper was often used in the windows. The oiled paper let in the light and kept out the wind. It was difficult to see through the oiled paper so it was not entirely satisfactory for windows. Sometimes a deer skin was stretched across the window. The deer skin kept out the cold but it did not let in much light. Wooden shutters were put on the windows in wintertime to keep out the cold. Shutters are window covers that can be removed. The early settlers in New England suffered greatly during the cold winters. They were not used to winters that were so severe.

OCCUPATIONS. Most of the people who settled in New England were farmers. Their farms were small. These New England farmers worked very hard. The land was filled with stones. The stones had to be cleared from the ground before crops could be planted. The farmers used the stones

to build foundations for their houses and to build fences. Many of these early stone fences may be seen today in New England. The farmers raised corn, grain, beans, and pumpkins. Often the people did not live on the farms. They lived in villages. They went out each day to work in the fields. The homes of the village were often built around an open space. This space was called the Village Green.

Every village had a blacksmith. His chief task was to put shoes on the hoofs of the horses. He made many useful iron articles. Iron pots and kettles for cooking, andirons for the fireplace, and tools for the farmer were made in the blacksmith shop. It was indeed a busy place.

Skilled carpenters took charge of the building of the houses. Settlers who lived near the sea became fishermen or ship builders. Some of the people who lived near the sea became sailors or sea captains. Then there were the lumbermen who went into the forests to cut trees. Some of the early settlers became fur trappers and fur traders. Shoes were made by cobblers. The women and girls spun thread and yarn. They wove both linen and woolen cloths. Of course, the women and girls made the clothing. Butter and cheese, candles, brooms, and furniture were often made in the homes. There was plenty of work to do. The New England colonists were hard working people.

THE CHURCH AND THE PEOPLE. The church was usually the largest building in the village. The colonists considered the church a meeting house. It was an important place. The church was supported by taxes.

Persons who failed to attend church were subject to a fine. The minister or the preacher was usually the most important man in the settlement. He preached at the morning services and again at the afternoon services on Sundays. The people sat on hard wooden benches. The men and boys sat on one side of the church. The women and girls were seated on the opposite.

Often the services were very long. A man was appointed to keep the boys and even the men awake. His method was to use a long stick to poke the sleeper. Sometimes he attached a feather to a long stick. Then he merely had to tickle a sleeper to awaken him.

THE SCHOOLS. The people of New England believed in education. They insisted that their children have schools. The church or meeting house was often used as a school. Some villages had a separate one-room school building. The minister often was the school master.

The children were taught to read, to write, and to do some simple arithmetic. There were few books in the New England colonial schools. Usually the children learned their lessons from a single page. This page was framed between two pieces of thin horn. This kept the page clean and helped to make it last a long time. Such a page was very valuable. It was often called a horn book although it was only one page.

Lessons were taught from a Protestant catechism. A book with questions and answers on the teachings of the Christian religion is called a catechism.

The school term was short. The schools were closed when the boys and girls were needed for work. Boys and girls helped with the planting and harvesting of crops.

AMUSEMENTS. Games and sports which were common in the South were not common in New England. Card playing was popular in the South but card playing was not allowed in New England. The colonists in the South were fond of dancing but dancing was not permitted in the New England colonies.

Men and boys in New England did enjoy hunting. Southern men and boys often went on a hunt for mere sport. They shot animals needlessly. Men and boys of New England hunted only when food was needed.

Drill exercises were looked upon as real sport. It was thought to be fun to drill as soldiers. Games as we know them were rare. Boys did have marbles to play with and girls did have dolls. The dolls were home-made but the girls enjoyed playing with them. Toys were very scarce.

STUDY SUMMARY

---

1. Terms to know. Be able to give the meaning of each term listed.

planks	catechism	village green
		horn book

ACTIVITIES

---

1. Make a list of at least four articles made in the early saw mills.
2. Make two posters to show the change that was made in the type of New England homes.
   a. The early log cabin.
   b. The frame colonial house.
3. Prepare an oral report on—THE EARLY SCHOOLS OF NEW ENGLAND.
4. Make a list of the chief occupations of the settlers in New England.

STUDY TEST 13—SCORE 15

Draw a circle around the correct ending.

1. The colonial homes in New England were made of wood brick.
2. Colonial houses were heated by a stove fireplace.
3. The fuel burned was coal wood.
4. The roofs of the houses were built very flat steep.
5. Glass was very common scarce.
6. Windows were made very large small.
7. Windows were made of glass oiled paper.
8. The colonists found the winters in New England severe mild.
9. Most of the settlers who came to New England were farmers weavers.
10. The early New England farms were large small.
11. Most of the people lived on farms in villages.
12. The church was supported by collections taxes.
13. The children of New England had many books few books.
14. Dancing in New England was forbidden encouraged.
15. Toys in New England were plentiful scarce.

THE MIDDLE COLONIES

Read to learn

1. How Henry Hudson helped Holland.
2. How Holland obtained Manhattan Island.
3. Who the patroons were.
4. What the patroon system was.
5. Why forts were built along the Hudson River.
6. How fur trading began in America.
7. Why Holland and England were rivals.
8. Why England did not let Henry Hudson return to Holland.

TRADERS FROM HOLLAND. The people of Holland in Europe were great traders. There was a time when the people of Holland were called Dutch. This nickname became displeasing to them. The government of Holland, a few years ago, passed a law that the term Dutch was no longer to be applied to their people. Holland is sometimes called The Netherlands.

Traders from Holland were eager to enjoy the rich trade of the East. Groups of merchants in Holland formed trading companies. These trading companies became very wealthy and very powerful.

One of the trading companies hired Henry Hudson. He was an able English seaman. The trading company gave Henry Hudson command of a small ship. This ship was called the *Half Moon*. It had a crew of twenty men. The trading company sent Henry Hudson on an exploring trip to find a route across North America to the East.

THE VOYAGE. Commanded by Henry Hudson the *Half Moon* set sail to find a short route to the East. Henry

Hudson believed that there might be a north-west passage across North America. The idea of a north-west passage was not new. Many men believed that there was some waterway leading from the Atlantic to the Pacific Ocean.

The *Half Moon* sailed from Holland. Hudson steered the boat across the Atlantic Ocean. Weeks later they reached the coast of North America.

EXPLORING. The crew led by Henry Hudson explored along the Atlantic coast. They searched from Chesapeake Bay to Long Island for an opening into the land. Their hopes were high when they noticed that a large river entered the sea just to the west of Long Island. Henry Hudson thought that this stream might be the entrance to the north-west passage for which he was looking.

THE HUDSON RIVER. The *Half Moon* was steered into a beautiful river. They sailed northward on up the river. Soon they saw a natural wall of rock. This cliff-like rock rose straight up from the river. They were looking at the Palisades. A line of lofty steep cliffs like those in the picture is called a palisade.

Before long the *Half Moon* was sailing near the high hills along the river bank. Henry Hudson named the stream the River of Mountains. Today, it is called the

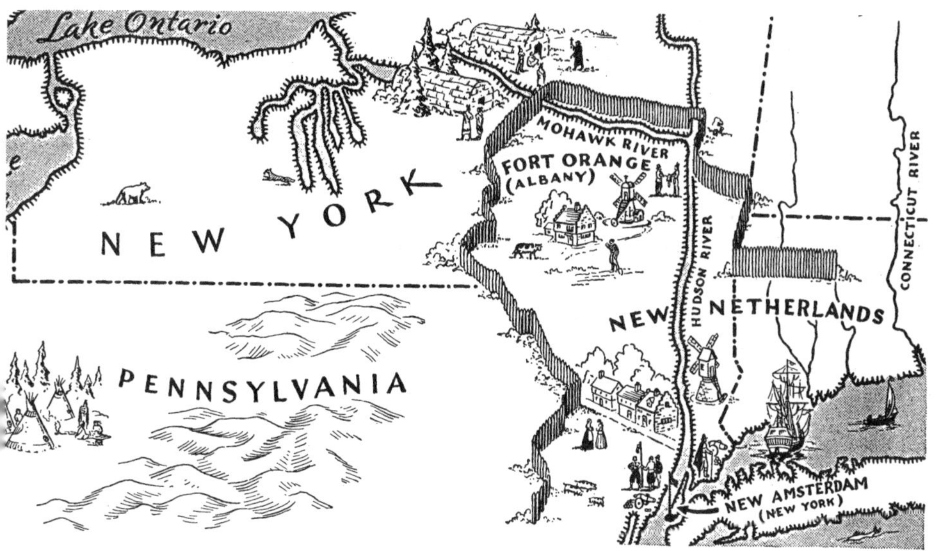

Hudson River in honor of the man who discovered it. Trace this river on the map.

The scenery along the river was very beautiful. It was late in the autumn of 1609. The autumn colors added great beauty. Henry Hudson steered the ship farther northward. The stream was becoming narrow and shallow. This showed Henry Hudson that this river was not a passage across the continent.

HENRY HUDSON AND THE INDIANS. Near the mouth of the river the crew had seen Indians. The Indians had never seen a sailing vessel. The Indians were curious. They wondered what kind of a thing this could be that was sailing on the river. They may have thought that the *Half Moon* was some great water fowl. The Indians were determined to learn about this strange thing. So they paddled their canoes right up to the *Half Moon*. The Indians climbed aboard the *Half Moon*. Henry Hudson gave the Indians gifts and showed them around the deck of the vessel. The Indians left the boat satisfied.

Usually when Hudson landed along the bank he met friendly Indians. They gave the white men gifts of corn, fruits, nuts, and tobacco leaves. The white men gave the Indians gifts of trinkets. There was some real trading between the Indians and the crew. The Indians traded some beaver furs for hatchets and knives.

Henry Hudson realized that the River of Mountains was not a north-west passage across North America. It was getting late in the year for any more exploring. So Henry Hudson steered the *Half Moon* on its return journey to Europe.

HOLLAND'S INTEREST IN AMERICA. The first voyage of Henry Hudson to America caused great interest in Holland. All the land that Henry Hudson explored while sailing under the flag of Holland was claimed by Holland. The merchants of Holland were greatly interested in the fact that the Indians had furs to trade. Traders from Holland came to the island at the mouth of the Hudson River. The traders wished to begin fur trading at once.

MANHATTAN ISLAND. The Indians called the island Manhattan. The Dutch West India Company had been formed to carry on trade with the Indians. Settlers came from Holland to found a colony on the island.

NEW NETHERLANDS. The settlers began to call the region in the New World claimed by Holland the New Netherlands.

Peter Minuit was the governor of New Netherlands in 1626. That same year he decided to buy the island of Manhattan from the Indians. He gave the Indians colored glass beads, brass buttons, gay ribbons, and little trinkets in exchange for the island. These articles were of little value. That is why it is sometimes said that the island of Manhattan was bought for twenty-four dollars. Manhattan is now part of the great City of New York.

A trading post was located in the lower end of Manhattan. A place where supplies were stored and where

goods like furs could be traded was called a trading post. The trading post on Manhattan island was called New Amsterdam. This settlement, which began as a trading post, grew to be the largest city in the New World. Another trading post was started up the Hudson River. It was called Fort Orange. The present city of Albany is on the site of Fort Orange.

THE PATROON SYSTEM. Holland was determined to have settlers in America. The scheme they made for settling in New Netherlands was not a very wise plan. Large tracts of land in New Netherlands were offered to members of the Dutch West India Company. There were only a few rules. 1. The merchant must take at least fifty settlers to the new land. 2. He must pay all the expenses. A merchant willing to undertake such a settlement was called a patron or patroon.

The patroon system did have some advantages. 1. It helped to bring settlers to America. 2. It held the land claimed by Holland. 3. It opened up rich farm lands. The patroon was very powerful. He had the powers of judge and ruler over the farmers on his estate. Some patroons became very stern and very unfair to the farmers. The patroon system had some great disadvantages. 1. The people under a patroon had practically no political rights.

2. Very large estates fell into the hands of a few wealthy patroons. 3. The patroons became interested in gaining great personal wealth.

STUDY SUMMARY

1. Terms to know. Be able to tell the meaning of each term listed.

patroon	Dutch West India Company
trading post	north-west passage
palisades	trading post

2. People to know. Be able to give one important fact about each person named on the list.

Henry Hudson	Peter Minuit

3. Places to know. Be able to locate on a wall map each place listed. Give one fact about the place as it is located.

Hudson River	New Netherlands
Manhattan	Hudson Bay

4. Dates to be remembered. Be able to give one fact about the Middle Colonies on each date listed.

1609	1626

ACTIVITIES

2. Write one paragraph about Henry Hudson.

THE PATROON SYSTEM
I. Advantages
1. 2. 3.
II. Disadvantages
1. 2. 3.

3. Make a list of the articles which were given in trade for Manhattan Island.

STUDY TEST 14—SCORE 20

This is a matching lesson. After each group of words in Column I put the letter of the term in Column II which makes a true ending.

Part I

Column I	Column II
1. The people of Holland were great . . .	*A.* passage
2. Henry Hudson was an English . . .	*B.* mutiny
3. The people of Holland used to be called . . .	*C.* friendly
4. Henry Hudson sailed in a ship called the . . .	*D.* fur trade
5. Natural walls of rock are known as . . .	*E.* seaman
6. Henry Hudson was searching for a north-west . . .	*F.* traders
7. The Indians whom Henry Hudson met were . . .	*G.* Palisades
8. Holland and England were great trade . . .	*H.* Dutch
9. The rebellion of soldiers or sailors is . . .	*I.* rivals
10. Holland established trading posts to protect the . . .	*J.* *Half Moon*

Part II

1. The trading fort in Manhattan was named . . .	*A.* patroons
2. Forts were built to protect the . . .	*B.* estates
3. The Dutch West India Company was a trading . . .	*C.* trading
4. Large tracts of land were given to the . . .	*D.* rights
5. People under a patroon had few political . . .	*E.* unjust
6. The patroons got control of very large . . .	*F.* New Amsterdam
7. Patroons were interested in gaining great . . .	*G.* company
8. Large profits were made in fur . . .	*H.* trade
9. Merchants were interested in the fur . . .	*I.* fur traders
10. Some of the patroons became very stern and . . .	*J.* wealth

LEADERS IN THE MIDDLE COLONIES

Read to learn

1. How New Amsterdam was settled.
2. About the government under Peter Stuyvesant.
3. Why they were called the "bread colonies."
4. How New Netherlands became New York.
5. About the "Charter of Liberties."
6. How William Penn helped the Quakers.
7. How the Quakers differed from other Englishmen.
8. The settlement of Pennsylvania.
9. How Delaware was settled.

PETER STUYVESANT

A STRONG CHARACTER. Among the famous men of New Netherlands was Peter Stuyvesant. He was born and spent his boyhood in Holland. His father was a minister. As a young man Peter grew tired of the quiet and orderly family life. He wanted to lead an active life. He became a soldier. While fighting a battle in the West Indies Peter Stuyvesant lost one of his legs. He suffered this great physical loss without complaining.

Peter Stuyvesant was a big man with a loud voice and a bad temper. He was a brave and an honest man. The fact that he was a very determined man sometimes caused trouble. People did not always understand why Peter Stuyvesant did certain things.

TROUBLE WITH ENGLAND. The English had colonies to the north and to the south of New Netherlands. It was

not very pleasant to have the two groups of English settlers separated by a rival colony. The English were jealous of the success of the colonists in New Netherlands. They had causes for this jealousy. 1. The traders in New Netherlands were becoming rich through fur trade with the Indians. 2. The farm lands held by the patroons yielded good crops. 3. New Amsterdam was an excellent harbor.

The English decided to take New Netherlands.

THE LETTER SENT TO STUYVESANT. An English fleet appeared in the harbor of New Amsterdam. It sailed to within cannon shot of the little fort. This was a very bold thing to do. The commander of the English fleet sent a letter to Peter Stuyvesant calling on him to surrender New Amsterdam. This would mean that Stuyvesant would give over the fort to the English. Peter Stuyvesant could not be frightened into a surrender. He tore the letter to pieces. He did this so that the messenger would report that Stuyvesant was angry and ready to defy England. Peter Stuyvesant made one mistake. He failed to destroy the pieces of the torn letter. Governor Stuyvesant called upon his people to fight against the English. He did not tell the people of New Amsterdam about the terms offered in the letter.

THE SURRENDER OF NEW AMSTERDAM. The people of New Amsterdam were not willing to fight. Many loved peace. The pieces of the letter from the English commander were found. The picture shows some of the men gathering the pieces of the torn letter and trying to put it together. That is how the people of New Amsterdam found out about the terms of surrender. The Dutch refused to fight. The people forced Governor Stuyvesant to surrender without a fight. New Amsterdam was surrendered to the English in 1664. This is an important date to remember because it marked the end of the rule of Holland in North America.

NEW NETHERLANDS BECAME NEW YORK. The English commander now took charge of New Amsterdam. All of New Netherlands was placed under English rule. The king of England gave this region to his brother. The new owner was known as the Duke of York and Albany. The settlement at New Amsterdam was re-named New York. Fort Orange on the Hudson River was re-named Albany. Later, the whole region which had been controlled by Holland came to be called New York.

The English were very happy about this victory. There was no longer a break in the English possessions. They now controlled all the land along the Atlantic Ocean, from Canada to Florida.

THOMAS DONGAN

A GOOD GOVERNOR. Later the King of England sent a very good man to rule New York as governor. Thomas Dongan, the new governor, was a very fine Catholic gentleman. He proved himself to be a very able ruler.

Thomas Dongan thought that the people should have some voice in the affairs of the colony. During his term of office he called an assembly of the people. An assembly is a meeting of law-makers. Governor Dongan guided the assembly. Some very important laws were passed by the New York assembly. One of the laws was known as the "Charter of Liberties." It provided for several changes in the government.

1. It provided for a trial by jury.

2. The people were given the right to vote on certain questions.

3. Freedom of worship was granted.

Freedom of worship would protect Catholics from being punished because of their religion.

Governor Dongan rendered another very fine service. He made a treaty with the Iroquois.

The Iroquois were a warlike tribe of Indians who lived near Lake Erie. Thomas Dongan was so wise in his dealings with the Iroquois that they always remained friends of the English.

SIR GEORGE CARTERET AND SIR JOHN BERKELEY

HOW NEW JERSEY WAS FOUNDED. New York was soon to have a new neighbor. The Duke of York did not seem to understand the value of his lands in New York. He gave a land gift to two of his friends. He granted them the land between the Hudson River and the Delaware River. His friends, Sir George Carteret and Sir John Berkeley, were interested in settling the land.

A band of thirty settlers was sent to establish a colony. At one time Sir George Carteret had been governor of the Island of Jersey. It seemed proper then to call his new colony New Jersey. Sir George Carteret is shown above carrying a hoe. He did this to impress people with the idea that only by honest toil could the colony be successful. A town was laid out and called Elizabethtown.

The next year some Puritans moved from Connecticut into New Jersey. The Puritans built a town, called Newark, on the Passaic River.

Settlers moved into New Jersey in large numbers. All was not pleasant in the new colony. Roman Catholics were denied freedom of worship there. The Indians were friendly and New Jersey became a prosperous colony.

WILLIAM PENN

YOUNG WILLIAM PENN. There lived in England a famous naval officer named Admiral Penn. An admiral is an officer of high rank in the navy. Admiral Penn was a very rich man. He was a good friend of the King of England. The King admired Admiral Penn.

Admiral Penn was very proud of his son, William. Young Penn was a student at Oxford University. William Penn was a thoughtful young man. He gave much thought to religious ideas and religious beliefs. His family and friends were greatly surprised when William Penn joined The Society of Friends. This was somewhat different from the other religious groups which had broken away from the one true religion. People who belonged to The Society of Friends believed that each person was capable of forming his own religious beliefs. They did not think that a church or priest or minister was needed. They believed that every person had what they called an "Inner Light." This light they thought would guide a person in his religious beliefs.

THE QUAKERS. The Friends insisted that in worshipping God there must be a very strong feeling or emotion. This feeling they thought of as a shaking or a quaking of the spirit. That is why the people belonging to this religion came to be called Quakers.

The Quakers were different in other ways than in religious ideas. 1. Quakers favored simple clothes and simple manners. 2. They believed it wrong to have titles. That is why they refused to bow before nobles or even before the king. 3. They did not believe in war. They declared that all men were friends and friends should not fight. 4. Quakers addressed everyone as "Friend." Every person, whether he was a nobleman or a laborer, was called "Friend."

FRIEND WILLIAM PENN. William Penn was not the kind of a young man to keep his new opinions secret. It was the school ruling at Oxford that students wear a cap and gown. Imagine how surprised everyone was when young William Penn appeared in class without his cap and gown. He was wearing the plain, strange clothes of a Quaker.

William Penn wanted all the students to give up the cap and gown. He wished them to wear plain clothes. Young Penn and his Quaker friends were very earnest. They tried to tear the gowns from the backs of the students. This act caused William Penn to be expelled from Oxford. It was considered a disgrace to be dismissed from Oxford.

THE KING OWES A DEBT. Some time later Admiral Penn died. He left a large sum of money to his son, William. Young Penn might have received a larger sum of money but for the fact that the Admiral had loaned money to the king. The king had no money to pay his debt to William Penn.

THE KING PAYS HIS DEBT. William Penn was very sorry for the Quakers. They were often punished because of their religious ideas. This was persecution. When people are treated harshly because of their religion it is called persecution. The persecution of the Quakers caused William Penn great sorrow. Then William Penn got an idea. He thought it would be a good thing to have a place in America for the Quakers. There they would be able to practice their religion.

William Penn went to the king and asked for a grant of land in America. The king liked young Penn. The king

knew that he owed a great debt to Penn. There was no way that the king could pay the debt with money. Penn's request for land seemed reasonable to the king. There was plenty of land in America. Then too, the land grant would cancel the debt. So the king gave William Penn a large grant of land. Every year William Penn was to send the king two beaver skins.

THE FOUNDING OF PENNSYLVANIA. The grant of land given to William Penn was just to the north of Maryland. It had one disadvantage. It had no seacoast. The king named the land Pennsylvania. This means Penn's woods. William Penn was shy and he feared that some of the Friends would think he was proud. They might think he had the land named in his honor. The king settled this worry. He said that the land was named to honor his friend, Admiral Penn.

William Penn set his mind to the task of making a colony in America. It was autumn in the year 1682 when William Penn and his Friends sailed up the Delaware River. He looked for a place to make a settlement. There was a little town located at New Castle. The settlers at New Castle were Quakers and Swedes. They had come to America earlier. The little party led by Penn sailed farther up the river. Here Penn found a place which he thought was suitable for a settlement.

PHILADELPHIA. William Penn chose a good name for the settlement. He called the little town Philadelphia. Philadelphia means brotherly love. The city was laid out on an orderly plan. All streets were at right angles.

THE GREAT TREATY. William Penn made a treaty with the Indians. The Quakers and the Indians promised to live together as neighbors and friends. The Quakers were always fair and just in their dealings with the Indians. This great treaty was never broken.

SUCCESS OF THE QUAKER COLONY. The fame of the colony spread far and wide. Settlers flocked to Pennsylvania. They came not only from England, but from Ireland, Scotland, and Germany. Philadelphia became a prosperous city. Today, Philadelphia is one of the most important cities in the United States. The success of the Quaker colony laid the foundation for Pennsylvania. This state is often called the Keystone state of the United States. It is a middle or key state along the Atlantic coast.

A SUCCESSFUL LEADER. William Penn proved himself to be an able leader in many ways:

1. He held the trust of his people.
2. He won the good-will of the Dutch, English, and Swedish settlers who were already in the region.

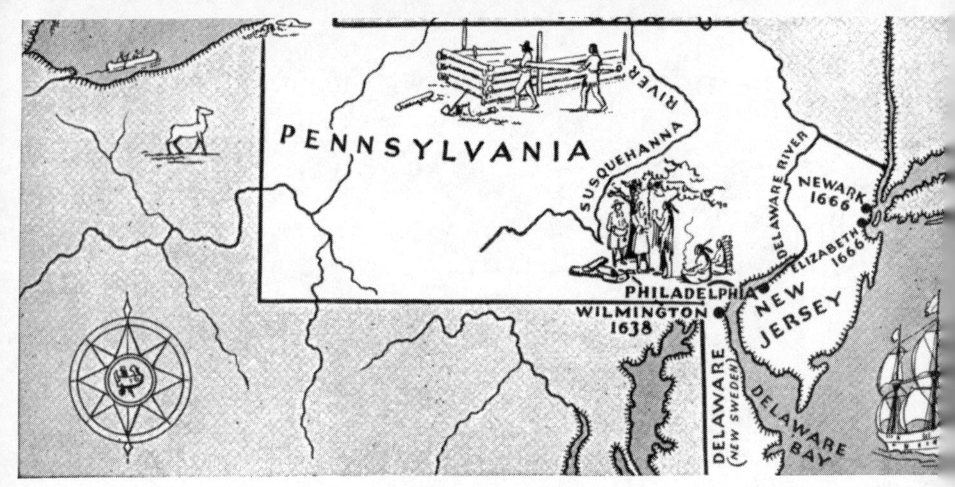

3. He made a great treaty of friendship with the Indians. The Quakers and the Indians never quarreled.

THE SMALLEST OF THE MIDDLE COLONIES

NEW SWEDEN. England and Holland were not the only countries to settle in the Middle Colonies. Sweden, too, sent out colonists.

The Swedes began their settlement not long after the Hollanders settled at New Amsterdam. Indeed the first governor of New Amsterdam, Peter Minuit, helped the Swedes found their settlement. The Swedes bought a tract of land from the Indians. It was located near the present city of Wilmington, Delaware. About five hundred settlers moved into the region which is now the state of Delaware.

When William Penn obtained the charter for his colony, he became the governor of the land occupied by the Swedes. Delaware was given its own government in 1712. Delaware was not really independent. The governor of Pennsylvania was also the governor of Delaware for many years.

STUDY SUMMARY

1. Terms to know. Be able to give the meaning of each term listed.

   "Charter of Liberties" persecution admiral
   "Society of Friends" surrender

2. People to know. Be able to tell one fact about each person or group of persons named.

   Iroquois
   Quakers
   Peter Minuit
   William Penn
   Admiral Penn
   Peter Stuyvesant
   Thomas Dongan
   Sir George Carteret

3. Places to know. Be able to locate on a wall map each place listed. Tell one fact about the place as it is located.

   New York City
   West Indies
   Albany
   New Jersey
   Delaware
   New Netherlands
   Pennsylvania
   Hudson River
   Philadelphia
   Delaware River

4. Dates to remember.

   1. 1664—New Amsterdam surrendered.
   2. 1682—Founding of Pennsylvania.

ACTIVITIES

1. Make a set of posters to show THE STORY OF NEW NETHERLANDS. Be sure to have a scene showing:

   a. Stuyvesant receiving a letter from the English commander.
   b. Settlers piecing the letter together.
   c. Surrender of New Amsterdam.

2. Character Study. Discuss in class the contrasts in the characters of Peter Stuyvesant and William Penn.

STUDY TEST 15—SCORE 20

Identify the great leaders of the Middle Colonies. Put *S* after each sentence which refers to Peter Stuyvesant. Put *P* after each sentence which refers to William Penn.

1. He was born in Holland. ______
2. His father was an admiral in the English navy. ______
3. He was a student at Oxford. ______
4. His father was a minister. ______
5. Everyone who met him liked him. ______
6. He became a soldier. ______
7. He lost his leg in a battle. ______
8. He became a Quaker. ______
9. He did not believe in war. ______
10. He had a very bad temper. ______
11. He was willing to suffer for his beliefs. ______
12. He asked for a grant of land in America. ______
13. He promised to send the king two beaver skins each year. ______
14. He was very strong willed. ______
15. He was forced to surrender New Amsterdam. ______
16. His people trusted him. ______
17. He was feared by many people. ______
18. He won the good will of settlers in neighboring colonies. ______
19. He made a great treaty. ______
20. His people would not fight for him. ______

UNIT III: THE ENGLISH COLONIES

LIFE IN THE MIDDLE COLONIES

Read to learn

1. About the homes built in the Middle Colonies.
2. The chief occupation of these colonists.
3. Why these were called the "bread colonies."
4. How furs were bartered.
5. How the children of the Middle Colonies were educated.
6. The sports and amusements of the colonists of this region.

HOMES IN NEW AMSTERDAM. The homes built in New Amsterdam were not like the log houses built in Massachusetts. Neither were they like the large frame houses built in the South. The Hollanders usually built their homes of black or yellow brick. They were comfortable homes. Gardens of gay flowers were planted around the house. Everything about the house was spotlessly clean. Brass knockers on the doors were kept brightly shining. The pots and kettles in the kitchen were polished. Pretty blue tiles were used to decorate the rooms. Tiles are thin pieces of baked clay. Tiles are now used for roofs, floors, and for ornaments. The Hollanders in America used the tiles to make the rooms look pretty. Picture tiles were set around the fireplace to make it look more attractive. As in New England, the cooking was done at the fireplace which also heated the house.

The furniture was large and comfortable. These people liked comfort. They also liked good things to eat.

The old colonial houses have disappeared in New York. Yet there are many reminders of the days of Peter Stuyvesant. There are reminders of the time when New York City was New Amsterdam and when New York State was New Netherlands.

OCCUPATIONS IN THE MIDDLE COLONIES. Farming and fur trading were the chief occupations of the people in the Middle Colonies.

Farming remained the most important occupation. The fur trade became the most profitable occupation in this region. The farmers in New York and in Pennsylvania worked hard. However, their work was not so hard as that of the farmers in New England. The land in the Middle Colonies was very fertile. The farmers raised wheat, corn, oats, rye, and some tobacco. The soil was rich and the climate was good for the growing of grain. The Middle Colonies came to be called the bread colonies. They raised much grain for the making of flour for bread. Many kinds of vegetables were raised. Fruit trees grew very well in this region.

There was plenty of good grazing land for sheep. The wool was spun into yarn and the yarn was woven into woolen cloth. Many cattle were raised in the Middle Colonies. The dairy products, milk, butter, and cheese were important products in this region.

The people living in the Middle Colonies had plenty of food. They also had a good variety of grains, fruits, vegetables, and dairy products. Food was more plentiful in the Middle Colonies than it was in New England or in the South.

Fur trading was the most profitable occupation in the Middle Colonies. Trading was chiefly by barter. This is a method of trading without the use of money. Usually in trade by barter, goods of great value are traded for goods of little value. Barter is quite different from exchange. Where trading is done by exchange the articles exchanged have an almost equal value. Articles traded by barter are usually of very unequal value.

The Indians trapped and hunted fur-bearing animals. The skins of these animals were taken to the trading post. The trading posts were really places where furs were traded and where furs were stored until they were sent to Europe. Here the Indians bartered the furs for things of little value. Valuable furs were bartered for beads, trinkets, hatchets, and for colored cloth. The trade by barter is what made the fur trade such a profitable business. The fur trade was so profitable that it caused much jealousy and many quarrels. The English quarreled with the Hollanders about the fur trade. At a little later date the fur trade was one of the chief causes of a great war between France and England.

TRADING IN THE MIDDLE COLONIES. Both New York and Philadelphia were good ports. Here ship owners and traders grew wealthy. The Middle Colonies were in an excellent location for trading. There was considerable trading by water between the Middle Colonies and the colonies of New England and of the South. Ships from the Middle Colonies carried on some trade with the West Indies. Cargoes were also sent to the ports of Europe.

The trading posts along the Hudson River were important centers of trade. Here the Indians brought valuable skins to be bartered. The trading posts served also as storehouses for supplies for the settlers.

EDUCATION. Schools were not so common in the Middle Colonies as they were in New England. The schoolhouses built in the Middle Colonies were small. Only a few subjects were taught. The settlers along the Hudson River set up what they called common schools. These schools were for all the children. The common school was founded on the same idea that we now have in public schools. There were public schools in Philadelphia. These public schools were supported by taxes just as public schools today are supported by taxes. There were some church schools. The minister was the teacher in the church school.

After the English captured New Netherlands the schooling of children was neglected for many years. Perhaps the English thought it best to let the children grow up without much schooling. Then it would be easier to teach them English ideas and English manners.

AMUSEMENTS. The settlers of the Middle Colonies enjoyed simple sports. They liked to go hunting and fishing. There was plenty of game in the forests and there were numerous fish in the streams. Skating and sleighing

were enjoyable winter sports. The colonists of this region liked games that they could play out of doors. During the winter it was enjoyable to gather around the fireplace for games and for the telling of stories. Story-telling was a real art among the settlers in the Middle Colonies.

ACTIVITIES

1. Make a table and fill in the items.

MIDDLE COLONIES		
Chief crops raised	Dairy products	Chief animals raised
1.	1.	1. ....
2.	2.	2. ....
3.	3.	
4.		

2. Write one sentence about each term listed.
   tiles   barter   trading post
3. Poster. Make a poster to show Indians bartering furs with the white man.

4. Write three sentences to explain why the Middle Colonies were called the Bread Colonies.

STUDY TEST 16—SCORE 15

This is a matching exercise. Underline the term which matches the first term.

1.	Homes in New Amsterdam	bricks	logs
2.	Homes in Middle Colonies	careless	very clean
3.	Chief occupation	farming	fur trading
4.	Soil	poor	fertile
5.	Bread colonies	New England	Middle Colonies
6.	Most profitable occupation	farming	fur trading
7.	Grazing lands	plenty	scarce
8.	Bread colonies	vegetable	grain
9.	Trade	money	barter
10.	Barter	equal value	unequal value
11.	Trading post	stores	forts
12.	Caused jealousy	hunting	fur trade
13.	Quarrels between the colonists	shipping	fur trade
14.	Ship owners	poor	wealthy
15.	Game	plentiful	scarce

UNIT IV: NEW FRANCE

THE FRENCH COME TO AMERICA

Read to learn

1. How Quebec was founded.
2. How the friendship of the Algonquins was won by Champlain.
3. Where the warlike Iroquois lived.
4. Why the Iroquois became bitter enemies of the French.
5. Why the Iroquois became friends of the English.
6. Why Champlain is called the Father of New France.

SAMUEL DE CHAMPLAIN

THE FOUNDING OF QUEBEC, 1608. One year after the English settled at Jamestown, a party of French colonists came to America. Samuel de Champlain led the party. He planned to start a settlement at Quebec. There were three reasons why this was a good place for a town: 1. The land on the bank of the Saint Lawrence River was nearly level. 2. Right behind the level place there was a high steep cliff or wall of rock. The cliff would be a fine place for a fort. Champlain knew that a fort would be necessary to protect the settlers from unfriendly Indians. 3. The St. Lawrence River would serve as an outlet to the Atlantic Ocean.

CHAMPLAIN, A GOOD LEADER. Samuel de Champlain was a good man to direct a settlement in America. He had been to the New World before. There were three reasons why Champlain was willing to serve as colonial governor of New France.

1. Samuel de Champlain knew that there was a great profit to be made in the fur trade. He was a patriotic man and he desired France to have some of the profit to be gained by the fur trade in America. Champlain was not very much interested in personal gain.

2. Champlain was a real patriot. He wished to extend the boundaries of the French colonies in America.

3. Champlain was a devout Catholic. He wished that the Indians might be converted to the Catholic Faith. He desired to serve his Church and his God.

FARMING IN NEW FRANCE. Governor Champlain knew that the winters of New France were long and cold, and that the summers were short and hot. This meant a shorter growing season than the French settlers were used to in France.

Many of the settlers who came to New France were farmers. It was well for them that the Governor had a knowledge of what crops could be grown in this new land. The soil was thin and rocky. This was not good soil for successful farming. The short growing season and the poor soil were the chief reasons why the colonists of New France were not successful farmers.

THE FRENCH AND THE INDIANS. Governor Champlain made every effort to win the friendship of the Indians. The Indians in the neighborhood belonged to the Hurons and the Algonquins. Champlain succeeded very well in making friends with the Algonquins. Notice that the Indian in the picture is holding out his peace pipe to the French leader. Warlike Indians named Iroquois lived in what is now the state of New York. The Iroquois were bitter enemies of the Algonquins. The Iroquois were angry when they learned that the French had made friends with the Algonquins whom they hated. This friendship with the Algonquins caused the Iroquois to hate the French.

This bitter hatred really checked French settlement towards the south. The French trappers and fur traders had to go far out of their way to reach the interior of America. They knew that the fierce Iroquois would attack them.

THE ENGLISH AND THE IROQUOIS. The English, when they came into the region of New York, found the Iroquois friendly and willing to trade with them. The Iroquois were also willing and eager to help the English in a fight against the French.

English fur traders usually paid more for skins than did the French traders. Of course, the skins were not paid for in money. The Indians were able to get more guns, powder, lead, woolen blankets, knives, and hatchets when they bartered furs with the English. It was more profitable for the Iroquois to take the furs to the trading post at Albany than to take them to the post at Montreal. Montreal was the great fur trading post of New France. Albany was the English fur trading post.

FATHER OF NEW FRANCE. Samuel de Champlain was a man of great courage. It was his courage as a leader that saved the French settlement during the first terrible winter. It was his courage that saved his Indian friends, the Algonquins.

He was a most unselfish man. He sacrificed his time and his ability in service for other people. He never tried to gain personal wealth or honor.

Samuel Champlain was a very patriotic man. He wished to serve France well. He labored hard to strengthen the power of France in America. The early fur trade was directed so that profits might go to his beloved France. He served as governor of New France until his death.

Governor Champlain was a zealous Catholic. A zealous person is eager and enthusiastic. Champlain was eager and enthusiastic about the conversion of the Indians.

The Father of New France was a great man. Perhaps he was so great because he was so good. He always said that a leader should be "a man of God."

STUDY SUMMARY

---

1. Terms to know. Be able to give the meaning of each term listed.
   - cliff
   - zealous
2. People to know. Be able to give three facts about each person or group of persons named.
   - Samuel de Champlain
   - Iroquois
   - Algonquins
   - French colonists
3. Places to know. Be able to locate on a map each place named. Give one fact about the place as it is named and located.
   - Montreal
   - Lake Champlain
   - Albany
   - St. Lawrence River
   - Quebec
   - New York
4. Remember the date when Quebec was founded—1608.

ACTIVITIES

1. Make a list of six articles which were bartered for furs.

2. Write a paragraph giving three reasons why Samuel de Champlain thought that Quebec would be a good place for a settlement.

3. Make a study showing the contrast between the Iroquois and the Algonquins. After each fact which refers to the Iroquois put I; after each fact referring to the Algonquins put A. Another way to arrange this activity would be to make a table listing facts under the headings: Iroquois—Algonquins.

   a. Made friends with Champlain.

   b. Were warlike.

   c. Were saved by the courage of Samuel de Champlain.

   d. Hated the French.

   e. Never forgot the kindness of Champlain.

   f. Remained loyal to the French.

   g. Took the furs to Montreal.

   h. Were defeated.

   i. Became bitter enemies of the French.

   j. Checked French settlement.

   k. Bartered furs at Albany.

4. Write a paragraph describing farming in New France.

STUDY TEST 17—Score 15

Draw a line under the word or the term which answers the question.

1. Was Quebec or Jamestown settled first?
2. Was the land on the river bank at Quebec rocky or level?
3. Was Samuel de Champlain a selfish or an unselfish man?
4. Was the climate in New France colder or milder than that of France?
5. Was the growing season for crops longer or shorter in New France than it was in France?
6. Were the colonists of New France unsuccessful or successful farmers?
7. Did the Algonquins become enemies or friends of the French?
8. Were the Iroquois peaceful or warlike?
9. Was Champlain an enemy or a friend of the Algonquins?
10. Were the Algonquins friends or enemies of the Iroquois?
11. Was the French settlement helped or checked by the Iroquois?
12. Were the Iroquois the enemies or the friends of the English?
13. Were French traders or English traders able to give the Indians better value for furs?
14. Did Champlain labor to strengthen or to weaken the power of France in the New World?
15. Which was more profitable in New France, farming or fur trading?

EARLY AMERICAN SAINTS

Read to learn

1. Meaning of the term pagan.
2. Why Governor Champlain sent for missionaries.
3. About some of the new tasks which the missionaries had to solve.
4. How Father Isaac Jogues was martyred.
5. About "The Lily of the Mohawks."

THE FIRST FRENCH MISSIONARIES. Samuel de Champlain, the Governor of New France, was a devout Catholic. It caused him great sorrow when he thought of his Algonquin friends as pagans. Persons who are not Christians are pagans.

Governor Champlain wished more than anything else that the Indians might be converted to Christianity. He sent an invitation to the Franciscans in France to come to New France. A little band of Franciscan fathers did come as missionaries. Persons who teach other people to know, to love, and to serve Christ are missionaries. They do not usually engage in any occupation because all their time is given to religion. That is why they are often spoken of as religious. Quebec became the center from which the missionaries started on their journeys. Franciscans, Jesuits, and Carmelites all labored among the Indians living in New France.

NEW TASKS. The missionaries made many sacrifices.

1. They gave up the comforts of life in France to live in the wilderness of New France. Unsettled regions are often called the wilderness.

2. They gave up their families and their friends to come among the pagan Indians.
3. It was necessary to learn the languages of the Indians. This was no easy task, because each tribe spoke differently. Indian languages were very different from the French language. It was very difficult to learn the strange language.
4. Missionaries who went into the wilderness found it necessary to prepare, and to eat strange foods.

SAINT ISAAC JOGUES, S.J.

A YOUNG JESUIT. Among the Jesuits who came to New France was young Father Isaac Jogues. He was sent to New France to labor among the Indians. Father Jogues made Quebec his headquarters just long enough to learn something about Indian customs and their languages.

Father Jogues set out for a Huron village. The priest made a hard trip of over nine hundred miles. He journeyed by canoes on the lakes and streams. He travelled many weary miles on foot over forest trails. A path across a wild, unsettled region is called a trail.

A LIVING MARTYR. Father Jogues helped the Hurons in many ways:

1. He visited and cared for the sick.
2. He taught the Hurons the great truths of the Catholic religion.
3. He spent six years helping these Indians.

Father Jogues hoped to be able to labor among the Iroquois. This tribe was not friendly toward the French. The Iroquois hated anyone who was friendly with the Hurons or with the French.

Father Jogues had a young friend, a doctor. The doctor begged to go with Father Jogues on the mission. The Iroquois captured Father Jogues and his friend. The Indians killed the doctor. Father Jogues had to suffer great torture from the Iroquois. Torture is great suffering and pain inflicted by an enemy.

THE ESCAPE. Somehow Father Jogues escaped. He made his way to the English settlement at Albany. The settlers were very kind to the good Jesuit. They sent him to New Amsterdam. Here he was able to get passage on a small ship going to France.

THE HUMILITY OF FATHER JOGUES. The missionary was the center of interest in France. People were eager to hear his story. The superiors of Father Jogues requested him to write the story of his experiences with the Indians. Father Jogues was a good priest, so he obeyed his Jesuit superiors. Their request for his story was fulfilled.

This humble priest wrote his story in Latin rather than in French. He wished to avoid publicity. He knew that fewer people could read the story if it were written in Latin.

People came long distances to honor the great Jesuit. They were eager to kiss the hands that had been tortured. The Queen of France is shown in the picture kissing the tortured hands of Father Jogues. He tried to avoid the praise that was showered upon him. His one wish was that his superiors would permit him to return to New France.

A MARTYR PRIEST. His superiors sent Father Jogues back to Quebec. After two years he was again captured by unfriendly Iroquois. Father Jogues died a martyr. A person who dies for the Faith is a martyr.

This good priest was a martyr and a patriot. He was a pioneer and a patriot. He was a pioneer because he moved into lands that were not settled. He was a patriot because he loved and helped his native land, France.

Father Isaac Jogues and several companions died deaths of martyrs. A chapel has been built on the spot where these martyrs died. Our Holy Father canonized these martyrs in 1929. When a person is canonized it means that the Church has declared the person to be a saint. Father Jogues became Saint Isaac Jogues.

LILY OF THE MOHAWKS

A SAINTLY INDIAN MAIDEN. An Indian girl was born not long after Father Jogues was martyred. Her name was Catherine Tegakwitha or Katerei. Quite often she is simply called "Lily of the Mohawks." This name fits her well. Her life was good and pure. The lily is the symbol of purity. She belonged to the Mohawk tribe.

Catherine was instructed by Jesuit missionaries. She was baptized a Catholic. The story of her life is a beautiful one. She set a noble example by her piety, purity, and faithfulness.

STUDY SUMMARY

1. Terms to know. Be able to give the meaning of each term listed.

torture	trail	"Black robe"
martyr	pagan	missionary
pioneer	canonized	wilderness

3. Places to know. Be able to locate on a wall map each place named. Give one fact as the place is located.

Quebec	Great Lakes
Albany	New Amsterdam

2. People to know. Be able to give at least one fact about each person or group of persons listed.

Father Isaac Jogues, S.J.	Franciscans
"The Lily of the Mohawks"	Jesuits
Hurons	Iroquois

ACTIVITIES

1. Write a paragraph on THE NEW TASKS WHICH THE MISSIONARIES HAD TO LEARN.
2. Character Study. Give one sentence about each of the character traits which Father Isaac Jogues possessed. Discuss only the character traits listed.

brave	humble	zealous
obedient		patriotic

STUDY TEST 18—Score 10

Put *T* after each sentence which is true; put *F* after each false sentence.

1. Samuel de Champlain was governor of New France for many years. . . .
2. Pagans are not Christians. . . .
3. Missionaries made no sacrifices. . . .
4. Indian languages were easy to learn. . . .
5. Quebec became a center for missionaries. . . .
6. Champlain was a devout Catholic. . . .
7. The Iroquois were savages. . . .
8. Father Isaac Jogues died the death of a martyr. . . .
9. Father Jogues wrote the story of his experiences in the French language. . . .
10. The Iroquois were friendly with the French. . . .

FATHER JAMES MARQUETTE, S.J. and LOUIS JOLIET

Read to learn

1. How Father James Marquette helped the Indians.
2. Why the Governor of New France sent Louis Joliet on an exploring trip.
3. How the Jesuit missionary became an explorer.
4. How the explorers reached the Mississippi River.
5. Why these French explorations were important.

JAMES MARQUETTE. James Marquette was born in France. His parents were important people in the town where they lived. They were known for their piety. His mother was related to the great Saint John Baptist de La Salle, the founder of the Christian Brothers. James Marquette was seventeen years old when he began his studies in the Society of Jesus. After completing his course he became a priest. He was sent to America. At Quebec he worked hard to learn the customs and language of the Indians.

MARQUETTE'S FIRST MISSION. Father Marquette was thirty-two years old when he was sent to his first mission. This was located on Lake Superior. Later, he moved to the Strait of Mackinac which connects Lake Huron with Lake Michigan. There he built a little chapel with walls of bark. The new mission was called Saint Ignace. There he instructed the Indians in the truths of religion. Father Marquette worked with all his strength to make the lives of the Indians happier and better.

THE SEARCH FOR THE GREAT RIVER. Several times Father Marquette had heard stories about a great river to the west. He thought that this river might be a passage to the Pacific Ocean. The English, Dutch, and French explorers were all searching for such a passage. Father Marquette heard something that made him very happy. On the feast of the Immaculate Conception, 1672, the Governor of New France had ordered Louis Joliet, a fur trader, to search for the great river in the West. Father Marquette was to go with Joliet. He was to act as chaplain and to report on everything they saw. The following spring they were able to begin their journey. The party was made up of Louis Joliet, Father Marquette, and four other Frenchmen. They took some smoked meat and Indian corn for food supplies. The expedition was placed under the protection of the Immaculate Conception.

THE ROUTE OF THE MISSIONARY. The little party, in two birch bark canoes, paddled along the west shore of Lake Michigan. Then they paddled up the Fox River as far as the portage to the Wisconsin River. A portage means a carrying place. There the canoes had to be carried

to the Wisconsin River. They paddled down the Wisconsin River and in a week's time they were on a great river. It flowed to the south. The Indians called this river Mississippi, which means "the father of waters." This was in 1673.

THE MISSISSIPPI. The canoes floated easily on this mighty river. The current was swift and strong. Almost without effort the party was carried mile after mile until they reached the mouth of the Arkansas River. Here Father Marquette notes, "there were scarcely any more woods or mountains. The islands are covered with shrubs but we could not see any deer, buffaloes, or swans." They were now sure that the Mississippi did not flow into the Pacific Ocean. They realized that it was not a passage to the Pacific. It would be useless to go farther south. It now seemed wise to return home.

THE RETURN TRIP. Going back was hard work. The travelers had to paddle their canoes against the current. Instead of returning by way of the Wisconsin River the party went by way of the Illinois River. The journey was hard on everyone. Father Marquette felt the hardship

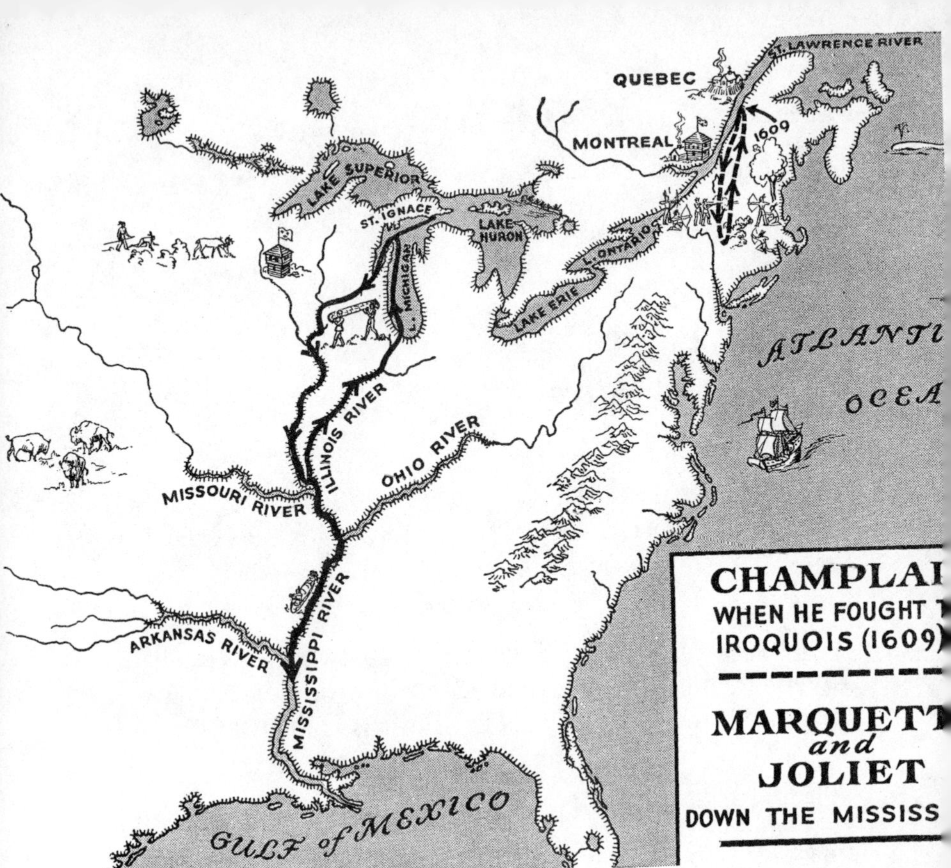

most of all. He was daily growing weaker. Louis Joliet left the party and went on ahead. He wished to report the discovery of the great river to the French governor at Quebec.

FATHER MARQUETTE'S LAST MISSION. Father Marquette at last succeeded in reaching one of the missions on Lake Michigan. There he hoped to rest and recover his health. He did improve for a time. While his strength lasted he traveled as much as he could among the Indian tribes. He felt his end was near and hoped for one last chance to speak to the Indians. He sent word that a meeting would take place.

The meeting took place in a large Indian village. Six hundred camp fires blazed. Father Marquette said Mass for the Indians on Easter Sunday. Then he set out for Saint Ignace, the place he loved to call home.

THE JOURNEY HOME. A number of the Indians went part of the way with him. The party could not travel very fast for Father Marquette was very ill. Finally, the little party had to halt. Father Marquette died saying, "Mother of God, remember me."

THE BURIAL. Father Marquette's worn-out body was buried near the banks of the river that now bears his name. The next spring some of the Indians placed his body in a birch bark coffin. They took it back to the old mission he loved. As they came near the chapel the party was met by two Jesuits. They recited the prayers for the dead. Father Marquette's body was buried beneath the floor of the chapel at St. Ignace.

THE IMPORTANCE OF THESE FRENCH DISCOVERIES. The report of the journey of Louis Joliet and Father Marquette caused great excitement. The explorers had gone far into unexplored territory. France claimed all the land discovered by Louis Joliet and Father Marquette. The value of this land would be great indeed if France could build up trade with the Indians.

STUDY SUMMARY

---

1. Terms to know. Be able to give the meaning of each term listed.

   strait portage

2. People to know. Be able to give five facts about
   a. Father James Marquette, S.J.
   b. Louis Joliet

3. Places to know.
   a. Be able to locate on a wall map each place listed. Give one fact about each place as it is located.
      Saint Ignace Montreal Strait of Mackinac
      Lake Huron Quebec Lake Michigan
   b. Trace the following rivers on a wall map. Be sure to trace a river from its source to its mouth.
      Mississippi River Wisconsin River
      Illinois River Fox River
4. Remember the date 1673, the year Louis Joliet and Father Marquette entered the Mississippi River.
5. CHARACTER STUDY. Give an example from the life of Father Marquette for each character trait listed.
   a. zealous c. devout e. unselfish
   b. kind d. patient f. faithful

ACTIVITIES

---

1. Plan a five day journal such as Father Marquette might have written during the journey.
2. Make a table to contrast the two great French explorers. Use only terms listed and put them under the proper headings.

A STUDY IN CONTRASTS

Father Marquette	Louis Joliet
1.	1.
2.	2.
3.	3.
4.	4.
5.	5.

Spirit of adventure Honor and glory of God
Spirit of service Honor and glory of France
fur trade interested in the Indians
Jesuit priest interested in exploring
patriotic buried at Saint Ignace

STUDY TEST 19—Score 15

Cross out the term or terms which do not belong under the heading. Put a period after the correct ending.

1. James Marquette was born in
   France England Canada
2. Saint John Baptist de La Salle founded
   New France Christian Brothers
3. James Marquette became a
   Franciscan Jesuit Carmelite
4. Father Marquette was sent to
   Montreal Quebec Albany
5. Father Marquette was anxious to
   explore new lands preach the gospel to the Indians
6. The mission house at Saint Ignace was built of
   bricks logs bark
7. The Strait of Mackinac connects
   Lake Erie with Lake Huron
   Lake Huron with Lake Michigan
8. Father Marquette was
   selfish unselfish
9. Louis Joliet was a
   priest fur trader
10. The journey of exploration began in
    spring autumn winter
11. The exploring party was under the protection of
    The Sacred Heart The Immaculate Conception
12. A portage is a place
    where goods are sold
    where goods are carried to another place
13. The explorers entered the Mississippi River in
    1673 1607 1593
14. The return journey was
    easy difficult pleasant
15. Father Marquette's body was buried at
    Quebec Saint Ignace Montreal

ROBERT DE LA SALLE

Read to learn

1. About Robert de La Salle's great plan.
2. How La Salle discovered the Mississippi River.
3. Why England, France, and Holland were such bitter enemies at this time.

A FRENCH ADVENTURE. Robert de La Salle was born in France. He was well educated in the Jesuit colleges. Robert de La Salle was a clever fellow but he was restless. Stories about New France especially attracted him. He came to Montreal as a young man ready to try his luck in the new land.

La Salle settled on a farm on the island of Montreal. He was too restless to be satisfied with the quiet, uneventful life of a farmer. The stories which the Indians told him about the land to the west appealed to him. He sold his farm and decided to go on a journey of discovery.

THE GREAT PLAIN. The country through which he traveled gave La Salle several ideas. One idea was that it should be easy to build up the fur trade of this part of the country. He expected to become rich by selling furs. The fur trade would also be a help to his native land, France. La Salle felt that as soon as the English learned of the money to be made in the fur trade they, too, would send traders into the region. Most Frenchmen felt keenly the rivalry between England and France.

Robert de La Salle was a thoughtful man. He thought out a plan to strengthen the claims of France in the Mississippi Valley. He believed that it would be wise for the French to build a chain of forts along the Mississippi.

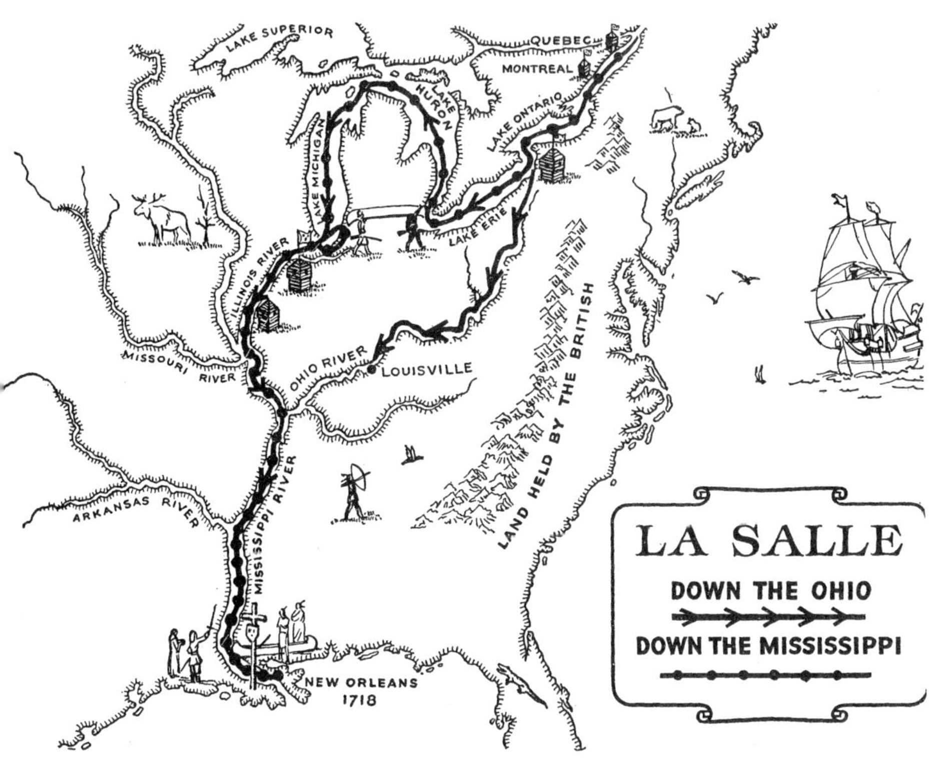

He felt that a strong fort should be built at the mouth or outlet of the river. He was sure that if this plan were carried out France would control almost all of North America. France would then be powerful.

At this time the English settlements were only along the Atlantic coast. All of the English settlements were east of the Appalachian Mountains. The English were not as yet very powerful in America. La Salle thought that it would be well to keep the English east of the mountains. This would help to check their power in North America.

GETTING THE KING'S APPROVAL. La Salle felt that his plan was a wise one for France to follow. So he decided to go back to France and explain his plan to the king.

The king listened to La Salle's plans and granted his requests. When this clever man left France he had the king's permission to do four things.

1. He had permission to explore the wilderness of New France. The wilderness was the unsettled region.

2. He was to explore for the outlet of the Father of Waters, as the Mississippi River was called.

3. He had permission to trade with the Indians for furs.

4. He had permission to build a chain of forts. These forts would serve the fur traders as places to store furs. Best of all the forts would protect the French from their rivals, the English, and the Spanish. These three nations were bitter enemies. They were each struggling for wealth and for power.

THE EXPLORING PARTY. The next step was to get back to New France. La Salle was eager to put his plans into action so he hastened back to America.

A good exploring party had to be organized. La Salle selected some trained backwoodsmen to go with him. Forests which have not been cleared are called the backwoods. There were no settlements near the backwoods. That is why men who lived in regions far from settlements were called backwoodsmen.

Robert de La Salle was wise to have backwoodsmen in the party. These men knew the wilderness region through which the exploring party was to travel. Backwoodsmen usually knew how to get along with the Indians.

A Franciscan missionary, Father Louis Hennepin, was a member of the exploring party. Father Hennepin became a discoverer in his own right. He is credited with the discovery of Niagara Falls. One time Father Hennepin, and two companions, left La Salle's party for a while. They went up the Mississippi on an exploring trip. They thought they would follow the river to its source. The place where a river begins is called its source.

Father Hennepin and his companions came to a waterfall in the Mississippi River. The Franciscan explorer

named it the Falls of Saint Anthony. This was in honor of Saint Anthony of Padua. The Falls of Saint Anthony is one of the reasons why the city of Minneapolis is today the world's greatest flour milling center.

TRIP ON THE MISSISSIPPI. Robert La Salle made two attempts to explore the Mississippi River. The second time his efforts were successful. A small party of French and a few Indians accompanied La Salle on this journey. They paddled along in birch bark canoes. At last they reached the mouth of the great river.

CLAIMING THE LAND. The explorer claimed all the land drained by the Mississippi River for France. Thus a great valley in the heart of the continent became a French possession. La Salle named the land Louisiana. He did this to honor Louis XIV, the King of France.

The act of taking possession of the land was very solemn. A great wooden cross was set in the ground. Then a wooden stake was erected. One of the kettles was used to make a plate bearing the king's arms. Nobles and persons of high rank often used pictures and designs on their shields. This was spoken of as a coat of arms. The metal plate with the king's coat of arms was fastened to the stake. This was a sign that the land had been claimed for France. It was the year 1682 when La Salle claimed the Mississippi Valley for France.

STUDY SUMMARY

1. Terms to know. Be able to give the meaning of each word listed.

   wilderness   source   backwoodsmen

2. People to know:
   a. Be able to give an oral report about
      Robert de La Salle   Father Louis Hennepin
   b. Be able to give two facts about King Louis XIV.

3. Places to know. Be able to locate on a wall map each place listed. Give one fact about the place as it is located.

   Green Bay   Minneapolis   Gulf of Mexico
   Montreal   Niagara Falls   Mississippi River

4. Date to remember. La Salle discovered the Mississippi River in the year 1682.

ACTIVITIES

1. Make a sketch map of North America. Locate and name each place in North America that is mentioned in this chapter.

2. Make a set of posters. Be sure to show
   a. Paddling on Lake Michigan
   b. La Salle explaining his plans to the king
   c. Taking possession of the Mississippi Valley

   Use the posters as oral reports are given.

3. Write a paragraph telling the four things King Louis XIV gave La Salle permission to do.

4. Make a list of the difficulties, disappointments, and trials that La Salle met.

5. Character Study. Give an example to prove that La Salle had each of the following character traits:

brave	thoughtful	good planner
daring	earnest	willing worker

STUDY TEST 20—Score 10

Draw a ring around the correct ending of each sentence.

1. Robert de La Salle explored for
   England Spain France

2. He went to explore for the outlet of the
   Mississippi River Gulf of Mexico

3. La Salle dreamed of building up a great
   fur trade farm region mill town

4. The king gave La Salle permission to explore the
   sea coast Hudson River wilderness

5. France, Spain, and England were
   good friends bitter enemies very neighborly

6. An unsettled region was often called a
   plain wilderness town

7. The place where a river begins is its
   mouth tributary source

8. The Falls of Saint Anthony were discovered
   by Robert de La Salle Father Hennepin

9. Robert de La Salle was not easily
   discouraged disappointed

10. All the Mississippi Valley was claimed by La Salle
    for England Spain France

UNIT V: THE GREAT STRUGGLE BETWEEN THE ENGLISH AND THE FRENCH

FRENCH TERRITORY IN AMERICA LOST

Read to learn

1. How the French strengthened their land claims.
2. Why the English settlements remained along the Atlantic Coast.
3. Three causes for the bitter rivalry between the French and the English.
4. Why the Ohio Company was formed.
5. Why the English colonies were not more united.
6. How the English captured Quebec.
7. The chief results of the French and Indian War.

THE FRENCH AND ENGLISH SETTLEMENTS. The early French colonists made their settlements along the St. Lawrence Valley. A few brave French settlers moved westward and settled along the Great Lakes. Later, the French began to settle in the Mississippi Valley.

The French were clever. They strengthened their claim to the Mississippi Valley. They did this by building a chain of forts from Quebec to New Orleans. The French possessions in North America formed a huge arm which blocked the English advance to the west.

The English settlements stretched along the Atlantic coast. They extended from Maine to Georgia. The English did not go farther than about one hundred-fifty miles inland from the coast. The Appalachian Mountains were like a great barrier between the English and the French lands. As long as the English colonists remained content on the Atlantic coast there was no difficulty.

The real trouble between the French and the English

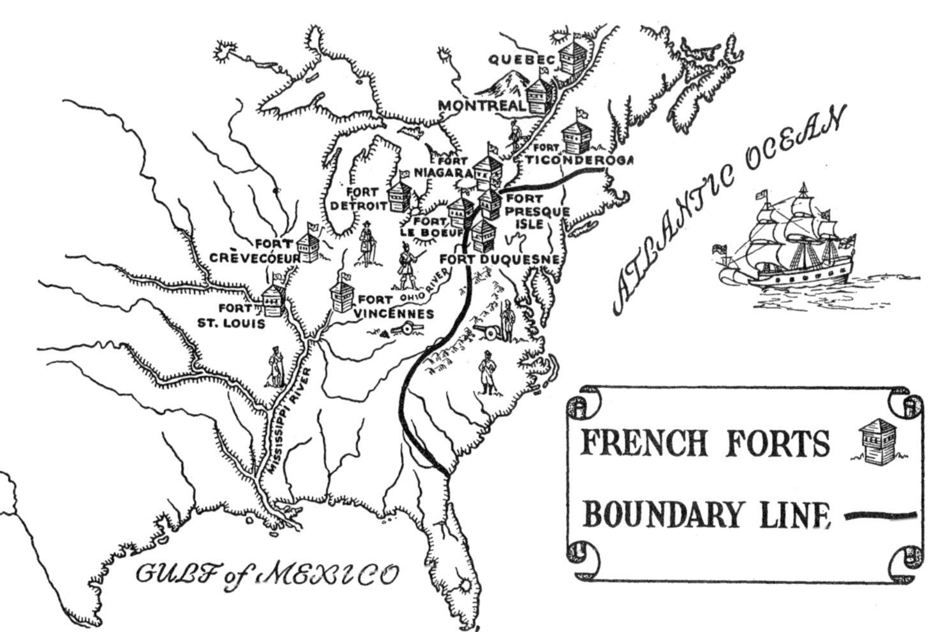

began when the English decided to cross the Appalachian Mountains. These daring English settlers paid no attention to the French land claims. They insisted that the whole territory from the Atlantic Ocean to the Pacific Ocean belonged to England. The daring English began to settle on the disputed territory west of the Appalachian Mountains. Several times the English colonists actually went to war with their French neighbors. It seemed that English and French settlers could no longer live in peace with one another.

CAUSES OF RIVALRY. There were three chief reasons why the English and the French were great rivals. 1. There was great rivalry between England and France in Europe. This rivalry naturally spread to the colonies in the New World. 2. The disputes over the land claims in America added to the bitter feeling between these two nations. 3. There was trouble over the fur trade. The French were very successful fur traders. Somehow the French trappers got along well with the Indians. This fact caused great jealousy on the part of the English fur traders.

THE OHIO COMPANY. The Ohio Valley was a most attractive place. Both England and France claimed this valley. The English tried to strengthen their claim by sending settlers into the region. The Ohio Company was formed for the purpose of settling the Ohio Valley. The French could not hope to send in as many settlers as the English. In America there were fifteen English settlers for every French settler. The French depended upon their forts as a means of strengthening their land claims. The forts were intended as a warning to the English. They were to show that the French intended to hold the Ohio Valley.

THE GOVERNOR OF VIRGINIA TAKES ACTION. The French had built Fort Presque Isle near the present site of the city of Erie, Pennsylvania. They also built Fort Le Boeuf on a branch of the Allegheny River. These two forts were in the region claimed by the English. Locate these two forts in the map on page 167.

Governor Robert Dinwiddie of Virginia heard about these French forts. He was very angry that the French had dared to build forts on land claimed by England. Governor Dinwiddie decided to notify the French to leave the Ohio Valley. He needed a reliable officer to carry the message to the French. Governor Dinwiddie chose George Washington to deliver the important message. Young George Washington was a major in the army of Virginia. The governor trusted the young major.

Major Washington delivered the message to the French Commander. The French refused to leave the Ohio Valley. Before long the French and the English were engaged in a great war. This war began in 1754. It came to be called the French and Indian War. During the time the great struggle was taking place in America a great war was being fought in Europe. In Europe this war was called the Seven Years' War. In America it was known as the French and Indian War.

THE FRENCH AND INDIAN WAR

THE WARRING COLONIES. The English believed that it would be easy to defeat the French. There were only a few thousand French in America when the war began. There were about fifteen times as many English people as there were French people.

There was one great weakness that the English had to overcome. The English settlers of the thirteen colonies were not united. English settlements were scattered all along the Atlantic Coast. The colonies were very jealous of one another. This weakened the English colonies.

Benjamin Franklin, a clever American, urged the people of the English colonies to unite. He realized the danger of a lack of union among the colonies. The colonies could not agree. This lack of union was a great disadvantage to the English. The French profited by the weakness of the enemy caused by the lack of union.

FORT DUQUESNE. Where the city of Pittsburgh now stands, two streams meet to form the Ohio River. The meeting place of these streams was called "the forks of the Ohio." The early explorers and settlers realized that this was a place of importance. It was really the key to the Ohio Valley. Whichever nation controlled "the forks" would also control the Ohio Valley.

The British started to build a fort right at the forks of the Ohio River. The French dared not permit the British to remain in control of this key position.

The French drove the British from the fort they were building. Then the wise Frenchmen finished the fort for themselves. The fort was named Fort Duquesne. This name was given to the fort in honor of Governor Duquesne, who was the governor of New France.

GENERAL EDMUND BRADDOCK. The King of England sent General Edmund Braddock to take charge of the English army in America. General Braddock planned to capture Fort Duquesne. The army under General Braddock was not well suited for the task of capturing Fort Duquesne. Neither the British soldiers nor their general knew anything about the way fighting was done in the New World. All of their training and fighting had been done in Europe.

General Braddock also had four hundred and fifty Virginians under his command. These Virginians were backwoodsmen. The uncleared forests, the unsettled region, was called the backwoods. The men who lived in these regions, far from the settled areas, were backwoodsmen.

The four hundred and fifty Virginian backwoodsmen were clad in buckskin. Skins of deer were made into strong leather called buckskin. The backwoodsmen were experienced Indian fighters. These men had their own way of fighting. They elected their own officers. The British never understood the backwoodsmen.

The British army was a three-fold army. 1. There were the well trained and well clothed British troops sent from England. 2. Next, there were the four hundred and fifty backwoodsmen from Virginia. 3. Last but

not least, there were about fifty Indians. These were brightly colored in their war paint.

General Braddock never seemed to realize the fighting value of the backwoodsmen and of the Indians. He did not believe in their methods of fighting. That is why it is said that General Braddock did not use his forces to the best advantage.

BRADDOCK'S DEFEAT. Suddenly General Braddock found his army caught in a regular backwoods fight. The French and Indians had taken him by surprise. The general was puzzled. He did not know how to direct the battle when the enemy fought from behind the trees and rocks. General Braddock was a man of courage. He tried to encourage his men. Four horses were shot under the brave general. Then he fell seriously wounded. The loss of the leader caused great disorder in the British ranks.

GEORGE WASHINGTON TAKES COMMAND. Young Major Washington took command of the British army. His uniform had been pierced by bullets, but he himself was unharmed. Major Washington succeeded in getting good order among the soldiers. He knew that the British were beaten so he planned an orderly retreat. A retreat

means that an army moves back to seek shelter from the enemy. By leading an orderly retreat Washington saved what was left of the British troops.

The French had won a great victory. They remained for the time the masters of the Ohio Valley.

FROM RETREAT TO VICTORY. After much fighting the tide of war changed. Little by little the French began to lose; little by little the British began to win.

The English in England began to take more interest in the war going on in America. William Pitt was a high official in the English government. He was a clever man because he realized the value of the colonies in the New World. He sent men and ships to aid the English army fighting in America. He also sent an able general, named James Wolfe.

THE LAST FRENCH STRONGHOLD. The French still had control of Quebec, the capital of New France. This was a strongly fortified city. The British General James Wolfe determined to capture Quebec. He knew that if he could take Quebec French power would be broken in the New World.

The French had two good reasons for believing that Quebec could not be captured: 1. Quebec was well protected by Nature. The upper town was built on top of the "Rock of Quebec." This was really a flat plain on top of a steep hill. This plain was called the Heights of Abraham. It would be difficult for an enemy to reach this city perched on top of the "Rock of Quebec." The city could be reached only by climbing steep and dangerous paths. 2. Quebec was defended by General Montcalm. He was a man of great ability and great courage. General Wolfe had a clever plan to capture Quebec.

General Wolfe ordered a picked force of men to embark upon the British warships. The act of getting on a ship is to embark. The warships were ordered to sail along the river quietly in the dead of night. A few days earlier General Wolfe had discovered a path. This path ran from the river up to the Heights of Abraham, where the city of Quebec was located. General Wolfe ordered a landing to be made at the proper place on the river bank. This was at the foot of the path. The British troops landed quietly.

The entire British force reached the Heights of Abraham safely and quietly. The British force numbered four thousand five hundred men. Quickly they arranged themselves in battle formation. The French were greatly surprised. They bravely came out to meet the enemy. The battle was desperate, but it was short. The French were forced to surrender Quebec. To surrender means to give up possession of a thing or place. It was a terrible blow to the French to be forced to give up their capital.

TWO HEROES. General Wolfe, the English commander, was seriously wounded in the Battle of Quebec. He died thanking God that his men had won the victory.

General Montcalm, the French commander, was also seriously wounded. His last words were, "Thank God, I shall not live to see the surrender of Quebec."

FRENCH POWER ENDED IN AMERICA

The surrender of Quebec marked the end of New France. The treaty of peace was signed at Paris in 1763. France was forced to give up her possessions in North America. England was now the strong power not only in the New World but also in Europe.

The map shows how North America was divided by the treaty of Paris.

(1) England took possession of New France. England also took the French territory east of the Mississippi River, except the port of New Orleans.

(2) Spain was given the city of New Orleans. Spain was also given the vast territory between the Mississippi River and the Rocky Mountains.

(3) France was allowed to keep a few small islands near the Gulf of St. Lawrence. These were good fishing stations.

UNEXPLORED
ENGLISH
SPANISH
CANADA
FRENCH ISLANDS
NEW ENGLAND
MIDDLE COLONIES
SOUTHERN COLONIES
OHIO RIVER
MISSISSIPPI RIVER
NEW ORLEANS (Spanish)
GULF of MEXICO
ATLANTIC OCEAN
GLISH
ANISH
ENCH

RESULTS OF THE FRENCH AND INDIAN WAR

The French and Indian War had several definite results.

(1) The power of France in the New World was forever crushed.

(2) The power of England was greatly strengthened in America and in Europe.

(3) The change in land ownership made England practically ruler of the North American continent. England now controlled:

a. The original thirteen colonies along the Atlantic coast.

b. Canada, the land which had been called New France.

c. The land between the Appalachian Mountains and the Mississippi River. This included the Ohio Valley and the Great Lakes region where the fur trade was so profitable.

(4) The American colonists had learned to fight as well as the British soldiers. Their experience as soldiers was to prove of great value to them later on.

(5) The colonists learned that war is expensive. Paying for the war later caused real trouble between the colonies and England.

(6) The war tended to unite the colonies.

THE BEGINNING OF UNION. Before the French and Indian War the colonies had little to do with one another. They were very jealous of one another. The war taught the colonists that they had the same interests. Fighting the French as a common enemy had really united the English colonies in America. This spirit of union became so strong a bond that the colonies were able later to make their great Declaration of Independence. This freed them forever from English rule.

STUDY SUMMARY

1. Terms to know.
   Be able to tell the meaning of each term listed:

embark	rear guard
retreat	buckskin
backwoodsmen	surrender

2. People to know.
   Be able to tell one worth-while fact about each person or group of people whose names are listed:

Benjamin Franklin	George Washington
General Braddock	Governor Dinwiddie
William Pitt	

3. Be able to locate on a wall map each place named. Give one fact about each place as it is located.

Great Lakes	Plains of Abraham
New Orleans	Saint Lawrence Valley
Quebec	Mississippi Valley
Pittsburgh	Ohio Valley

4. Dates to remember:
   a. 1754—Beginning of the French and Indian War.
   b. 1755—British army arrived from England.
   Braddock defeated by the French.
   c. 1763—Treaty of Paris signed at close of war.

ACTIVITIES

1. Make a large sketch map of North America.
   a. Letter in the names of the following places:
   Louisiana Quebec New France
   Acadia New Orleans
   b. Color the areas claimed by England and France about the year 1750.
   c. Draw a circle on each of the following rivers and enclose the number as listed:
   (1) Mississippi River.
   (2) St. Lawrence River.
   (3) Ohio River.

2. Make a large sketch map of North America. Shade or color the territory belonging to each nation after the Treaty of Paris.
3. Write a paragraph telling about THE RIVALRY BETWEEN THE ENGLISH AND THE FRENCH.

STUDY TEST 21—Score 20

Word answers:

1. Settled along the St. Lawrence Valley ....
2. Settled along the Atlantic coast ....
3. Were very successful fur traders ....
4. Settled in the Mississippi Valley ....
5. Began to settle in the disputed territory ....
6. Were far outnumbered by their enemy ....
7. Founded the Ohio Company to settle the Ohio Valley ....
8. Notified the French to leave the Ohio Valley ....
9. Sent by Governor Dinwiddie to carry the message to the French ....
10. Refused to give up the fort ....
11. When the French and Indian war began ....
12. American who urged the colonists to unite ....
13. Sent by the king to command the British army in America ....
14. Planned to capture Fort Duquesne ....
15. British general defeated by the French ....
16. Led an orderly retreat after the British defeat ....
17. English official who realized the importance of the colonies in America ....
18. Decided to capture the capital of New France ....
19. Forced to surrender Quebec ....
20. Thanked God that his men had won a great victory ....

UNIT V: THE GREAT STRUGGLE BETWEEN THE ENGLISH AND THE FRENCH

GEORGE WASHINGTON

Read to learn

1. Something about the boyhood of George Washington.
2. Lessons his mother taught him.
3. Washington, the surveyor.
4. The part George Washington took in the French and Indian War.
5. The valuable services Washington gave to his native country.
6. Some of his fine character traits.

EARLY LIFE. Every twenty-second of February we honor the memory of a great American. George Washington was born on February 22, 1732. His birthplace was Bridges Creek in Virginia. The parents of George were fairly well off. They lived on a very fine estate.

WASHINGTON'S EDUCATION. There is little known about the early education of George Washington. His father died when George was about twelve years old. The father's death caused some changes in the family plans. As a result, George did not receive as good an education as his older brothers did. They had been sent to England to be educated. George was educated in Virginia.

The colonial schools at that time were few and they were poor. However, George Washington was serious about his school work. He attended a country school. There he learned reading, writing, and arithmetic. He also learned some geography and a little grammar. His favorite study was arithmetic. He learned to keep accounts. The boy, George Washington, took great pride in his penmanship. Some of the very neat copy books that he made have been kept as treasures.

A YOUNG SURVEYOR. The real wealth of the people of Virginia in those days was in land. Some of the land owners had so much land that they really had no idea how much they did own. This was because of three reasons: 1. The country was still new. 2. There were very large areas of unexplored land. 3. Not much of the land had ever been measured. There was plenty of work for surveyors in Virginia. A surveyor is a person who makes an exact measurement of land. George Washington decided to study land surveying. It was well that he liked arithmetic because a surveyor must do a great deal of figuring.

A LAND OWNER. His experience as a surveyor gave George Washington a real interest in land ownership. His brother Lawrence became the head of the family when their father died. When Lawrence Washington died George became the owner of the plantation. Lawrence Washington had called his home Mount Vernon. George became very fond, and very proud of Mount Vernon. He was a thrifty man. He began to buy more land. By the time he was twenty-one years old George Washington was one of the large land owners of Virginia.

MAJOR WASHINGTON. Governor Dinwiddie appointed George Washington a major in the Virginia militia. A militia is a band, or group of citizens trained for military service. The militia is not a regular army. Only in times of serious difficulty is the militia ever called upon to serve.

A TRUSTED MESSENGER. About the time that George was twenty-one years old trouble between the English settlers and the French began. The French decided to build forts in the Ohio Valley. Governor Dinwiddie was the governor of Virginia. He decided that the French needed to be warned that the Ohio Valley belonged to the English. Governor Dinwiddie chose Major Washington for the task. This proved to be a wise choice.

Major Washington finally reached the French commander. The letter from Governor Dinwiddie was delivered. The French received Major Washington kindly. They were most polite to the young messenger. Major Washington was given a sealed reply to carry back to Governor Dinwiddie. After a difficult return journey Major Washington delivered the reply to the governor. It was not a satisfactory reply because the French refused to move from the Ohio Valley. This was one of the causes of the French and Indian War. You remember how well

George Washington fought in this war and how he saved what was left of Braddock's army. After the war George Washington left the army and returned home.

Later, when the American colonies rose in rebellion against England, George Washington became the Commander-in-chief of the American army. This great leader served in three armies: 1. The Virginia militia. 2. The British army during the French and Indian War. 3. The American army during the Revolutionary War.

Historians sometimes refer to George Washington as the link between the French and Indian War and the Revolutionary War. Later on you will study about the Revolution and how the United States became a nation. You will learn that George Washington also took an active part in the Revolution.

STUDY SUMMARY

1. Terms to know. Be able to tell the meaning of each term listed:

   plantation surveyor militia

2. People to know. Be able to give one fact about each person named:

   Governor Dinwiddie Lawrence Washington
   General Braddock

3. Places to know. Be able to locate each place listed on a wall map. As the place is located give one fact about the place:

   Virginia Ohio Valley
   Bridges Creek Potomac River
   Mount Vernon Blue Ridge Mountains

4. Date to remember. Be able to give an important fact about the date of February 22, 1732.

ACTIVITIES

1. Make a list of five of the subjects George Washington studied. Underscore his favorite study.
2. A character study. Discuss in class and prove that each term listed can be applied to George Washington.

courteous	thrifty	careful worker	honorable
obedient	trusty	respectful	leader

STUDY TEST 22—Score 15

This is a completion exercise. Fill in each name, date, or term that is missing.

GEORGE WASHINGTON

1. Date of birth ....
2. Birthplace ....
3. Cause of change in family plans ....
4. Where older brothers were educated ....
5. Washington's favorite study ....
6. What Washington did with great pride ....
7. A person who measures land ....
8. Name given to Washington's great estate ....
9. A group of citizens trained for military service ....
10. Where the French were building forts ...... Valley
11. Governor who warned the French ....
12. Intrusted to carry the letter of warning ....
13. Armies in which George Washington served:
    a. ....
    b. ....
    c. ....

UNIT VI: THE BIRTH OF OUR NATION

HOW BAD LAWS CAUSED TROUBLE

Read to learn

1. How the French and Indian War was to be paid for.
2. Some strange English notions about the American colonists.
3. About the House of Burgesses and the Stamp Act.
4. How the colonists began to discuss their rights.
5. How Patrick Henry defended the rights of the colonists.

RELATIONS BETWEEN THE COLONIES. The English colonies did not have much need for contact with one another before the French and Indian War. Each colony had its own problems to solve. There was little reason for knowing, or for trying to understand each other's problems. The colonies dealt with England rather than with one another. Roads were poor and there was little traveling between the colonies. There was some contact through trading. So few people were affected by trade that trade was not important in helping the people of one colony to become acquainted with the people of another colony. During the French and Indian War the colonists really met and had a chance to know each other. England was later to feel the influence of this contact between the colonists.

A CHANGE OF FEELING. The French and Indian War had some very important effects on the American colonists. Some of these effects were:

1. The war gave the colonists a more united feeling. They had all faced the same dangers in the war. They had fought together. They had come to know and to like one another.
2. The colonists had fought well. They knew that they fought just as well as the trained English troops.
3. The colonists felt more free after the close of the French and Indian War. They no longer had to depend upon England to protect them from the French.
4. The war had cost a great sum of money, as wars always do. England thought that the colonies should help to pay the costs of the war.

THE COST OF THE FRENCH AND INDIAN WAR. England was deeply in debt. She paid out huge sums of money to conquer the French in America. Even after the war was over an army was kept in the conquered territory. This cost a great sum of money. The Indians had to be watched and the country had to be kept peaceful.

Who was to pay for the war? Who was to pay the expense of keeping an army in America? These questions came up in the English Parliament. This is the law-making body of the English government. Parliament makes the laws of the land. There was much discussion about the costs of the war. Parliament decided that the American colonies should help to pay the debt. This money was to be raised by taxes. At first Parliament attempted to enforce some old tax laws. This plan failed. Parliament then passed a new tax law called the Stamp Act.

THE STAMP ACT. This law was passed by Parliament in 1765. This was only two years after the end of the French and Indian War. According to this new law the colonists were required to place stamps on all important papers. The storekeeper had to stamp his bills. The banker had to stamp his checks. Every college diploma had to be stamped. Deeds and leases to property, pamphlets, and even news sheets were stamped.

THE EFFECT OF THE STAMP ACT. The Stamp Act made most of the colonists very angry. Although they did not live in England the colonists felt that they should have the same rights as Englishmen. They became aroused and began to discuss the matter even on street corners. The colonists knew that no Englishman would let himself be taxed without having something to say about the tax.

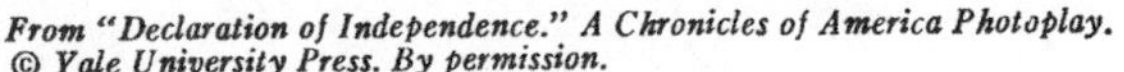

From "Declaration of Independence." A Chronicles of America Photoplay.
© Yale University Press. By permission.

© *International Newsreel Photo.*

Few of the English people living in England thought very highly of the colonists. The English had some queer notions about the American colonists.

1. The English, more or less, looked down upon the colonists.
2. Englishmen thought that it was the duty of the colonies to help to make the mother country rich.
3. They considered it the duty of the colonies to trade only with England and to buy only from England.
4. The English felt that the colonists should do everything that Parliament told them to do.

There were wise men in America who began to see that it would be better if the colonies had a chance to manage their own affairs. Patrick Henry, of Virginia, was one of the first Americans to protest against the unjust laws passed by Parliament.

Patrick Henry had been elected a member of the House

of Burgesses. This was the law-making body of the Virginia colony.

THE RIGHTS OF THE COLONISTS. The meeting of the House of Burgesses was being held and Patrick Henry was there. Patrick Henry rose to speak. He said that the Stamp Act was unjust. He declared that the right to tax the people of Virginia belonged to their own assembly, the House of Burgesses, and not to Parliament. He became more earnest as he spoke. He condemned the methods of the English Parliament and of the King of England. Some of the members of the House of Burgesses were frightened; others were shocked. They thought that Patrick Henry was threatening the King. An attack upon the ruler, or the government is an act of treason. Members of the House of Burgesses cried out, "Treason! Treason!" "If this be treason, make the most of it," answered Patrick Henry. The picture on page 187 shows how this scene looked.

THE BEGINNING OF THE UNION. Time went on and the feeling against the English government grew stronger in America. Wise men saw that the colonies ought to form some kind of a union. They realized that England was taking away their rights.

The colonies were called upon to send delegates to meet in Philadelphia in 1774. This meeting was called the First Continental Congress.

Virginia sent Patrick Henry as a delegate to the First Continental Congress. At this meeting Patrick Henry's good sense was of great value. He explained to the delegates that they needed to become more united. This is the plain way he put the fact of union: "The distinctions between Virginians and Pennsylvanians, New Yorkers, and New Englanders, are no more. I am not a Virginian, but an American."

ENGLAND'S BAD MANAGEMENT. The speeches of Patrick Henry should have been a warning to the English that trouble was brewing in the colonies. The English were stubborn. They could not understand why the colonists were unhappy. They could not understand that the colonists might even fight for their rights.

REPEAL OF THE STAMP ACT. The Stamp Act was repealed by Parliament. It was cancelled not because the English Parliament was willing to admit that the Stamp Act was unjust, but because the law was hurting English merchants.

OTHER BAD LAWS. England made some bad mistakes. Bad laws were forced upon the colonists. The people in Boston were angered by the presence of the king's troops. The royal governor in Virginia dared to interfere with one of the dearest rights of free men. It is an unwritten law that free men have the right to meet. The governor of Virginia would not permit the House of Burgesses to meet in their capital, Williamsburg.

AN IMPORTANT MEETING. The Virginians were determined men. Since they could not meet at Williamsburg they met at Richmond. Old Saint John's Church was chosen as the meeting place. The men who met on March 23, 1775, knew that there was serious business ahead. There was less joking than usual as they stood in little groups waiting for the time of the meeting. The men thoughtfully took their seats in the church. Patrick Henry sat toward the front, in the fifth pew.

A GREAT SPEECH. The meeting opened. Patrick Henry arose and declared that Virginia must arm herself. He plainly said that Virginia must be ready to go to war, if necessary, for her rights.

Try to picture him standing there as the earnest tones of his voice rang on the air: "Gentlemen may cry, 'Peace! Peace!'—but there is no peace! The war is actually begun. The next gale that sweeps from the north will bring to our ears the clash of resounding arms! Our brethren are already in the field. Is life so dear, or peace so sweet as to be purchased at the price of chains and slavery? Forbid it, Almighty God! I know not what course others may take; but as for me, give me liberty, or give me death!"

STUDY SUMMARY

1. Terms to know. Be able to give the meaning of each term listed.

pioneers	Stamp Act	Continental Congress
orator	treason	Parliament
repealed	planters	House of Burgesses

2. People to know. Be able to tell one important fact about each person.

   Patrick Henry　　royal governor

3. Dates to remember. Be able to give one important event which took place on each date listed.

   1763　　1765　　1774

4. Places to know. Be able to locate on a wall map each place listed. Tell one important fact about the place as it is located.

Philadelphia	Appalachian Mountains
Richmond	Williamsburg
Virginia	Boston

5. Character study. Give an example to prove that each of the following sentences might refer to Patrick Henry.
   1. He was very earnest.
   2. He had great courage.
   3. He was a very determined man.

ACTIVITIES

---

1. Give a two-minute oral report on the Stamp Act. Be sure to tell:
   a. Why the British Parliament passed this law
   b. Date
   c. Some of the things which had to be stamped
   d. How the colonists received the news about the Stamp Act
   e. A great American orator who opposed this law
   f. Why the English Parliament repealed the Stamp Act
2. Make a poster showing Patrick Henry making his great speech opposing the Stamp Act.

STUDY TEST 23—Score 20

EITHER—OR. Underscore the word or the term which answers the question.

1. Did the colonies have much or little contact with one another before the French and Indian War?

2. Was the French and Indian War a means of helping the colonists to know one another less or better?
3. Did the colonists fight well or did they fight poorly in the French and Indian War?
4. Do wars seldom or always cost large sums of money?
5. Did Parliament or the House of Burgesses pass the Stamp Act?
6. Was the Stamp Act passed in 1765 or in 1763?
7. Were the colonists overjoyed or were they angry about the Stamp Act?
8. Did Englishmen think that it was the duty of the American colonists to make themselves or the mother country rich?
9. Were the colonists forced to trade only with England or with other countries?
10. Was Patrick Henry a Virginian or a New Yorker?
11. Was Patrick Henry elected to the House of Burgesses or to Parliament?
12. Did Patrick Henry call the Stamp Act an unjust or a just law?
13. Did Patrick Henry think that the House of Burgesses or Parliament had the right to tax Virginians?
14. Was the British Parliament and the King praised or condemned by Patrick Henry?
15. Did Patrick Henry defend or oppose the Stamp Act?
16. Was the First Continental Congress held in New York or in Philadelphia?
17. Was the feeling of the colonists towards England growing better or more bitter?
18. Were English merchants helped or were they hurt by the Stamp Act?
19. Did the royal governor encourage or prevent the meeting of the House of Burgesses?
20. Did Patrick Henry deny the right of the Virginians to arm themselves or did he encourage them to take up arms against England?

BREAKING WITH ENGLAND

Read to learn

1. How James Otis guided the thinking of the colonists.
2. Why the colonists resisted the "Writs of Assistance."
3. About the new taxes.
4. Why the colonists needed the Committees of Correspondence.
5. How Benjamin Franklin served the colonists.

THE BOSTON MASSACRE. Dislike of the British was growing in America. The feeling against England was very bitter in Massachusetts. Two regiments of British troops had been sent to Boston. These soldiers acted like conquerors. The people of Boston became more bitter.

Finally one day there came a real clash between the British troops and the townspeople. This fight was called the Boston Massacre. The cruel killing of people, who are unable to defend themselves, is called a massacre. Several Americans were killed. This was too much for the colonists. Leaders who were thoughtful men began to assume the direction of the colonists.

THREE STRONG LEADERS

LEADERS FOR FREEDOM. Men like Benjamin Franklin, Samuel Adams, and James Otis began to guide the thinking and the activities of the colonists. Samuel Adams and James Otis were about the same age. Both had studied at Harvard College. Both of these men were in-

terested in political questions. Any question relating to government is said to be political because politics is the art or science of government. Men who are active in directing government are sometimes called politicians.

Early in the quarrel between England and the colonies both James Otis and Samuel Adams began to show leadership. James Otis made many splendid speeches. He encouraged the colonists to resist all unfair laws passed by the British Parliament. He was called a rebel because he defied the government. All the colonists who opposed the English were rebels.

Otis was very much against one particular thing that the British did. The English had been very stern about collecting taxes on certain goods coming into the country. Such goods are called imports. The colonists often tried to evade the import tax. This was done by bringing in the goods secretly. This act was called smuggling. It is dishonest to smuggle anything into the country and thus avoid paying the tax. The English determined to stop the smuggling.

The king's officers were given "Writs of Assistance." Written orders are called writs. These "Writs of Assistance" gave the English officers the authority to enter any house and to search for smuggled goods.

THE PROTEST OF OTIS. James Otis was a gifted orator. He made a speech protesting against the "Writs of

Assistance." He declared that "a man's home is his castle." The speech made a deep impression on all who heard it. One man remarked that "then and there American independence was born."

Samuel Adams was strongly influenced by the attitude of James Otis. Adams had advised the colonists not to buy goods made in England while the Stamp Act was in force. Many people followed the advice of Adams. The British merchants soon found that their goods would not sell in the colonies. It was British merchants who forced Parliament to repeal the Stamp Act.

NEW TAXES. King George III of England was very angry about the repeal of the Stamp Act. George III was a very stubborn man but he was not a very wise ruler. He made a very bad mistake when he determined to make the colonists obey his royal will.

A new tax was placed on certain goods imported into the colonies. A special tax was placed on lead, glass, paint, and tea. Samuel Adams rose up in a great protest against this new tax. He advised the colonists not to buy any of those articles which were taxed, no matter how much they thought they needed them.

TEA SENT TO BOSTON. Several shiploads of tea had been sent to Boston. The English tea merchants made the price of the tea very low. Even with the tax the tea was cheaper in America than in England. This was done because the king wished to trick the colonists into buying the tea and paying the tax. Samuel Adams heard of the arrival of the tea. He sent a guard to see that the tea was not unloaded at the Boston wharf. Several meetings were held to decide what should be done. The colonists in other cities to which tea had been sent, said that the tea must be shipped back to England. The matter was not to be settled so easily in Boston. A meeting was held in the Old

© *International Newsreel Photo.*

South Church. The representatives of six towns attended. They resolved that the tea should be sent back to England. The tea merchants, by this time, were willing enough to take the tea back to England. The royal governor at Boston refused to allow the tea to be returned to England. He felt that this would be a sign of weakness because it would be giving in to the colonists. The royal governor believed that the will of the king must be enforced.

THE BOSTON TEA PARTY. The matter was finally settled in a most unpleasant manner. A party of sixty men dressed as Indians marched through the streets of Boston one night. They hurried down to Griffin's wharf. Here three ships loaded with tea were docked. The men shattered open the three hundred and forty-two chests of tea. All the tea was hastily thrown overboard. This was a most unjust act because the tea which was destroyed belonged to English merchants. The colonists had no quarrel with these merchants. Their quarrel was with the king and Parliament. This thoughtless act, which took place in 1773, is often called the Boston Tea Party. It was the beginning of the fight against the English government. A fight against the established government is a rebellion.

COMMITTEES OF CORRESPONDENCE. Samuel Adams realized that there was only one way to resist the harsh English laws. The Americans must be united. They must think and act together. The first thing to do was to let people know exactly what was happening. Someone, or some group, had to take over the job of spreading news.

A Committee of Correspondence was formed in Boston by Samuel Adams. This committee sent news letters by special messenger to all the nearby towns. Soon this idea spread and Committees of Correspondence were formed in all the colonies. The Americans began to feel a bond of union. They knew what was going on in the other colonies. This was the first step in united action. When small groups of colonists met, as shown in the picture, the common subject talked about was the bad English laws.

Photo from International Newsreel Photo.

© Photo from International Newsreel P

ANOTHER GOOD LEADER. The American colonists had another splendid leader in Benjamin Franklin. During the French and Indian War, he advised the colonists to unite. Franklin's advice was of great value as the quarrels between the English government and the colonists grew more bitter.

A GREAT PATRIOT. Benjamin Franklin's greatest work was done in the dark days when the colonists were fighting England. Franklin was an old man by the time Congress sent him to ask France to aid the American colonies. He made the long trip in a sailing vessel. He remained in France for some time. The picture shows Franklin standing before the throne of the King of France.

It was partly through Franklin's efforts that France helped the American colonies. France sent money, guns, ships, and men to help the Americans in their fight against the English.

Benjamin Franklin lived to be eighty-four years of age. His useful life did not end until he had the happiness of seeing America free from English rule.

STUDY SUMMARY

1. Terms to know. Be able to tell the meaning of each term listed.
   massacre repeal rebel Writs of Assistance
   rebellion politics imports smuggling
2. People to know. Be able to give one important fact about each person named.
   Benjamin Franklin George III
   James Otis Samuel Adams
3. Places to know. Be able to locate on a wall map the following places. As the place is located tell one important fact about it.
   Philadelphia France Boston New York
4. Date to remember. Tell the important event which took place in 1773.
5. Character studies.
   a. Prove that King George III had the following character traits.
      quick temper stubborn
6. Discuss in class.
   a. Why smuggling is a dishonest act
   b. Why the destruction of the tea in the Boston Tea Party was unfair.
7. Word study. Be able to give sentences correctly using each word listed.
   a. import imported
   b. politics politician political

ACTIVITIES

1. A dialog. Write a short dialog which might take place between two American colonists just after the Boston Tea Party.
2. A drama. Make a one-act play around the theme of the Writs of Assistance.

STUDY TEST 24—Score 15

MATCHING. After each term in Group I put the letter of the matching term in Group II.

Group I

1. Massachusetts ( )
2. Rebellion ( )
3. Boston Harbor ( )
4. Smuggling ( )
5. Samuel Adams ( )
6. Rebel ( )
7. Stamp Act ( )
8. George III ( )
9. Boston Tea Party ( )
10. James Otis ( )
11. Writs of Assistance ( )
12. British merchants ( )
13. Committees of Correspondence ( )
14. Benjamin Franklin ( )
15. Old South Church ( )

Group II

A. a person who defies the government
B. protested against the Writs of Assistance
C. where meeting to protest the special tax was held
D. a fight against the government
E. stubborn ruler of England
F. harbor where tea was destroyed
G. a law repealed by Parliament
H. forced Parliament to repeal the Stamp Act
I. sent to France to seek aid
J. where hatred for British was very bitter
K. written orders to search homes
L. sent news letters to nearby towns
M. led protest against Stamp Act
N. the beginning of the rebellion
O. bringing goods in secretly to avoid tax

Photo from "Eve of the Revolution." A Chronicles of America Photoplay.
© Yale University Press. By permission.

UNIT VI: THE BIRTH OF OUR NATION

THE FIGHT FOR FREEDOM

Read to learn

1. Why the port of Boston was ordered closed.
2. How the fighting between the British and the colonists began.
3. About the Declaration of Independence.
4. The British plan to cut off New England from the other colonies.
5. The hard winter at Valley Forge.

BOSTON PORT BILL. The Boston Tea Party made the British very angry. The owners lost their tea and the government lost its tax. Worst of all the affair was an act of defiance. An act of defiance is a refusal to obey an order or command. King George III would not overlook that. The people of Boston must be taught to obey. The port of Boston was therefore declared closed. No ships were

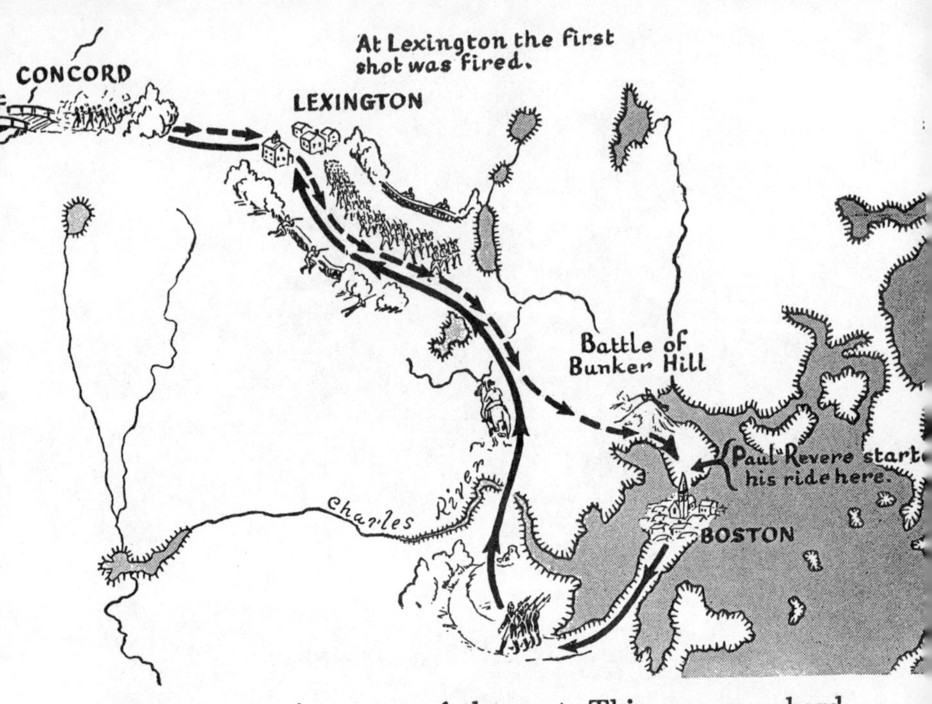

allowed to go in or out of the port. This was very hard punishment because some of the food supply came by way of Boston harbor. It hurt, too, because commerce was very important to Boston. Many people suffered when commerce was stopped.

When the people in the other colonies heard of the trouble of their friends in Massachusetts they planned to aid them. Food supplies were sent overland to Boston so that the people would not have to go hungry.

GENERAL GAGE'S MEASURES. General Thomas Gage was the British commander in charge of the troops at Boston. He began to fear serious trouble. His main quarrel was with the Massachusetts Assembly. He knew that as long as the Assembly was allowed to meet it would find ways to outwit orders from England. General Gage told members of the Assembly that they could no longer meet. The patriots had no intention of obeying this order. Men who were loyal to the colonies were called patriots. They not only met, but they planned to arm the colonists and to fight, if necessary.

PAUL REVERE. The patriots got together a supply of guns, powder, and shot. These supplies were hidden at Concord, near Boston. Companies of men were brought together secretly and they were drilled as soldiers. They were called "Minute Men" because they would fight at a minute's notice. Despite all the care to keep these matters secret, the British learned what was happening. A force of British soldiers was sent from Boston to Concord to capture the Americans' supplies. The Americans had been watching the British closely. The night before they marched out news of their plan was signalled to the patriot, Paul Revere. Paul Revere mounted a fast horse. He galloped along the road over which the British planned to march. At each patriot's home he cried out a warning—"The British are coming!"

LEXINGTON, APRIL 19, 1775. The Minute Men hurried to their secret meeting places. At Lexington, seventy silent, determined men were drawn up on the green just as the sun was rising. The British marched on proudly, their red coats were brilliant in the sun. Captain John Parker of the Minute Men spoke a few words to his sol-

From "Eve of the Revolution." A Chronicles of America Photoplay.

diers. "Stand your ground! Don't fire unless fired upon, but if they mean to have war let it begin here," he said.

The British meant war. Major John Pitcairn, the British commander, called out, "Disperse, ye rebels, disperse!" Not a man moved. The English commander then gave the order, "Fire!" Eight Minute Men fell dead. The Americans fell back, but the fight for freedom had begun. It was to be a long bitter fight.

BATTLE OF CONCORD. The British marched on to Concord. Four hundred Minute Men guarded the bridge leading to that town. The Americans were determined; they held their ground. The British became alarmed. The whole countryside made ready to fight. Every man and boy who could use a rifle was ready to do his part. From behind fences and farm yard walls they fired at the retreating British. The British regulars finally turned and fled. They were badly beaten.

THE CAPTURE OF TICONDEROGA. The news that fighting had commenced spread rapidly throughout the colonies. Bands of patriots from Connecticut and Massa-

From "Declaration of Independence." A Chronicles of America Photoplay.

chusetts took up arms. They got together with the "Green Mountain Boys" from Vermont. This force led by Ethan Allen made an attack upon Fort Ticonderoga in New York. They surprised the British in the middle of the night and forced them to surrender the fort. Valuable cannon and supplies were also surrendered. The Americans needed these supplies.

THE BATTLE OF BUNKER HILL. The first thing for the Americans to do was to get the British out of Boston. The American commander gave orders that the heights above Boston should be taken. The British could not safely stay in the city if the Amercians held the hill overlooking it. One night the Americans started to fortify the hill. They dug trenches and built earthworks. The night passed and with dawn the British understood that they would have to face a hard fight. Three thousand British soldiers charged up the hill. After a bitter struggle the British took the hill, but only after the Americans had used their last grain of powder. The British had the hill; the Americans had the glory.

GEORGE WASHINGTON, COMMANDER-IN-CHIEF. Two days before the Battle of Bunker Hill George Washington had been made Commander-in-Chief of the American Army. He was on his way from Philadelphia to Boston when the news of the battle reached him. Anxiously he asked, "Did the militia fight?" "They did," was the answer. "Then the liberties of our country are safe," he said. American liberty was indeed safe. It was in the care of the immortal George Washington.

Boston was in the hands of the Americans within a year. General William Howe sailed away from Boston to Halifax taking the British army with him. A few months later the American colonies declared their independence from England.

© *Vale University Press. By permission.*
Photo from "Declaration of Independence." A Chronicles of America Photoplay.

THE DECLARATION OF INDEPENDENCE

THE CONTINENTAL CONGRESS. We have already learned that important men from the different colonies met in Philadelphia. The idea of this meeting was to get the colonies to unite. Wise men in America saw clearly that the colonists must stand together and refuse to obey all unjust laws. This meeting of the colonists was called the First Continental Congress. It met in 1774.

AMERICAN FREEDOM. Once the war had begun, it became clear to many American leaders that America ought to be forever free from England. At the Second Continental Congress the question was debated. Finally a committee was appointed to draw up a document. Thomas Jefferson wrote it in simple language. The document is the Declaration of Independence. It contains ideas about rights of the people and it lists many complaints against the King of England. The Declaration of

© International Newsreel Photo.

Independence was adopted July 4, 1776. This date, then, is really the birthday of the United States of America.

The war was now fought for independence. That is why it is often called The War For Independence. Many people refer to this war as the Revolutionary War, or the Revolution. Revolution means change. The American Revolution means a change in government.

THE LONG STRUGGLE

THE FORTUNES OF WAR. The British at first thought that General Washington could easily be defeated. They planned to capture New York and bring the war to a swift end. They did defeat Washington badly at the Battle of Long Island. General Washington met defeat bravely. He kept his little army together and escaped from Long Island during the night.

Day after day Washington and his army had to retreat. The British chased Washington's army all the way across New Jersey. Everything seemed lost for the American cause when Washington suddenly turned on the enemy.

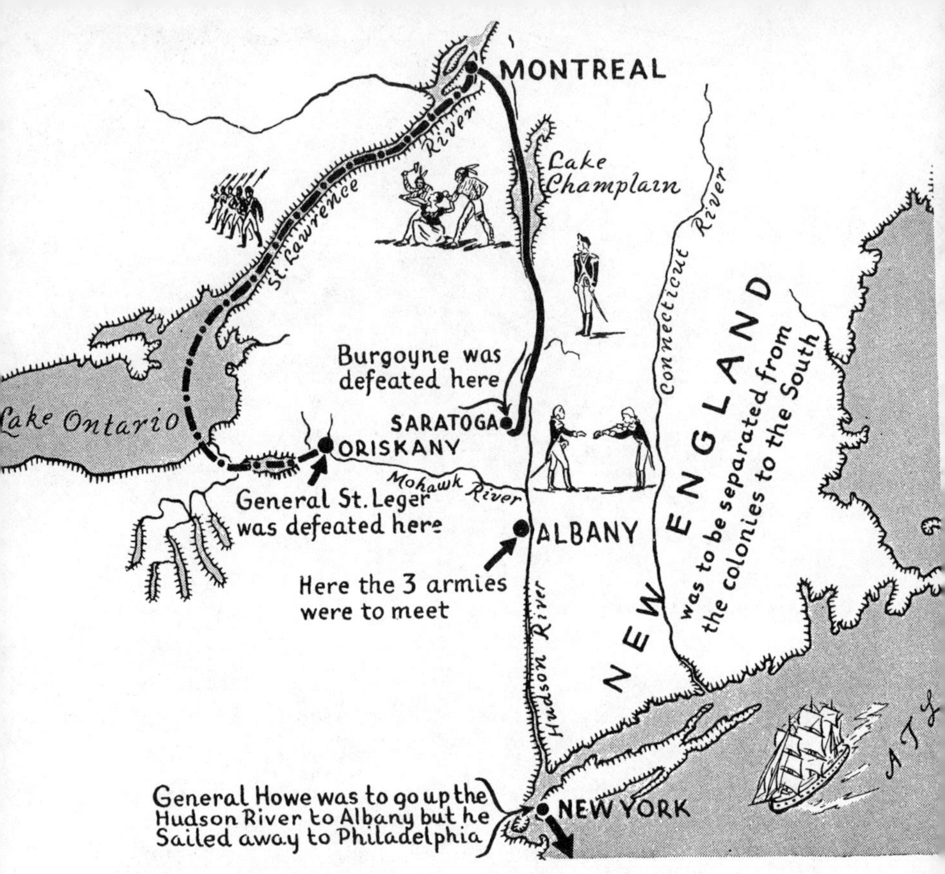

On Christmas night, 1776, Washington led his army across the Delaware River. They attacked the British at Trenton and won a famous victory. Later the Americans won a most important battle at Saratoga.

THE FAMOUS VICTORY AT SARATOGA. The British had failed to end the war quickly. War had been going on for two years. Then the British thought they had a plan by which they could finally beat the Americans. Under this plan three British armies were to invade New York. The first was to come down from Canada. The second was to go up from New York City. The third was to come across the Mohawk Valley from Lake Ontario. All three armies were to meet at Albany. The idea was to cut off New England from the other colonies. The British thought that each section could then be beaten separately. The

plan looked well on paper but it turned out to be a failure. The army that was to cross the Mohawk Valley was beaten by the Americans near Fort Stanwix. The army that was to march north from New York City never got started. This army moved south and captured Philadelphia. General John Burgoyne, who led the main army, was badly beaten at Saratoga. He had to surrender his entire force.

This American victory meant more than just winning a battle. After the American victory at Saratoga, France began to think that the Americans might win. France now helped openly with an army and a fleet. Victory for the Americans seemed nearer, yet Washington's troubles were by no means over.

VALLEY FORGE. Before the winter of 1777 Washington led his army into Valley Forge, Pennsylvania. Here the army set up winter quarters. What winter quarters they were! The men lived in rude shacks, or shelters, made of dead branches of trees. The winter was terribly cold so that the miserable huts gave little protection. There was very little food. Even the animals fared badly. The horses starved to death. Men had to be harnessed to wagons to bring in the little food that could be obtained. Most of the soldiers were poorly clothed. Many were without shoes. Washington saw all this and it nearly broke his heart. Yet he never gave up hope. He prayed for help and victory.

STUDY SUMMARY

1. Terms to know. Be able to give the meaning of each term listed.

Minute Men	rebel	patriot
defiance	retreat	winter quarters

2. People to know. Be able to give one interesting fact about each person named.

General George Washington	General William Howe
Major John Pitcairn	General John Burgoyne
Paul Revere	Thomas Jefferson
General Thomas Gage	Captain John Parker
Ethan Allen	

3. Places to know. Be able to locate on a wall map each place listed. Give one fact about each place.

Lake Ontario	Boston	Ticonderoga
Lexington	Halifax	Bunker Hill
Saratoga	Trenton	Mohawk Valley
Concord	Albany	Valley Forge

4. Dates to remember. Be able to tell one important event which took place on each of the following dates.

   April 19, 1775 July 4, 1776 Winter of 1777-1778

ACTIVITIES

1. Dialog. Have a dialog such as might take place between a patriot and a Tory after the English Parliament passed the Boston Port Bill.
2. Make a poster showing how Paul Revere served his country in the hour of need.
3. Make a sketch map of the North Atlantic coastal lands. Indicate by a dot, and letter, the name of each place listed.

Boston	Concord	Lexington	Saratoga
Halifax	Philadelphia	Ticonderoga	Albany

   Below the map write one sentence about each place located. Tell why it was important.

STUDY TEST 25—Score 25

SELECT THE CORRECT ENDING. Place a period after the correct ending of each sentence. Cross out the endings which are not correct.

1. The Boston Tea Party made the British very
   happy angry jovial
2. King George III decided that the people of Boston should be
   punished praised encouraged
3. The Port of Boston was declared
   open for trade closed to all trade
4. People in the other colonies sent food to the people in
   Massachusetts New York Pennsylvania
5. The British troops at Boston were commanded by
   General George Washington General Thomas Gage
6. General Gage refused to permit the meeting of the
   House of Burgesses Massachusetts Assembly
7. The Massachusetts Assembly planned to arm the
   British American colonists Tories
8. The patriots hid the guns, powder, and shot at
   Boston Concord Halifax
9. Men who were loyal to the American colonies were called
   Tories patriots Britishers
10. The British learned that the Minute Men were
    drilling resting loafing
11. Paul Revere spread the alarm that the British were
    going to Halifax coming to Concord
12. The Minute Men were under the command of
    Captain John Parker General Thomas Gage

13. The fighting began at
    Saratoga   Boston   Lexington

14. The British Commander called the Minute Men
    heroes   rebels   patriots

15. The Battle of Lexington, beginning the Revolution was fought
    July 4, 1776   April 1774   April 19, 1775

16. The Green Mountain Boys captured supplies at
    Ticonderoga   Boston   Lexington

17. Bunker Hill was fortified by the
    Americans   British   French

18. George Washington was made Commander-in-Chief of the
    Minute Men   American army   British troops

19. General Howe moved the British forces to
    Boston   Halifax   Lexington

20. The purpose of the Continental Congress was to get the colonies
    to unite   to quarrel   to defend the king

21. The Declaration of Independence was written by
    Thomas Jefferson   Samuel Adams   George Washington

22. The British decided to end the war by capturing
    Boston   New York   Ticonderoga

23. Washington won a great victory over the British at
    Boston   Trenton   Concord

24. General Burgoyne, a British Commander, met defeat at
    Saratoga   Trenton   Halifax

25. After the Battle of Saratoga the Americans were helped by
    Canada   England   France

UNIT VI: THE BIRTH OF OUR NATION

NAVAL HEROES

Read to learn

1. About the beginning of the American navy.
2. How John Barry served the American colonies.
3. How Congress honored John Barry.
4. About the adventures of John Paul Jones.

BEGINNING OF THE AMERICAN NAVY. The Americans had no navy when the war began. The British had a large fleet of the best ships. Americans had one good thing to start with. American sailors were skillful seamen.

Congress ordered thirteen small ships to be fitted out during the first year of the war. They were small but they were swift sailing vessels. Their crews and officers were bold and skillful seamen. They could not give battle to the great English warships. The best chance the Americans had was to spread out over the seas and to capture British merchant ships. They sailed far and wide. They even dared to cruise into British waters. They entered British harbors and they burned British ships at their own docks. Within three years the little American navy captured five hundred ships. Two of the greatest American commanders were an Irishman and a Scotchman. These men were John Barry and John Paul Jones.

JOHN BARRY

A GOOD SEAMAN. John Barry was born in Ireland. He went to sea and became a good sailor. When he was thirty-six years old he had command of a fine merchant ship. Just then the American Revolution broke out and Barry asked Congress to let him fight for America. The offer was accepted. Barry was given a ship named the *Lexington*. The *Lexington* met and captured the *Edward,* a man-of-war belonging to the British navy.

THE BRITISH BLOCKADE. After this victory Barry went back to Philadelphia. He was given a new ship but the ship was not yet ready. Barry was impatient because he knew that there were British war vessels in the Delaware River. These ships stopped all American boats. They also were bringing supplies for the British army. Barry planned to outwit the British.

A DARING FEAT. Barry started down the Delaware River at night with four boatloads of trusted men. The oarlocks had been muffled so that not a sound was heard. At sunrise Barry found that he was almost alongside a British man-o'-war. Nearby were four supply ships. Everything happened quickly. Barry and his little boats rowed for the man-o'-war. Barry's men were on the decks of the British vessel in a few minutes. The British were so taken by surprise that they forgot to fight. The warship surrendered. Barry captured the four supply ships almost as easily. Both the British and the Americans agreed that Barry's plan was a perfect success. The Americans were delighted with the work of John Barry but the English hated him for his daring deed.

THE FATHER OF OUR NAVY. All through the war Barry continued his good work. Toward the close of the Revolution John Barry was given command of the *Alliance*. She was the finest ship in the American navy. Barry was sent on a mission to France. Going and coming he captured four British warships. Sometimes when Barry could not fight at sea he joined the troops and fought on land. He was a good soldier.

Congress established the regular United States Navy Department after we won our independence. The first officer in the new navy was Captain John Barry. Barry had charge of the building of the American warship, the *United States*. He was in command of her until he left the navy to spend his last days in Philadelphia. Americans gratefully remember Captain John Barry as the "Father of the American Navy."

JOHN PAUL JONES

AN ADVENTURESOME LAD. Another great name in the history of our navy is that of John Paul Jones. Jones was born in Scotland. At first he called himself John Paul. Later he added Jones. He was two years younger than John Barry. The early home of John Paul Jones was near the sea. He was only a boy when he joined a ship. His first long voyage took him to America. He liked it here and decided to stay.

SERVICES TO AMERICA. John Paul Jones went to sea for America after the Revolution broke out. He fought bravely on several ships. At last he found himself in command of a ship that could hardly float. She was an old and almost useless French merchantman. Jones decided to turn the ship into a battleship. He got together a battery of forty guns, most of them as poor as the vessel itself. The guns in a warship are often referred to as a battery. He renamed the ship *Bon Homme Richard,* which means "Poor Richard." This was in honor of Benjamin Franklin. The name was the only good thing about the ship. Jones used this old craft to capture several English prizes. Then he found himself in a fierce naval battle against the fine new British frigate *Serapis.* A frigate was a three-masted war vessel carrying many guns.

AMERICAN PLUCK. The two vessels came close together. They were so close that the muzzles of their big guns almost touched. Only about three of the American

guns were in working order. The American ship took fire. The British captain, thinking that Jones was ready to surrender, called to him, "Have you struck your colors?" "I have not yet begun to fight" answered the daring Jones. The British soon learned that he spoke the truth. The fight was a fierce one. The British were getting the worst of it. At last the British captain surrendered. Jones and his crew worked with might and main to move their wounded men onto the captured British ship. Hardly had the last man left the American vessel when she sank.

STUDY SUMMARY

1. Terms to know. Be able to tell the meaning of each term listed.

frigate	man-o'-war
battery	merchant ship

2. People to know. Be able to give a good description of the services rendered by the two great American naval heroes.

John Paul Jones	John Barry

ACTIVITIES

1. Game of Naval Heroes. Two teams are necessary. Leader will give a short statement of some fact in the life of either John Barry or John Paul Jones. Play this game on the same plan as a spelling bee.
2. Write an imaginary letter. Pretend you were a sailor aboard one of the ships in Barry's fleet. Write a letter to the folks at home telling:
   a. Something about the commander.
   b. How your companions fought the British.
   c. How Barry broke the British blockade.
3. Make a five-point outline of the life of John Paul Jones. Use the outline as a guide in an oral report.

STUDY TEST 26—SCORE 20

TRUE OR FALSE. Put T after each sentence which is a true statement. Put F after each false statement.

1. The Americans had no navy at the beginning of the Revolution. ____
2. There were many skilled seamen in America when the Revolution began. ____
3. The British had no navy. ____
4. American seamen sank British merchant ships. ____
5. Congress ordered thirteen ships built. ____
6. Five hundred British ships were captured by the Americans during the first three years of the war. ____
7. John Barry was an English seaman. ____
8. John Barry asked Congress to let him fight for America. ____
9. Many British war vessels formed a blockade in the Delaware River. ____
10. John Barry led a surprise attack on the British war vessels in the Delaware River. ____
11. The British saw John Barry and his men. ____
12. John Barry succeeded in capturing the four supply ships on the Delaware River. ____
13. Captain John Barry was declared to be the first officer in the navy established by Congress. ____
14. John Barry is called the "Father of the American Navy." ____
15. John Paul Jones was an American-born seaman. ____
16. An old French merchant ship was made into a war vessel by John Paul Jones. ____
17. Battery is a name that is given to a group of guns on a warship. ____
18. John Paul Jones forced the British commander of the *Serapis* to surrender. ____
19. The British learned that the American seamen lacked pluck. ____
20. John Barry and John Paul Jones were the greatest American naval heroes of the Revolution. ____

UNIT VI: THE BIRTH OF OUR NATION

THE TIDE OF WAR TURNS

Read to learn

1. How the winning of the Battle of Saratoga helped the Americans.
2. About the fighting in the South.
3. Foreign friends who helped the American colonists win their freedom.
4. How the Revolution came to an end.

BRIGHTER DAYS. Winning the important Battle of Saratoga was most helpful to the Americans. Its most important result was that France made up her mind openly to help the Americans. Before long the French sent over a fleet of ships and an army. They loaned Congress money and sent us supplies. They kept English ships and English troops busy in other parts of the world. We needed the help of France. Without the French we could hardly have won the war.

WAR IN THE SOUTH. The English were badly beaten in the North so they turned to the South. There they were successful for some time. Savannah, in Georgia, and

Charleston, in South Carolina, were captured by the British. General Cornwallis was in command of a fine army. It was made up of British troops and American Tories. Americans who remained loyal to the British government were called Tories. Cornwallis gave the Americans a bad thrashing at Camden, South Carolina. General Gates, perhaps the poorest American officer, was in command in the South. Cornwallis sent out his troops to conquer the South.

THE COUNTRY RISES. The fight in the South became a grim and a cruel one. It was war between American Patriot and American Tory. Brother fought brother and no mercy was shown. The Patriots had few troops but they had fine leaders. Daniel Morgan was there with his riflemen. No enemy was safe within gunshot of Morgan's men.

Francis Marion was a splendid guerrilla fighter. They called him the "Swamp Fox." He was a terror to the Tories and to the British. He moved swiftly and secretly, and fell on the enemy savagely.

Thomas Sumter, the "Carolina Game Cock," was another keen fighter. Leading a few hundred irregulars he would dash in and attack a British post. He might be beaten off but he soon struck again.

FOREIGN FRIENDS. Americans during the long years of the war had had the help of men from Europe. These men loved liberty and they were willing to help the Americans win their liberty. The brave Marquis Robert Lafayette of France had come to America. "As soon as I heard of American independence my heart was enlisted," he said. Washington loved this brave young Frenchman. He trusted him and found him to be a splendid soldier. Baron de Kalb was a friend of Lafayette's. De Kalb fought bravely for America. He met an heroic death at the Battle of Camden where he was leading the Continentals. The Americans were sometimes called Continentals.

Baron von Steuben came from Prussia. He was a trained officer who had fought with the finest troops in Europe. He became the drill master of the American troops. He taught them how to act in battle, how to fire volleys, and how to make a bayonet charge. He soon turned the American Continentals into well-trained troops.

Thaddeus Kosciusko came from far-off Poland to help the Americans win their freedom. He was an engineer and showed the Americans how to fortify important places, how to build bridges across streams and how to erect earthworks behind which the soldiers could hide.

Photo from "Yorktown." A Chronicles of America Photoplay.

Casimir Pulaski was another brave fighter from Poland. He was an experienced fighter in the wars in his native land. He was exiled to America and offered to fight for his new country. His troops, called "Pulaski's Legion," fought splendidly.

GENERAL GREENE. The American leader, General Horatio Gates, was the pet of some of the men in the Continental Congress. General Gates had been badly whipped at Camden. So Congress now asked Washington to name a commander for the South. Washington gladly appointed Nathanael Greene. Next to Washington, Greene was the finest officer in the Revolution. Greene's army was not large but he had a splendid body of officers. He proved himself to be a good leader.

A series of fights started between Cornwallis and Greene. They fought from South Carolina north to Vir-

© *Yale University Press. By permission.*

ginia. Greene might lose a battle but he never lost his army. He retreated, drew on the enemy and then turned and fought the enemy. Finally, Cornwallis left Greene and went to Virginia. It was a fatal move for the British. Washington sent Lafayette with a small army to oppose Cornwallis. Cornwallis destroyed as much property as he could and then camped at Yorktown. Lafayette was soon in front of Cornwallis. At his back was the York River.

THE END. Washington saw his chance. He urged General Rochambeau, the commander of the French army, to go with him to capture Cornwallis. The two American armies rushed to Virginia. Cornwallis was hemmed in. A French fleet under Admiral de Grasse prevented escape on the water side. The final battle was on.

One of the first Americans to take a British defense was young Captain Alexander Hamilton. The fighting became furious. The Americans and their friends, the French, fought with fine courage. The British fought bravely too,

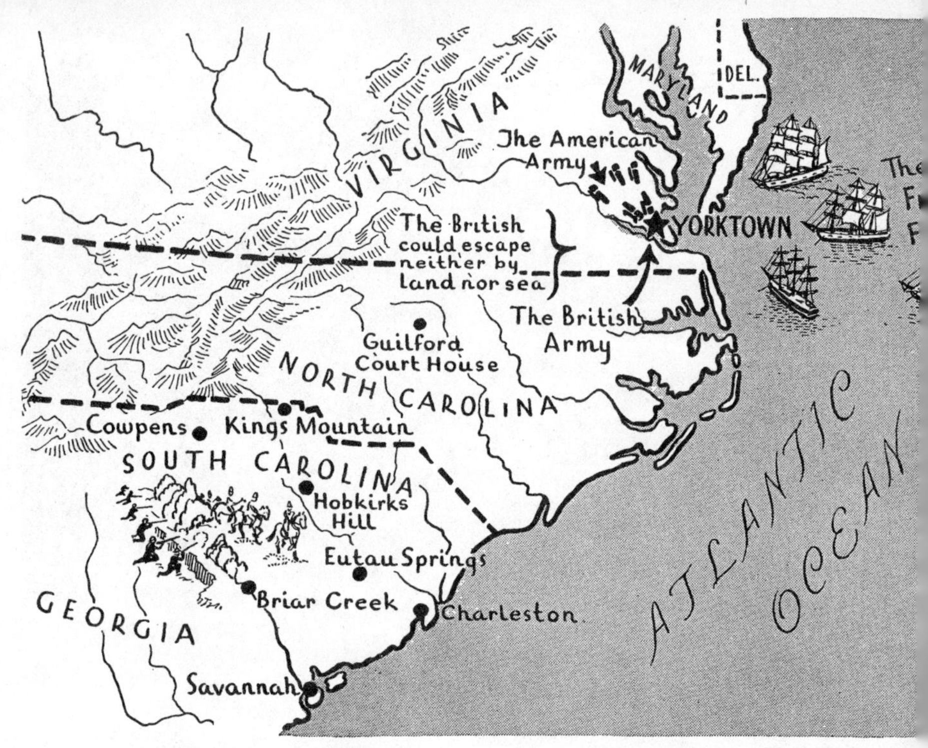

but theirs was a lost cause. Cornwallis saw that he could not win; nor could he escape. Only surrender was left. This took place on October 19, 1781. A British statesman said, "It is all over." He was right. Washington had brought victory to the American armies.

END OF THE REVOLUTION. Fighting ended with the surrender of Cornwallis at Yorktown. The Revolutionary War was over. Americans and English both wanted peace. Each side wanted to say what the terms of peace would be. Another kind of battle had to be fought. It was a battle of wits, a battle to gain every possible advantage in a peace treaty.

America sent some of her cleverest men to Paris where the peace treaty was to be planned. John Adams, Benjamin Franklin, and John Jay represented the new republic. The treaty was finally signed on September 3, 1783. The three most important terms of the treaty were:

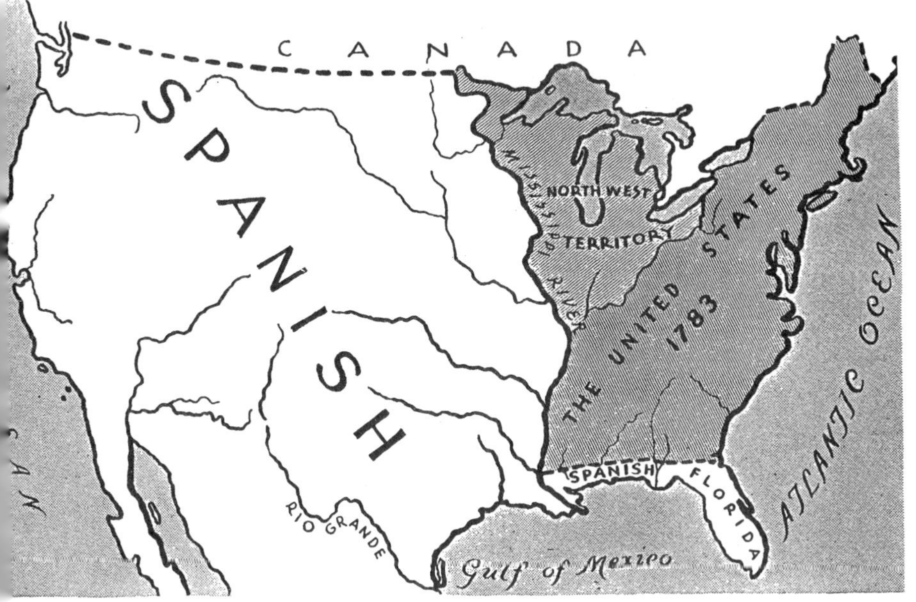

1. The independence of the United States was acknowledged by England.
2. The new nation extended from the Atlantic to the Mississippi and from Canada to Florida.
3. American rights to fish off the banks of Newfoundland were acknowledged.

GEORGE WASHINGTON'S FAREWELL. One of the saddest events in Washington's life was his parting with his officers. General Washington and his men had fought together during the long bitter years of the Revolution. They had learned to understand and to respect one another. The officers were very fond of their leader.

There were tears in Washington's eyes as he said, "Good-by" to his officers. He was very sorry to part from these fine men but he was happy that the war was over.

George Washington felt that now he could return to his home. His beautiful home, Mount Vernon, was on the bank of the Potomac River. Here Washington planned to live in peace and happiness. He could not foresee that ahead of him was yet a great work to be done for his country. George Washington had saved the American colonies. Soon he must save the new nation.

STUDY SUMMARY

1. Terms to know. Be able to give the meaning of each term listed.

   Continentals | Tories

2. People to know. Be able to give an important fact about each person named.

Alexander Hamilton	Francis Marion
Harry Lee	Robert Lafayette
Nathanael Greene	Baron de Kalb
Thomas Sumter	Baron von Steuben
Daniel Morgan	Thaddeus Kosciusko
	Casimir Pulaski

3. Places to know. Be able to locate on a wall map each place listed. Give a fact about the place as it is located.

Philadelphia	West Point	Savannah
Long Island	Charleston	Yorktown

4. Dates to remember. Be able to give the most important event which took place on the following dates.

   October 19, 1781 | September 3, 1783

5. Character study. Give an example to prove that each of the following is true.
   a. Marquis de Lafayette was a loyal friend.
   b. Nathanael Greene was a determined leader.
   c. George Washington was a leader of great courage.

ACTIVITIES

1. Make a list of six foreign friends who came to America and helped the colonists in their fight against England. Tell one important thing each of these foreigners did to help the colonists.

2. Make a sketch map of the land east of the Appalachian Mountains. Locate with a dot and name each place listed.

Trenton	Saratoga	Philadelphia
Camden	Savannah	New York Bay
Yorktown	Charleston	

   Under the map write one sentence about each place listed. Be sure to tell why the place was important in the Revolution.

3. Draw a diagram sketch to illustrate how Cornwallis was surrounded by George Washington and his army, General Rochambeau and the French army, and the French fleet under command of Admiral de Grasse.

STUDY TEST 27—Score 15

IDENTIFICATION. Below each statement put the name of the person you identify with the event. Use only names listed. Cross out each name as you use it. There are two names which you will need to use twice.

1. He sent his troops to conquer the Americans in the South.

   . . . .

2. He was one of the poorest of the American commanders in the Revolution.

   . . . .

3. He led his riflemen against the British in the South.

   . . . .

4. He was a fierce guerrilla fighter.

   . . . .

5. He was called the "Carolina Game Cock."

   . . . .

6. He was a French noble who came to help the Americans win independence.

. . . .

7. He died an heroic death fighting for the Americans at Camden.

. . . .

8. He was the Prussian who drilled the American troops.

. . . .

9. He was the Polish engineer who taught the Americans how to build fortifications.

. . . .

10. He was a Polish exile who fought bravely with the Americans.

. . . .

11. He met a very bad defeat at Camden.

. . . .

12. He was one of the finest officers who served under Washington.

. . . .

13. He fought bravely in the Battle of Yorktown.

. . . .

14. He led the Americans to victory at Yorktown.

. . . .

15. He was forced to surrender his army at Yorktown.

. . . .

Francis Marion	Casimir Pulaski
Daniel Morgan	General Horatio Gates (2)
George Washington	Gen. Charles Cornwallis (2)
Alexander Hamilton	Nathanael Greene
Thaddeus Kosciusko	Baron von Steuben
Baron de Kalb	Marquis Lafayette

Thomas Sumter

THE WINNING OF THE WEST

Read to learn

1. Where the West was.
2. How Daniel Boone explored the wilderness.
3. Why a search for salt was made.
4. Why the Ohio Valley was worth fighting for.
5. How George Rogers Clark won the Northwest.

THE "WEST" OF THE EARLY DAYS. People living at the time of the Revolution thought of the "West" as the country just beyond the Appalachian Mountains. The "West" was only a few hundred miles from the seacoast. Few people had seen the land beyond the mountains. Soon, however, this country was to become better known because of Daniel Boone, George Rogers Clark, and other pioneers. People who move into unsettled lands are known as pioneers.

DANIEL BOONE

THE BOONE FAMILY. Daniel Boone's father was a Quaker who lived in England. Having heard fine reports of America, Friend Boone decided to come to America to make his home here. He settled in the wilderness of Pennsylvania. The unsettled area was referred to as the wilderness. There were few homes in the wilderness so the Boones lived rather lonely lives. The soil was not much good for farming but the woods were full of game. There was plenty to eat for the eleven Boone children, all of whom had good appetites.

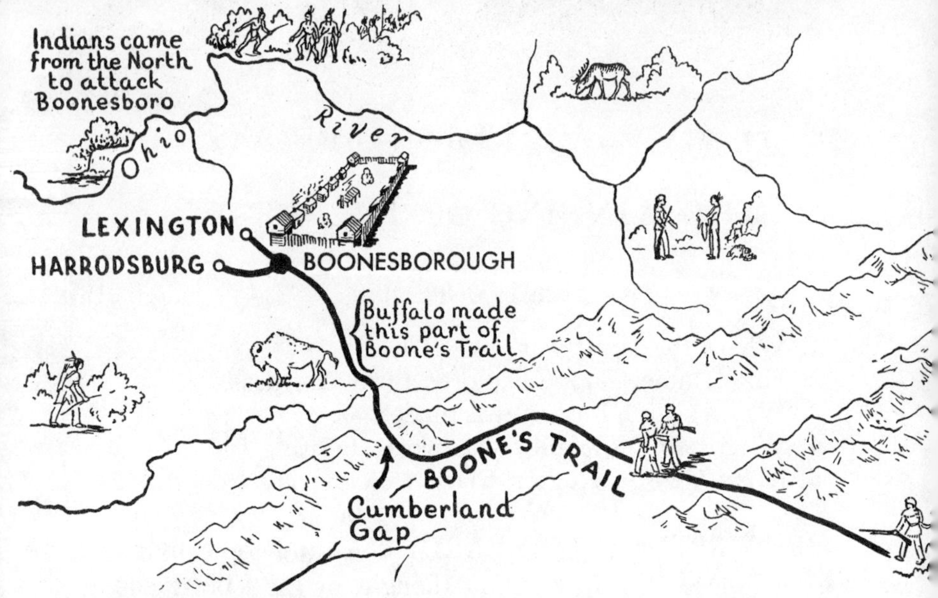

After a time the Boone family left the wilderness of Pennsylvania. They moved to North Carolina where they settled. Here Daniel met a young lady who was willing to marry him. The young couple went to live on a small farm but Daniel Boone was not suited to the quiet, uneventful life of a farmer.

LOVE FOR EXPLORING. Daniel Boone did not like farm life in North Carolina. He would rather go off on exploring expeditions. Most of his time was spent away from home. One time Boone and a companion made their way westward into the wilds of Kentucky.

BOONESBOROUGH. Daniel Boone loved Kentucky. He hoped that he would be able to get several families to form a party for the settlement of this new country. First he succeeded in persuading his two brothers to move to Kentucky. The Boone brothers began their journey into the wilderness in the year 1773. The path by which they went into Kentucky became known as the "Wilderness Road." It was the first road across the mountains. Later the Boones were joined by five other families. Their party had to keep constant watch lest the Indians

attack them. This caused delay. It was nearly two years after leaving Carolina before the party reached the banks of the Kentucky River. They found a good place for a settlement which they called Boonesborough. Borough means a small town. This town was named in honor of Daniel Boone.

THE SEARCH FOR SALT. The little settlement managed somehow to exist in spite of many dangers. During one winter the people suffered much from the lack of salt. Boone knew where salt could be found. With a party of backwoodsmen he set out for a place which was called "Lower Blue Lick." The place was so named because herds of buffalo went there to lick the salt rocks. There were also many springs of salt water in the neighborhood. Boone planned to get salt by boiling away the water until only salt remained. He decided to lay in a large supply.

A CAPTIVE. One day Boone and some of his men were surprised by a large party of Shawnee Indians. Boone was captured by the Indians. He advised the men of his party to surrender. He knew that if they fought they would all

© Yale University Press. By permission.
Photo from "Daniel Boone." A Chronicles of America Photoplay.

be killed. Boone feared that the Indians would move on to Boonesborough and kill the people there. Boone was marched through the woods to the Indian camp at Detroit. Meanwhile he had planned to escape. He made believe he liked the Indians and their ways. The old Indian chief took a great fancy to Boone. He offered to adopt him into the tribe. Boone politely accepted the honor though it took great courage to do so.

THE WHITE INDIAN. The ceremony of adoption was not too pleasant. Boone's hair was pulled out of his head in small bunches. Only the scalp-lock on the top of his head was spared. He was given a bath, Indian fashion. Next the Indians gave Boone's face a thick coat of war paint. When the ceremony was over the Indians allowed Boone to go hunting. He never went back to the Indian camp. Instead he pushed on for Boonesborough. He had no food. He did not dare shoot game for fear the Indians would hear his gun. Boone knew the Indians would follow him. They would try to trace his footsteps. Boone covered his tracks by crossing and recrossing streams.

The whole distance between the Indian camp and Boonesborough was more than one hundred and sixty miles. Boone covered this distance in less than five days.

Daniel Boone warned the little settlement of the danger of an Indian attack. The men prepared for the coming fight. The Revolutionary War was still going on so the Indians had English help. Soon they moved against the fort. The Americans were ready for the attack. They drove off the Indians and their English allies.

THE LURE OF THE WEST. After the war Boonesborough enjoyed peace, but Daniel Boone did not care to remain. Kentucky was becoming too crowded to please Boone. He still loved the wilderness. He decided to move farther west where he could have more "elbow-room." Packing up his belongings he moved to what is now the state of Missouri. Here he continued to roam the wilds he loved so well.

Daniel Boone died in his eighty-seventh year. The westward movement, which he had helped to start, was opening a new frontier. Many settlers were moving into the West, there to build up one of the richest sections of our country.

GEORGE ROGERS CLARK

THE NORTHWEST TERRITORY. The valley of the Ohio River was rich country. France had claimed it, England had taken it from France, and now the Americans wanted it. This is how it all happened:

1. The English, helped by the American colonists, had won the Ohio Valley from France in the French and Indian War. The colonies thought they now owned the land beyond the mountains.
2. England and her colonies commenced to quarrel and England took the Ohio Valley away from the colonies. She made it part of Canada.

3. During the Revolution the Americans made up their minds to get the Ohio Valley from England.

That part of America was well worth fighting for. A brave young soldier from Virginia, named George Rogers Clark, became friendly with the famous orator, Patrick Henry.

George Rogers Clark was born in Virginia, twenty years after the birth of Washington. As he grew to be a man, Clark, was the leader who helped win this fine country for the Americans.

Clark was anxious to do his share in the War for Independence. He thought the best thing he could do for his country would be to capture the British territory in the Northwest. This land was east of the Mississippi River and north of the Ohio River. There were few settlements in that vast territory. They were mostly the old French trading-posts. These settlements were under English rule. A few forts held by English soldiers were placed throughout the territory. Though the forts were rudely made of logs they were fairly strong. They had been placed at points where they would be easy to defend. The fort at Vincennes was built near the Wabash River. Another fort at Kaskaskia was located on the Mississippi River. Detroit was also defended by a fort.

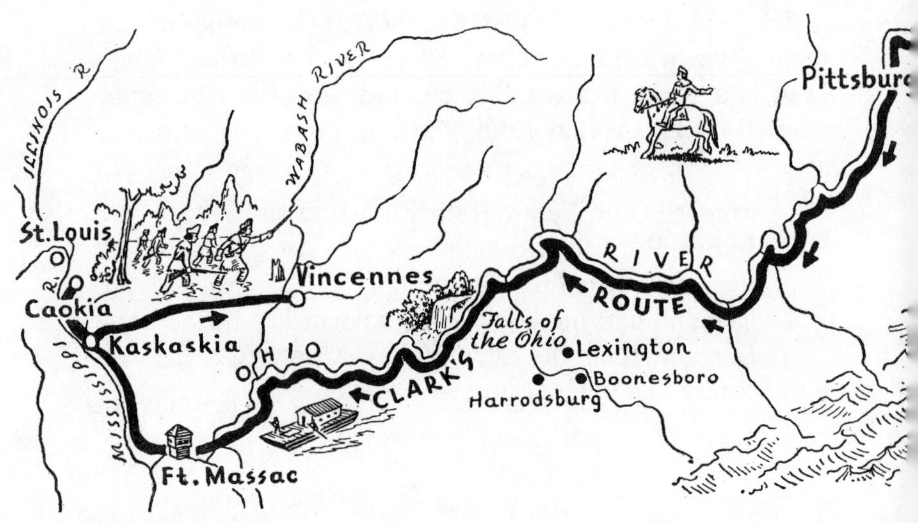

Photo from "Vincennes." A Chronicles of America Photoplay.

A PICKED FORCE. Clark took a small picked force of less than two hundred men. Then began the journey in boats. The men rowed day and night to make all possible speed. They went down the Ohio River to a point where the journey had to be continued by land. They hid their boats carefully in a creek. Clark and his force then started the overland march to Kaskaskia.

THE MARCH TO KASKASKIA. This part of the journey was hard. The party had to carry as little luggage as possible so that they could travel quickly. Food was not plentiful and, of course, there was no shelter. After pushing through the woods and fields, Clark came to a spot within four miles of Kaskaskia. The little band of backwoodsmen moved forward with great care. Clark knew that the fort and town must be captured by a surprise attack. Everything favored Clark's plan. The British did not dream that there was even one American within many miles of Kaskaskia.

A PLEASANT EVENING. There was a dance at the fort on the night of July fourth. Most of the British officers were there. Many of the young ladies of the village had come dressed in their summer finery. Some Indians

friendly to the English were also present. No doubt they were delighted with the graceful dancing of the ladies and the music of the fiddle. So interested were they all that no one noticed that the door had opened and that a man had entered the room.

Suddenly one of the Indians saw the stranger. He cried out. The music stopped. All was confusion. The candlelight fell on a tall figure clad in buckskin. His arms were folded across his chest and a smile played about the corners of his mouth. Clark was the only person who was enjoying himself. He made a little speech, something like this: "Go on with your fun. Only remember that you are now dancing under the flag of Virginia and not that of England." The dance stopped and the dancers hurried to their homes. The fun was over. Clark's men had taken the town and its fort before the British could collect their wits. The commander of the fort had been enjoying his sleep in a comfortable bed. Clark had to awaken him to tell him that the fort had been captured and that he was a prisoner.

A PEACEFUL SETTLEMENT. The next day Clark brought together the leaders of the town to settle the matter of surrender. Father Pierre Gibault, the pastor of the village church, was also invited. He proved to be the best friend of Clark and the American cause. Father Gibault was able to convince the people of the town that the Americans would be their real friends. He did more than this to prove his friendship.

FATHER GIBAULT'S HELP. Clark knew that he must take the other towns in this neighborhood. Father Gibault offered to do what he could to help Clark. The priest went to the town of Vincennes to ask the people there to join with the Americans. They took the priest's advice. Remember that most of the settlers of this region were French, who came under the rule of England at the close of the French and Indian War. They had not been very happy about some of the ideas the English had forced upon them. That is why they were willing to give up English rule and come under the rule of Virginia.

Later, the British recaptured Vincennes. They forced the people to remain for a while longer under British rule. This made the people unhappy.

THE FALL OF VINCENNES. The British were able to hold Vincennes only for a short time. The winter of the year 1779 was nearly over when Clark set out from Kaskaskia to capture Vincennes. Clark's men had to cross swollen streams, swamp lands, and stretches of deep snow to reach the town. They lived on buffalo meat, elk steak, venison, and rabbit meat. Towards the end of February, Clark was at the edge of Vincennes. The English had built a strong log fort. They did not have a full force of soldiers because the British commander did not dream Clark would make that terrible winter march. He was not expected until spring.

Clark's men opened fire on the British. They were well covered and were able to pick off every enemy that showed his head. The British commander soon saw that defense

Photo from "Vincennes." A Chronicles of America Photoplay.
© Yale University Press. By permission.

was useless. Vincennes surrendered once more to Clark. The great Northwest Territory was now under the control of the Americans. It is well to remember that Ohio, Indiana, Illinois, Wisconsin, and Michigan were the states made from the Northwest Territory.

STUDY SUMMARY

---

1. Terms to know. Be able to give the meaning of each term listed.

   pioneer   borough   frontier

2. Places to know. Be able to locate on a wall map each place listed. Give one fact about the place as it is located.

Kaskaskia	The West	Northwest Territory
Vincennes	Kentucky	Boonesborough
Detroit		North Carolina

3. People to know. Be able to give an important fact about each person named.

Daniel Boone	Father Pierre Gibault
Patrick Henry	George Rogers Clark

4. Dates to remember. Be able to give one important event which took place on each of the following dates.

1773 1779

5. Character study. Prove the following statements.
   a. Daniel Boone was an adventurer.
   b. George Rogers Clark had the qualities of a great leader.

ACTIVITIES

---

1. Make a set of six or seven panel posters to illustrate the life of Daniel Boone. Use the posters to guide oral reports on the life of Boone.
2. Give an oral report telling how George Rogers Clark saved the Northwest Territory for the United States.
3. Make a sketch map of the United States.
   a. Block off with heavy lines the Northwest Territory.
   b. Put in with light lines the present boundary lines of the states made from this territory.
   c. Letter on the map the names of the states made from the Northwest Territory.

STUDY TEST 28—Score 25

COMPLETION. Fill in each missing letter to complete the words. The initial letter of each missing word will help you. Re-read each sentence as the word is completed.

1. The colonists called the land beyond the Appalachian Mountains the W – – –.
2. People who move into unsettled lands are called p – – – – – – – –.

3. Daniel Boone's father was a Q—————.
4. The Boone family first settled in P———————————.
5. The woods were full of g———.
6. Daniel Boone did not enjoy being a f—————.
7. Boone liked to explore in the w—————————.
8. The Wilderness Road was the first road across the m————————.
9. Settlers at Boonesborough suffered because of a lack of s———.
10. Daniel Boone was captured by the I——————.
11. Salt was found by following the path made by herds of b——————.
12. Daniel Boone really helped to start the westward m———————.
13. The Americans were anxious to control the O——— V—————.
14. George Rogers Clark was a daring young s——————.
15. Patrick Henry was the governor of V———————.
16. Clark wanted to capture the Northwest Territory from the B——————.
17. The N———————— was under British rule at this time.
18. Clark planned to capture Kaskasia on the M—— ———————— River.
19. The Americans made a surprise attack on the British at K————————.
20. Father Pierre Gibault convinced the settlers that the Americans were f———————.
21. Clark set out in 1779 to capture Fort V————————.
22. The British commander at Vincennes did not expect Clark to attack the fort before s—————.
23. The Americans forced the British commander at Vincennes to s————————.
24. The daring of George Rogers Clark helped win the Northwest Territory for A——————.
25. The United States of America extended from the Atlantic Ocean to the Mississippi River and from the Great Lakes to F——————.

FORMING A GOVERNMENT

Read to learn

1. Why the government under the Articles of Confederation was weak.
2. Five things which wise men realized were needed.
3. About the branches of our government.
4. The oath a president takes.
5. How political parties arose.

HOW THE UNITED STATES CAME INTO BEING. Each of the thirteen colonies had now become a state. The original thirteen colonies passed out of existence as the United States came into being. The states were not really united. They acted like thirteen little nations. Each one was jealous of the other. Sometimes one state made laws that would hurt another state. Only a very weak written agreement held the states together. This agreement was called the Articles of Confederation. A confederation is a union. The union of the thirteen states under the Articles of Confederation was weak. Congress had no power. This was indeed a most dangerous time.

Wise men saw that something must be done if the nation was to hold together. These wise men saw that some things were very necessary.

1. A strong government was needed.
2. Congress must be given certain powers.
3. A set of written laws must be made. This would give the nation a Constitution to guide its government.
4. The rights of each state must be protected.
5. The central government, or Congress, must be stronger than any state.

Finally, a meeting was called at Philadelphia in 1787 to solve these problems. All the states, except Rhode Island, sent delegates. George Washington was elected president of the Convention. This Convention presented a Constitution to the nation. That is why this is often called the Constitutional Convention.

THE CONSTITUTION. Each state wanted its own way about the Constitution. There were many, many quarrels during the Convention. George Washington, the president of the Convention, was wise and calm. The delegates were thoughtful men. They wanted the new nation to succeed. That is why the delegates, after four months, decided to accept the Constitution. Their next task was to present the Constitution to the people. Each delegate had to explain the Constitution to his own state. The Constitution was presented to the states. Nine states ratified the Constitution. That is, the nine states agreed to accept this new form of government. The Constitution became the law of the land in 1787.

The Constitution was strong. It gave the nation the three great branches of our government.

1. A President to execute the law. To execute the law means to see that the laws are obeyed. Therefore, the President heads the *executive* branch.
2. A Congress to make the law. Those who make the law are said to legislate. Therefore, Congress is the *legislative* branch of the government.
3. A Supreme Court to explain the law. Explaining the law is called a judicial act. So the Supreme Court is the *judicial* branch of the government.

At last our country was a real nation. Congress could raise money to pay our debts. Congress was given power to coin money. We could make treaties with other countries. A treaty is an agreement between nations. We could show the world that we were united in more than name.

CHOOSING OUR FIRST PRESIDENT. There was no trouble in choosing a President. Americans thought of only one man. Every vote was cast for George Washington, of Virginia. John Adams of Massachusetts was elected the Vice-President.

Washington had been living the happy life of a farmer for two years. His lovely home at Mount Vernon meant much to him. Once again he must leave his beloved home. The first time he had torn himself away to fight a war and win our freedom. A second time he had been called away to lead the struggle for the Constitution. Now he must undertake his third great duty. He must go to New York, the capital of the nation. There he would become the First President of the United States.

As Washington rode on his way to New York each town along the way turned out to honor him. Bells rang out with joy. Houses were gayly hung with bunting. There was a gay display of flags. People lined the streets to cheer the great man. Young girls scattered flowers in his path.

BECOMING PRESIDENT. One of the most solemn scenes in our history took place in New York when Washington was inaugurated in 1789. That is, he took the oath as President of the United States. An oath of office is a solemn promise made before God. The President of the United States makes a solemn promise to uphold the Constitution. Washington was driven to Federal Hall in a fine carriage drawn by four white horses. Crowds of people stood along the way to cheer him as he passed. The ceremony of inauguration took place on the balcony of Federal Hall. Thousands of people stood in the street and listened in silence as Washington took this oath: "I do solemnly swear that I will faithfully execute the office of President of the United States, and will to the best of my ability preserve, protect, and defend the Constitution of the United States." As he finished Robert Livingston,

who had just administered the oath, cried out, "Long live George Washington, President of the United States." The people, as shown in the picture, took up the joyful cry. They were thankful that there was a president to govern the United States. They were also thankful that this president was George Washington.

WASHINGTON'S CABINET. Washington asked some good men to enter his cabinet. The President's cabinet is a group of men who help him to govern the country. There were but four people in Washington's cabinet. The first of these was the Secretary of State. His duty was to take charge of all business with foreign governments. Thomas Jefferson served as Secretary of State under Washington. Then there was a Secretary of the Treasury. He had charge of the nation's money. Washington invited young Alexander Hamilton to fill this post. There were two other men in the cabinet. Henry Knox, who had served under Washington in the army, became the Secretary of War. Edmund Randolph, a Virginia lawyer, served as the first

Attorney General. Alexander Hamilton was perhaps the most helpful member of Washington's cabinet. He served as Secretary of the Treasury. This was indeed a difficult job. There was no money in the nation's treasury. Hamilton's first task was to plan ways of raising money.

POLITICAL PARTIES

AMERICA'S DEBTS. As head of the treasury Hamilton had his great chance. He did many things of great value. The best thing he did was to arrange to pay all the debts of the nation. There were plenty of debts. During the Revolutionary War Congress had borrowed whenever possible. France, Holland, and Spain had loaned money. Wealthy citizens had loaned all the money they could spare. The army had taken supplies without money to pay for them. Even the soldiers had not been paid in full. Our money became worth very little. Hamilton knew that a country that did not pay its debts would lose the respect of everyone. He wanted America to stand high in the eyes of the world. This was a splendid ambition but where was the money to come from? There was not a

penny in the treasury. Hamilton might well have been called the Secretary of the Empty Treasury. The money that had been issued by the states now had little or no value. Shop keepers refused it. They wanted only money made by the United States Government.

THE START OF POLITICAL PARTIES. Thomas Jefferson was Washington's Secretary of State. Jefferson and Hamilton were members of the cabinet. These two men were unlike in almost every way. Jefferson was born very rich. Nevertheless, he favored the poorer people. He wanted to be democratic. In fact, he liked to be called "the man of the people." Hamilton was born very poor but he favored richer people. His ideas were aristocratic. An aristocrat is the opposite of a democrat.

Hamilton wanted a strong central government. He did not believe that the states should be given much power. He thought that the nation should be ruled by a President and a Senate. Further, he thought that these officers should rule for life. Hamilton's ideas were feared by people who believed it unwise to give too much power to the President. Jefferson fought against Hamilton's ideas. Jefferson said these ideas were dangerous to liberty. He wanted the states to have most of the power. Jefferson trusted the ordinary people to rule. He believed in a government by the people.

Some people followed Jefferson, others thought Hamilton was right. So two political parties were formed. Those who believed with Hamilton were called Federalists. Jefferson's friends formed the Democratic-Republican party.

WASHINGTON ELECTED AGAIN. Washington finished his first term. He wanted to go home to Mount Vernon but the people said "No." They elected him President again. Later on, they would have elected him a third term but then it was his turn to say "No." He wrote that ordinarily two terms of office were enough for a President.

PHILADELPHIA THE CAPITAL. Washington's second inauguration took place in Philadelphia. Washington liked William Penn's old city. It held many memories of the fight for liberty. The Continental Congress met there. In its Independence Hall the Declaration of Independence had been signed. There, too, the Constitution had been drawn up. But New York and Philadelphia were only temporary capitals. Everyone felt that our government should have a fine city of its own.

THE CITY OF WASHINGTON. A lovely piece of land on the Potomac River was chosen for the new capital. Virginia and Maryland each gave part of the land needed for the capital city. These states ceded the land to the national government. Land is ceded when it is given by one state, or country to another. In this case the states ceded the land to the United States. This land became known as the District of Columbia. President Washington thought that Federal City would be a good name for the new capital. Hardly anyone agreed with him. Most people thought it should be named after the "Father of Our Country," so the capital is called Washington.

A great French engineer set to work to plan the new capital. He started with almost a wilderness. Today, Washington is one of the most beautiful cities in the world.

George Washington, himself, laid the cornerstone of the capitol in 1793.

You have just read two words that are much alike, capital and capitol. Capital, as used here, means the city in which the government of a state or country is carried on. Capitol means the building in which the laws of the country are made.

George Washington did not live to see this beautiful city completed. After his second term he went home to his beloved Mount Vernon. There he died in the year 1799.

A MAN OF IDEALS. The city of Washington is a lasting monument to the greatest of Americans. Even if there were no city named for him, George Washington would always be remembered. He was truly great and truly good. Perhaps there is an explanation of his splendid character and noble soul. It can be found in a motto that he kept before his mind: "Labor to keep alive in thy breast that little spark of celestial fire called conscience."

STUDY SUMMARY

1. Terms to know. Be able to give the meaning of each term listed.

Continentals	capital	Constitutional Convention
judicial	oath	Articles of Confederation
ratified	cabinet	aristocrat
legislate	capitol	inaugurated
execute	ceded	treaty

2. People to know. Be able to give at least one interesting fact about each person named.

George Washington	Edmund Randolph
Henry Knox	Robert Livingston
Alexander Hamilton	Thomas Jefferson
John Adams	

3. Places to know. Be able to locate the following places on a wall map. Give one fact about each place.

   New York   Washington   Philadelphia

4. Dates to remember. Be able to tell the important event which took place in 1787   1789

ACTIVITIES

1. Write a paragraph explaining why the government under the Articles of Confederation was weak.
2. Write two paragraphs about the Political Parties. Write one paragraph on Hamilton's ideas and one paragraph on Jefferson's political ideas.

3. Make a table showing Washington's cabinet. Use the following form.

WASHINGTON'S CABINET

Name	Office
1.	
2.	
3.	
4.	

4. Make a table to show our form of government. Use the following form.

BRANCHES OF THE UNITED STATES GOVERNMENT		
Name of Branch	Officer or Body	Duty
1.		
2.		
3.		

STUDY TEST 29—Score 25

A. After each term which you associate with George Washington put the letter W; with Thomas Jefferson put J; with Alexander Hamilton put H.

1. Led the war for freedom from British rule. —
2. Favored the poorer people. —
3. Had democratic ideas. —

4. Was born poor but favored the rich people. —
5. Served as president of the Constitutional Convention. —
6. Was born rich but favored the poorer people. —
7. Had aristocratic ideas. —
8. Favored a strong central government. —
9. Trusted the people to rule the nation. —
10. Elected the first President of the United States. —
11. He feared to give the states too much power. —
12. He did not trust the people to rule themselves. —
13. Chose strong men to serve in his cabinet. —
14. Wished much power to be given to the states. —
15. He was a strong Federalist. —
16. Was a leader in the Democratic-Republican party. —

B. After each fact which you associate with government under the Articles of Confederation put A; under the Constitution put C.

1. Government was very weak. —
2. Set of written laws ratified by nine states. —
3. Congress had but little power. —
4. Congress had no power to raise money. —
5. Became the law of the land in 1787. —
6. Government under this set of laws is strong. —
7. Provided for three branches of government. —
8. Gave Congress power to raise money. —
9. Gave Congress power to make treaties. —

THE CHURCH AND THE NEW REPUBLIC

Read to learn

1. How John Carroll served his country.
2. The importance of the "Bill of Rights."
3. Changes during Archbishop Carroll's life.
4. The founding of the Sisters of Charity.

MOST REVEREND JOHN CARROLL

THE EARLY LIFE OF JOHN CARROLL. The Catholic Church started a new life in our country when America became free. The first great Catholic leader in the new nation was John Carroll. He was a native of Maryland.

The Carroll family was well known. One branch of it had a homestead at Upper Marlboro, Maryland. There in 1735 a boy was born, who at baptism was named John. John Carroll was three years younger than George Washington. Their birthplaces were not far apart.

As young Carroll grew up he was given his first lessons by his mother. She had been educated in France. John was fortunate in having so good a teacher. It was hard in those days to get a Catholic education in America. The laws in most of the colonies did not permit Catholic schools. If one Catholic school opened it was almost sure to be closed, yet they did open at times. One of these was a Jesuit Academy in Maryland. There John Carroll was sent. He was quite fortunate because he was able to study with the Jesuits long enough to get ready for college.

AT ST. OMER'S COLLEGE. There were no Catholic colleges in the colonies in those troubled times. Catholics

sent their sons to Europe to be educated, if they could afford to do so. Saint Omer's was a college in a part of France called Flanders. There John Carroll was sent. He found other boys there from the fine old Catholic families of Maryland. The boys received a splendid training under the Jesuits who taught at Saint Omer's.

John Carroll enjoyed his student days at college, in spite of the hard work. The boys rose at five o'clock in the morning and went to bed at nine o'clock at night. There was hardly an idle moment during the day. They had much studying to do. Not all the time, however, was spent at work. There were games to play. The favorite game was called trap ball as shown in the picture. It was not nearly as much fun as baseball or football.

FATHER CARROLL. John Carroll felt that God wanted him to be a priest. He joined the Society of Jesus. He studied long and hard and he prayed much. Finally he was ordained a priest. Then Father Carroll returned to his beloved Maryland. He had been away twenty-seven years. That was a long time. He returned just before the Revolution. Father Carroll found his fellow Catholics had many trials and troubles.

Maryland had been settled by Catholics, but now the Protestants were in control and the Catholics had few rights. The Puritans had taken control of Maryland. They made unjust laws which made it very hard for people who did not believe as they did. The Puritans would permit no Catholic schools, no Catholic churches. Mass had to be offered in private homes for the few Catholics who had the courage to remain in this colony.

A MISSION TO CANADA. During the American Revolution Father Carroll came to know Benjamin Franklin. Father Carroll went with Franklin on an important journey to Quebec, Canada. Father Carroll's cousin, the great Charles Carroll, was also a member of the party. Congress sent these Americans to ask the people of Canada to join in our fight against England. Father Carroll and the others could not persuade the Canadians to help us. England had been very clever. She treated the Catholics very badly in some parts of the world, but in Canada she

treated them very well. Catholics had full liberty in Canada. The Canadians, on the other hand, were afraid to trust the Americans. They knew that the people of New England looked on the Catholic religion with contempt. So the French Canadians would not risk taking part in our struggle.

BISHOP CARROLL. After the Revolution, the Pope put Father Carroll in charge of all Catholics in the United States. The Catholics numbered about 30,000 persons. The Church kept on growing. Soon it needed a bishop and Father John Carroll was chosen to be the first bishop in the United States. This was in 1789, the same year in which George Washington became the first President. Bishop Carroll's diocese was Baltimore. It took in the whole United States. The Church continued to grow. More bishops were needed. Dioceses were set up in New York, Boston, Philadelphia, and Bardstown. Bishop Carroll became the Archbishop of Baltimore in 1808.

ARCHBISHOP CARROLL. For seven years after he became Archbishop, John Carroll lived to see the Church grow. It moved forward with great strides. The Archbishop could look back upon some wonderful changes. When he was a boy he could not even get a Catholic education in his native land. In most of the colonies priests were forbidden to say Mass. This began to be changed after freedom had been won.

THE BILL OF RIGHTS. The first Amendments to the Constitution protected the Catholics very much. To amend the Constitution means to change part of it or to add something to it. There were ten Amendments to the Constitution. They are called the "Bill of Rights." (More Amendments have since been added.) The first of these Amendments granted freedom of worship. Catholics could now have their own churches and their own schools.

CHANGES IN ARCHBISHOP CARROLL'S TIME. Before he died, Archbishop Carroll saw Georgetown College founded. He saw a seminary raised up in Baltimore. A seminary is a school to train young men to be priests. He lived to see Catholics gain the respect of their countrymen. He lived to see Jefferson make the Louisiana Purchase. Many Catholics came into our country through the purchase of Louisiana. The good nuns were ready to begin their work in schools and hospitals. Archbishop Carroll had lived in a wonderful time.

MOTHER SETON AND THE SISTERS OF CHARITY

ELIZABETH ANN BAYLEY. A baby girl was born in New York City when that city was hardly more than a village. Her name was Elizabeth Ann Bayley, and her birthday was August 28, 1774. This was just before the American Revolution. At that time there was no Catholic Church and very few Catholics in New York. Today, the Church in America is strong partly because of this wonderful woman and her work. Elizabeth Ann Bayley's father was a famous doctor in New York. Neither of her parents was a Catholic.

EARLY LIFE. Elizabeth's childhood was like that of other children whose parents had wealth. She lived in a large comfortable house and was carefully educated by her father. Her mother died, but a very kind stepmother took her place so that Elizabeth's youth was happy.

Elizabeth Bayley married a splendid young man named William Magee Seton. Ill health soon forced Mr. Seton to take a long vacation. He decided to visit Italy where he had friends. Mr. Seton did not recover his health; he died while abroad. That was a very sad experience for Elizabeth Ann Seton. However, there was a comforting side. In Italy she first learned about the Catholic Church. She received the grace of the true Faith. She became a Catholic when she returned to New York.

EARLY CONVERT YEARS. At that time Catholics were not highly respected by their neighbors. Mrs. Seton soon learned that she had to suffer for her Faith. The years following her conversion were filled with hardships. Many of her friends and even the members of her family would have nothing to do with her. It was most difficult in those days for a woman to make a living. The fact that Elizabeth Seton was a convert to the Catholic Church made it even more difficult. Finally, she went to Baltimore, where she had her first success.

MOTHER SETON'S WORK. Elizabeth Seton's ambition was not to make a comfortable living, but to help others. She was very much interested in the care of the young and the poor. Another ambition of hers was to dedicate her life to God. This she did when she took her vows as a nun before Archbishop Carroll. Meantime a number of splendid women came to her to share in her work of helping children and those in need. Elizabeth Seton's group formed themselves into a community. They followed the rule Saint Vincent de Paul wrote for his nuns in France. Elizabeth Seton was elected the first Superior of the new community.

THE SISTERS OF CHARITY. Mother Seton's sisters moved to Emmetsburg in Maryland. This became the first American headquarters of the Sisters of Charity of Saint Vincent de Paul. Soon their work extended far beyond Maryland. They founded schools, homes for children, hospitals, homes for the aged, and began many other important works. The great holiness of Mother Seton's life seemed to bring a special blessing upon the work of the Sisters of Charity. Indeed Mother Seton was so holy that some day she may be declared to be a Saint.

STUDY SUMMARY

1. Terms to know. Be able to give the meaning of each of the following terms.

   Bill of Rights   seminary   amend

2. People to know. Be able to give at least one interesting fact about each person named.

   John Carroll   Elizabeth Ann Seton
   Benjamin Franklin   Saint Vincent de Paul

3. Places to know. Be able to locate on a wall map the places listed. Give a fact about the place as it is located.

Baltimore	Maryland
Quebec	Flanders

4. Character study. Prove the following statements.
   a. Father John Carroll served his country well.
   b. Mother Seton was a most charitable woman.

5. Word study. Be able to use correctly the following words.

amend	amended	amendment

ACTIVITIES

---

1. Discuss the growth of the Catholic Church in America.
2. Make a booklet on the life of Bishop Carroll. Make pen and ink, or pencil sketches to illustrate the important events in the life of this great American.
3. Give a brief biography of the founder of the Sisters of Charity of Saint Vincent de Paul.
4. Make a list of at least four types of works of charity begun by the Sisters of Charity.

STUDY TEST 30—Score 20

YES or NO. Answer each question with YES or NO.

1. Was the Carroll family one of the leading families of Maryland? ——
2. Did all of the colonies permit Catholic schools? ——
3. Was John Carroll educated in France? ——
4. Did Father Carroll return to Maryland just before the Revolution? ——

5. Did the Puritans permit the Catholics to have their own schools? ______
6. Did Father Carroll go to Quebec to persuade the Canadians to help the American colonists? ______
7. Were Catholics in the American colonies treated unjustly? ______
8. Were Catholics in Canada allowed to practice the Catholic religion? ______
9. Did the Catholic Church in America grow after the Revolution? ______
10. Did the French Canadians trust the Americans? ______
11. Was Father Carroll made the first bishop in the United States? ______
12. Were the first ten Amendments to the Constitution called the "Bill of Rights"? ______
13. Does the first Amendment to the Constitution grant freedom of worship? ______
14. Was Elizabeth Bayley born of Catholic parents? ______
15. Did Elizabeth Seton become a convert to the Catholic Church? ______
16. Were Catholics highly respected by their neighbors at that time? ______
17. Did Elizabeth Seton desire to accumulate wealth? ______
18. Did Elizabeth Seton dedicate her life to the service of others? ______
19. Were the Sisters of Charity of St. Vincent de Paul established in the United States by Elizabeth Seton? ______
20. Did Mother Seton lead a holy life? ______

UNIT VII: OUR NATION GROWS

THOMAS JEFFERSON

Read to learn

1. Why John Adams was not a successful leader.
2. How Thomas Jefferson learned about politics.
3. Why Jefferson was chosen to write the Declaration of Independence.
4. Why the United States purchased Louisiana.
5. What a bargain Louisiana was.
6. How the Lewis and Clark Expedition helped people to know about the West.

AFTER WASHINGTON'S TIME. John Adams followed Washington as President. John Adams had served his country long and well. He was a member of the First Continental Congress. Adams spoke strongly in favor of the Declaration of Independence. After the Revolution, Congress sent John Adams to England to help make a peace treaty. Adams was the first man elected Vice-President of the United States. He served two terms while Washington was President.

John Adams certainly understood the problems of the country. Yet he was not the sort of a man that people easily followed. He was not always patient. He liked to have his own way. That is one reason why he was not a successful leader. The people were glad to have Thomas Jefferson as third President of the United States when Adams' term was over. As President, Thomas Jefferson did great things for his country.

BOYHOOD OF THOMAS JEFFERSON. Thomas Jefferson was born on a large farm or plantation in Virginia. As soon as he was old enough he went to school. There were few schools in Virginia in those days. Thomas Jefferson was a good student. As a boy he learned to love books. During his long life books always were important to him. He also learned to play the violin. He was very faithful about practicing and soon learned to play quite well.

FIRST LESSONS IN POLITICS. After his school days Jefferson went to William and Mary College, which was located in Williamsburg, Virginia. Williamsburg was then the capital of Virginia. The Virginia House of Burgesses, where the laws for the colony were made, met in Williamsburg. During his college days Thomas Jefferson learned something about politics. Many times this tall, freckled lad listened to the debates in the House of Burgesses. He began to understand politics. He heard the burning words of Patrick Henry in defiance of the English king. The experiences which young Thomas Jefferson had in the House of Burgesses were preparing him to serve his country.

A YOUTHFUL STATESMAN. Soon after he left college Thomas Jefferson returned to Williamsburg. This time he came as a member of the House of Burgesses. Entering public life was quite a sacrifice for Jefferson. He had many excuses for staying at home. He had an immense plantation to look after. He owned nearly one thousand acres of land. More than three hundred slaves worked for him. He left all this because he believed that he owed a duty to his country. The stirring days of the American Revolution gave Thomas Jefferson many opportunities to be helpful to his country.

© Yale University Press. By permission.
Photo from "Declaration of Independence." A Chronicles of America Photoplay.

AUTHOR OF AN IMPORTANT DECLARATION. The First Continental Congress met at Philadelphia. Virginia sent Thomas Jefferson as a representative. He took an active part helping the Continental Congress do its work. Thomas Jefferson was not a fine speaker. He lacked the skill of his friend Patrick Henry, but there was one thing Jefferson did very well. He was able to write clearly on different subjects. He used words that ordinary people could understand. He was able to tell the people about their government and their rights as citizens. So he was chosen to write one of the most famous papers that was ever written. This is the Declaration of Independence. In the Declaration of Independence Thomas Jefferson wrote:

1. That each and every person has certain rights;
2. That governments should defend the rights of the people;
3. That the American people should be free from England because of her denial of their rights.

Jefferson put his whole soul into writing the Declaration of Independence.

PRESIDENT THOMAS JEFFERSON. Years passed and Jefferson was elected President of the United States. Towards noon of March 4, 1801, he left his boarding house in Washington and walked to the new Capitol. There was no parade, no fuss. The inauguration was to take place in the room used by the Senate. The building was hardly completed. Few people noticed the unfinished building. They were more interested in the new President. The man they looked at was slender and tall. His face was covered with freckles. His dress was plain; he seemed to be just a man of the people. Even today we speak of Jefferson's simplicity.

THE WESTERN COUNTRY. Jefferson will always be remembered for two things:

1. He wrote the Declaration of Independence
2. He made the Louisiana Purchase

At one time France owned a very large amount of land in North America. The French Territory stretched from the west bank of the Mississippi River all the way to the Rocky Mountains. The map on page 265 shows this land. It was called the Louisiana Territory.

About the time Jefferson became President, hundreds of families were moving to the West. West of the Appalachian Mountains they found plenty of free land. They raised corn and wheat, cattle, and hogs. They raised more than they needed for themselves and they looked around for a place to sell the surplus. It cost too much to send their products across the mountains to the East. So they floated their surplus goods down the Ohio and the Mississippi rivers in flat-boats to New Orleans. Find New Orleans on the map on page 291. New Orleans was a source of trouble. The Mississippi River marked the western boundary of the United States at that time. Our country owned only the eastern bank of that river. Worse still, the United States did not own the city of New Orleans.

This port belonged to France. The ships from Europe docked at New Orleans. The Americans had trouble in getting to these ships. President Jefferson and other Americans saw that the United States ought to own New Orleans. Ownership of New Orleans would solve the trying problem of shipping on the Mississippi River.

THE LOUISIANA PURCHASE. President Jefferson sent James Monroe to France. He was told to see if New Orleans and the land around the mouth of the Mississippi River could be bought. Monroe met Robert Livingston, another American, in Paris.

Napoleon Bonaparte was then the ruler of France. His worst enemy was England. When Napoleon heard that the Americans wanted to buy New Orleans, two thoughts came to his mind: (1) He needed money, (2) He hated England. If he made a deal with the Americans he would get a large sum of money and he could block England's growth forever in America. Napoleon did not realize the real value of Louisiana. So unwisely Napoleon offered to sell not only New Orleans but also the whole Louisiana

Territory. The Americans accepted Napoleon's offer. The price was $15,000,000. It was the biggest piece of land that was ever sold. The Louisiana Purchase was made in 1803. This is an important date in American history because it marks the real beginning of our growth.

THE GREAT BARGAIN. What a bargain that was! It almost doubled the size of our country. The Rocky Mountains became the western boundary of the United States. There were great and fertile plains; thousands of acres for farms; immense grazing lands for cattle. There were forests of the finest woods. In the mountains gold and silver were waiting for the miners. The map on page 417 shows the states that were later made from the Louisiana Territory.

EXPLORING THE LOUISIANA TERRITORY. Even before the United States had bought the Louisiana Territory, President Jefferson wanted to know more about this great section of North America. So no time was lost. Congress gave the money and a party of explorers was formed. Two men were in command of the exploring party. Captain Meriwether Lewis was one of them. He was Jefferson's secretary. The other leader was William Clark. He was a younger brother of George Rogers Clark.

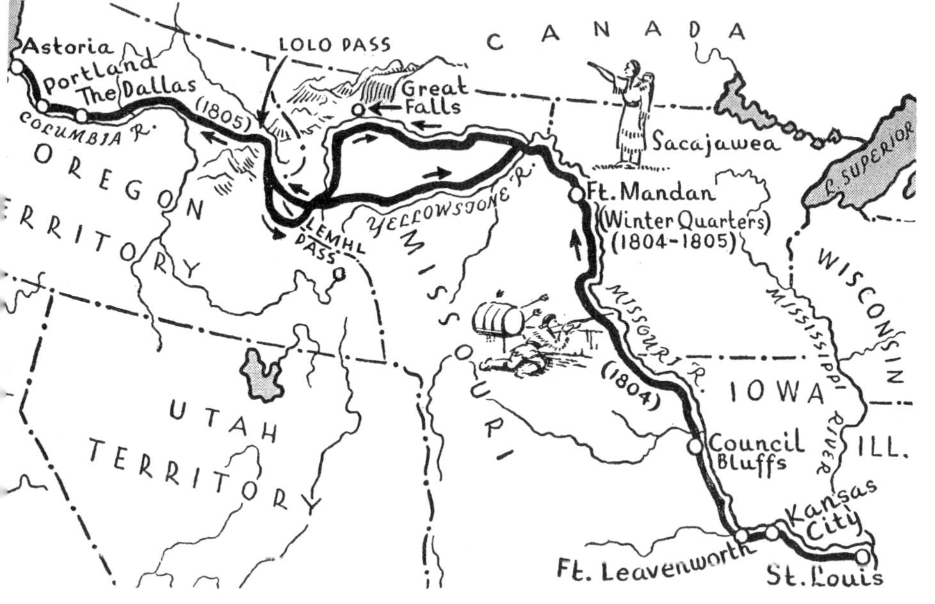

LEWIS AND CLARK EXPEDITION. Lewis and Clark's small force met at Saint Louis. It was then only a small fur-trading post on the Mississippi River. Some of the band had been explorers. Others were Indian fighters or fur-traders. Still others went for high adventure. The leaders were young, but they were wise. Before starting the difficult trip six months were spent in preparation. The men did much marching; they practiced with their rifles; they learned how to handle their boats.

The party began its long journey in the spring of 1804. There were forty-five men in three boats. Up the Mississippi River they went to the mouth of the Missouri River. Then they started up the "Big Muddy," as the Missouri River is called. It was hard work to make the boats go against the strong current. The boats were heavy and they were loaded with supplies. There were many snags in the river. A snag might be a log, a half sunken tree, or a sand bar. The party slowly pushed on up the river. The river wound through great grassy plains. Thousands of buffalo were seen. It was autumn before they reached the present state of North Dakota. The time had come to settle down for the winter.

THE BIRD WOMAN. They met an Indian squaw in Dakota. This Indian woman was to be of great help to the American explorers. She was called Sa-ca-je-we-a, which means Bird Woman. She had been born in the mountains. She offered to lead the Americans across the mountains. When the second spring came the party started on again, with the Bird Woman leading. They had many adventures. Their food ran low and game was scarce and hard to shoot. The party left the Louisiana Territory and crossed the high Rocky Mountains. Here it was hard to find their way. At length the men and their guide came to another great river. It was the Columbia River. They built boats Indian fashion by burning out logs. Soon they were floating down the Columbia River. Finally, they came in view of the Pacific Ocean which they had been anxious to see. They had reached the Oregon Country.

The journey back was a hard and a dangerous one. There were grizzly bears, rattlesnakes, insects, and some unfriendly Indians. Yet, through it all only one man deserted and one man died. After more than two years, and an eight-thousand-mile trip, Lewis and Clark reached the Mississippi River again.

THE JOURNAL OF LEWIS AND CLARK. Lewis and Clark kept a journal. It was a day-by-day account of their famous journey. Their journal is full of bad spelling and bad grammar. It is also full of the most useful information. It told all about the lands they visited, the trees, the shrubs, and the grasses. The journal described the life of the Indians and told where minerals could be found. Best of all, for those times, it told where fur-bearing animals lived. Soon the trappers were moving into the Louisiana Territory. Trappers took the first step in opening up the country. President Jefferson was delighted with the results of the Lewis and Clark Expedition. The President and his Cabinet began to realize what a bargain they had obtained from France.

ZEBULON PIKE AND THE SOUTHWEST. Another expedition to explore the western part of North America was sent out. It was under Zebulon Pike, a young army lieutenant. This expedition went beyond the Louisiana Territory into the west and the southwest. Pike had done some exploring but this time he had to be very much on guard. The country he was going into belonged to Spain. Lieutenant Zebulon Pike learned that he must be very careful not to offend the Spanish. His party of picked men reached the present state of Colorado. There they discovered the high snow-capped mountain we now call Pike's Peak. Pike went farther to the south into the Spanish territory and was arrested by Spanish soldiers. Later he was freed. He too, wrote an account of his journey. The West was being made known to Americans.

STUDY SUMMARY

---

1. Terms to know. Be able to give the meaning of each term listed.

   plantation   snag   squaw   journal

2. People to know. Be able to give an important fact about each person named.

   Sa-ca-je-we-a   Thomas Jefferson
   William Clark   Meriwether Lewis
   Napoleon Bonaparte   Zebulon Pike

3. Places to know. Be able to locate on a wall map each place listed. Give one fact about each place.

   Louisiana Territory   Philadelphia
   Williamsburg   Saint Louis
   Colorado   Paris

4. Trace each river named. Be sure to trace the river from its source to its mouth.

   Mississippi   Columbia   Missouri

5. Date to remember. Tell the most important event in American history in the year 1803.

ACTIVITIES

1. Make an outline of the LIFE OF THOMAS JEFFERSON. Use the outline to guide you in giving an oral report.
2. Make a sketch map of the United States. Shade or color the part of the land purchased as Louisiana Territory. Below the map write one sentence about each of the following facts:
   1. Country from which Louisiana Territory was purchased.
   2. Date.
   3. Price paid.
3. Make a list of the natural resources of Louisiana Territory which made its purchase a good bargain.
4. List the states later made from the Louisiana Territory.
5. Make a poster illustrating the Lewis and Clark Expedition. Use the poster to illustrate an oral report.

STUDY TEST 31—Score 25

EITHER—OR. Underscore the term which answers the question.

1. Did John Adams favor or oppose the Declaration of Independence?
2. Was John Adams a poor or a successful leader of men?
3. Is a plantation a large or a small farm?
4. Did Thomas Jefferson dislike or love books?
5. Did Jefferson attend Harvard or William and Mary College?
6. Was Jefferson or Patrick Henry the more able speaker?
7. Does the Declaration of Independence deny, or does it explain the rights of the people?

8. Did John Adams, James Monroe, or Thomas Jefferson write the Declaration of Independence?
9. Was Thomas Jefferson inaugurated when New York, Philadelphia, or Washington was the capital of the nation?
10. Did Spain or France own the land west of the Mississippi River when Jefferson became President?
11. Was New Orleans in 1800 under the rule of the United States, Spain, or France?
12. Did Americans offer to buy Louisiana Territory or New Orleans?
13. Were England and France friends or enemies during the rule of Napoleon?
14. Did Napoleon offer to sell New Orleans or Louisiana Territory?
15. Was Louisiana Territory purchased by the United States in 1800, 1803, or in 1805?
16. Did the purchase of Louisiana Territory help or block England's power in North America?
17. Was seven, fifteen, or ten million dollars paid for the Louisiana Territory?
18. Did the Lewis and Clark Expedition set out from Chicago, Saint Louis, or Saint Paul?
19. Was Sa-ca-je-we-a helpful or did she hinder the work of the expedition?
20. Did the Lewis and Clark Expedition reach California or Oregon?
21. Was Thomas Jefferson disappointed or pleased with the report of the Lewis and Clark Expedition?
22. Were farmers, miners, or trappers the first to move into the newly purchased land?
23. Did Zebulon Pike lead an expedition into the Northwest or into the Louisiana Territory?
24. Was the land where Zebulon Pike explored under the control of the United States, Spain, or France?
25. Did the expedition of Lewis and Clark, or the one under Zebulon Pike obtain the greater information about the land purchased from France?

UNIT VII: OUR NATION GROWS

THE SECOND WAR OF INDEPENDENCE

Read to learn

1. What the Embargo Act was.
2. How the Embargo Act and the Non-Intercourse Act helped us to begin manufacturing.
3. Why we fought against England and not against France.
4. What the War of 1812 taught Americans.
5. About the Monroe Doctrine.

WAR AND THREATENED WAR. During Jefferson's time we had a small war. It was with the pirates of Tripoli. Pirates are robbers who stop ships. Tripoli is a country in northern Africa on the Mediterranean Sea. The pirates of Tripoli sometimes captured our ships and made slaves of our sailors. President Jefferson sent a fleet to bombard the city of Tripoli. This frightened the ruler who was glad to make peace.

France and England were fighting a terrible war at this same time. It looked as though we might be drawn into it at any time. Both countries were committing crimes against our ships and our seamen. Jefferson did not believe that the United States should go to war. He did want to do something to show disapproval of the things these countries were doing to Americans. So a new law was passed known as the Embargo Act. An order forbidding ships to leave or to enter ports is an embargo. This act forbade American ships to leave our ports. In this way our ships would escape being fired upon or captured. Jefferson also hoped by this law to cut off food supplies from England and from France. The Embargo Act was bad. It ruined our trade. Those who hated it spelled it backwards and called it the "O-grab-me Act."

The Embargo Act was replaced by another law. This was the Non-Intercourse Act. Under this law our ships could trade with all the world, except with England or with France. Our country would have no intercourse with these countries.

There was one good thing that these laws did for us. We could not get manufactured articles from Europe first because of the Embargo and later because of the Non-Intercourse Act. So we started in building factories and making things for ourselves. Today, we are one of the greatest manufacturing nations in the world.

DEATH OF HAMILTON. Politics sometimes causes bitterness and anger. For example, Alexander Hamilton and Thomas Jefferson did not believe alike in politics. They were both fine men and they respected each other. A politician of another kind was Aaron Burr who was Vice-President under Jefferson. Burr wanted to be President but Hamilton opposed him. Hamilton did not trust Aaron Burr. Alexander Hamilton even supported his old foe, Jefferson, rather than let Burr be President. Aaron Burr became angry. He forced Hamilton to fight a duel. This duel, which means a private fight between two people, was fought with pistols. Hamilton was badly wounded and died in a short time. The United States lost a very fine statesman when Alexander Hamilton met his death.

THE WAR OF 1812

LEADING UP TO WAR. Thomas Jefferson, like George Washington, refused a third term as President. James Madison, of Virginia, was elected. Like Jefferson, he was a Democrat.

During these times our country was growing very fast. People were moving to the West by hundreds. People in the East were making money and building up business. The East was indeed prosperous. American shipbuilders were turning out fine ships. Our seamen were sailing to Europe and to distant places. We were taking some of the trade from European merchants.

The terrible wars in Europe continued. England and France were fighting on land and on sea. They were trying to cripple each other. This often injured us. France captured and plundered our ships. England did that, and she did still more. She needed seamen so she went so far as to impress American sailors from our own ships. To impress a seaman means to take him by force. English ships would stop American ships on the seas and take off any sailors that the English captain thought were Englishmen. English sea captains made the excuse that these men had been born on the British Isles. The English said, "Once an Englishman always an Englishman."

THE DECLARATION OF WAR. The United States could not fight both England and France. Which nation would we fight? It was less than thirty years since the Revolution. People still remembered how France had helped us. They still had hard feelings against the old enemy, England. It was also true that England seemed to be hurting us more than France. England was impressing our seamen. It was also thought that England was trying to get the Indians to attack our settlements in the West.

Then there was a selfish reason why the United States should choose to fight England. Many of our politicians thought we could easily capture Canada. Although we had plenty of land we wanted more. Americans were "land hungry." There was a band of young men in Congress who wanted war. They were called the "War Hawks." By 1812 they were able to bring about a war with England.

THE WAR ON LAND. Our first thought was to take Canada. That job seemed easier than it really was. Several times our armies crossed the border. Every time they met with miserable failure. Not only that, but the British turned around and invaded our land. They captured the city of Washington and burned our capitol. Then their ships and army made an attack on Baltimore.

THE STAR SPANGLED BANNER. Francis Scott Key was a young Baltimore lawyer. The forts protecting Baltimore were being bombarded by the English fleet. Young Key carried a message, under a flag of truce, to one of the British ships. A flag of truce is a white flag. In war it protects the one who carries it from being killed or taken prisoner. The British Admiral kept Key on board ship until after the bombardment was over.

All during the night young Key kept watch. He saw shot and shell fall like rain on the American fort. As the bombs burst in the air he could see that the American flag was still flying. Could it last through the night? With the coming of dawn would it still fly on high? As he watched, Key put his thoughts into words. These are the words of the "Star Spangled Banner." It will be sung as long as our flag is flown. When morning came "our flag was still there" flying above the fort as shown in the picture on page 276. The fort was not taken. Then the British sailed away.

THE WAR AT SEA. During the war our little navy did wonderful work. Our finest ship, the *Constitution,* is shown to the right in the picture on page 277. This ship is also called *Old Ironsides*. After a brief hour's fight she captured one of Britain's finest ships. That was a great shock to the English. Many other American victories followed. Over three hundred ships were captured in one year by our navy.

One naval battle was lost. The American *Chesapeake* was beaten by the British *Shannon*. The *Chesapeake* was commanded by Captain Lawrence. Captain Lawrence was mortally wounded. His dying words were, "Don't give up the ship!" These words have become the motto of the American Navy.

BATTLES ON THE LAKES. Another important naval battle was fought far from the sea. It was fought on Lake Erie. Whichever side could hold Lake Erie could hold the West. Young Oliver Hazard Perry of the American Navy was sent to take Lake Erie. He cut down trees from the forests on the shores of the lake. He built a small fleet. From the masthead of his flagship Perry flew the words of Lawrence, "Don't give up the ship!" His little fleet met the British ships in battle. The British fought hard and Perry's ship started to sink. He was rowed to another vessel. After a bitter battle the Americans won a complete victory. The British fleet was captured. The West was saved for America.

The British tried to invade New York from Canada. First the British fleet had to wipe out the American fleet on Lake Champlain. Captain Thomas McDonough was the American commander. The ships met in battle. It was the British fleet that was wiped out. McDonough won a fine victory and the English army went back to Canada.

THE BATTLE OF NEW ORLEANS. The one great American victory on land took place at New Orleans. It might be called the "battle of slow news." A peace treaty had already been signed when the battle was fought. News traveled slowly in those days. It took six weeks for news to come from Europe. Had there been a cable or a fast steamer there would have been no battle.

The Americans at New Orleans were commanded by General Andrew Jackson. His men called him "Old Hickory." Hickory is a very strong hard wood. The men under him were backwoodsmen. They were all good rifle shots. Jackson placed them on high ground. He put bales of cotton in front of them. The British were splendid soldiers. They had fought and beaten Napoleon. They marched up against the Americans without fear. But they stood no chance. Jackson's riflemen picked them off. The American victory was complete and New Orleans was saved.

A QUEER TREATY. A treaty of peace was signed on Christmas Eve, 1814. It was indeed a queer treaty because it did not mention the causes of our war against England. However, England quit impressing our seamen. Since the War of 1812 the United States and England have been on friendly terms.

WHAT THE WAR OF 1812 TAUGHT US. Sometimes we call this "our second war of independence." We gained no land by it. Many things remained as before the war. Nothing was decided about England taking our seamen from our ships. Indeed, the British had already stopped impressing our sailors.

The war did help us in ways we had not foreseen. It changed some of our ways of living and of thinking. It taught us that we must depend upon ourselves. We must manufacture our own goods. We must build our own factories. We must be able to get along without Europe.

AMERICA FOR AMERICANS. After the War of 1812, America got right down to work. Times were good. People were busy and happy. The United States felt sure of remaining free and independent. We wanted no more interference of European countries in America.

About this time important changes were taking place in the Spanish colonies in America. These colonies were separating from their mother country, Spain. Mexico was already free. New republics were springing up on every side in South America. The Americans wanted to be free from Canada to Cape Horn.

The United States was very glad to see these new free nations. A strong feeling of friendship for the new American republics grew up among our people.

THE MONROE DOCTRINE. When Congress opened in 1823 President James Monroe read an important message. This famous message became known as the Monroe Doctrine. It declared:

1. Nations of Europe must not increase their territory in America.
2. They could keep the colonies which they already had.
3. The independence of any country in America must not be interfered with.

What this message really meant was that "America for Americans" was to be the future policy of the nations in the Western Hemisphere.

STUDY SUMMARY

1. Terms to know. Be able to give the meaning of each term listed below.

Old Ironsides	pirate	Non-Intercourse Act
Embargo Act	impress	Monroe Doctrine

2. People to know. Be able to give an important fact about each person named.

James Madison	Oliver Hazard Perry
James Monroe	General Andrew Jackson
Alexander Hamilton	Francis Scott Key
Thomas Jefferson	

3. Places to know. Be able to locate on a wall map each place listed. Tell one fact about the place as it is located.

Canada	Baltimore	Lake Champlain
Tripoli	Lake Erie	New Orleans

4. Dates to be remembered. Be able to tell one important event which took place on each of the following dates.

1812 1814 1823

ACTIVITIES

1. Make a poster illustrating the event of the writing of the Star Spangled Banner.
2. Make a sketch map of the United States. Locate and name the following places on the map.

Canada	Washington
Lake Erie	Baltimore
New Orleans	Lake Champlain

   Below the map write one sentence about each place located. Tell why the place was important in the War of 1812.
3. Explain why the Battle of New Orleans might be called "the battle of slow news."
4. Make a list of three policies declared by the Monroe Doctrine.
5. Explain the meaning of the slogan of "America for Americans."

STUDY TEST 32—Score 30

TIME PLACEMENT. After each event you identify as happening during the time Thomas Jefferson was President put J; after each event which you identify as happening while James Madison was President put M.

1. Embargo Act. —
2. War of 1812. —
3. War with Tripoli. —
4. Pirates on the Mediterranean Sea captured American ships. —
5. Non-Intercourse Act. —
6. England was impressing American seamen. —
7. American ships not permitted to leave port. —
8. Manufacturing in America was increased due to the wars in Europe. —
9. The East was enjoying prosperity. —

10. United States declared war against England. —
11. British captured Washington, our capital. —
12. American army crossed Canadian border. —
13. United States attempted to cut off food supplies from England and France. —
14. Francis Scott Key wrote the Star Spangled Banner. —
15. Oliver Hazard Perry won a great victory on Lake Erie. —
16. British tried to invade New York. —
17. United States sent a fleet to bombard Tripoli. —
18. Andrew Jackson saved New Orleans. —
19. President did not believe that the United States should go to war. —
20. *Old Ironsides* captured one of England's finest ships. —

DATE PLACEMENT. After each term which you identify with the War of 1812 put the date 1812. After each term which you identify with the Monroe Doctrine put the date 1823.

1. Second war of independence. ———
2. Nations of Europe no longer permitted to increase their territory in America. ———
3. Checked British impressment of American seamen. ———
4. West was saved for the United States. ———
5. European nations were permitted to keep colonies in America which were already under their control. ———
6. President Monroe presented his doctrine to Congress. ———
7. There must be no interference with the independence of any country in America. ———
8. Taught Americans to depend upon themselves. ———
9. Taught Americans the necessity of manufacturing own goods. ———
10. The policy of "America for Americans" was established. ———

A MAN OF THE PEOPLE

Read to learn

1. How General Jackson won Florida.
2. About the "spoils system."
3. Why South Carolina objected to the tariff.
4. How Andrew Jackson defended the Federal Union

ANDREW JACKSON. The men who had done most for America up to this time had come from the thirteen original states. Most of them came from very comfortable homes. The first presidents were well educated men. Now we are to learn of a great American who was born very poor. He was a man who had lived in the rough Tennessee Country, beyond the mountains. This interesting person was Andrew Jackson. He was the hero at the Battle of New Orleans in the War of 1812.

WINNING FLORIDA. After the War of 1812, Jackson was a hero to the people. He remained in the army and had many exciting experiences. One of his experiences resulted in adding a large piece of country to the United States. At this time, Georgia, our most southern state, had a very bad neighbor. The bad neighbor was Florida. Spain owned Florida but paid little attention to it. Florida was filled with troublemakers. The Seminoles lived there. They were a fierce Indian tribe and often made raids into Georgia. It was quite safe for these Indians to attack the settlements in Georgia. The Seminoles could run back into Florida when they got into trouble. They were safe in the swamps and the forests.

Slaves often escaped from their masters by crossing over from Georgia into Florida. Pirates had their hiding places along the coast of that country. Florida was really a very bad neighbor.

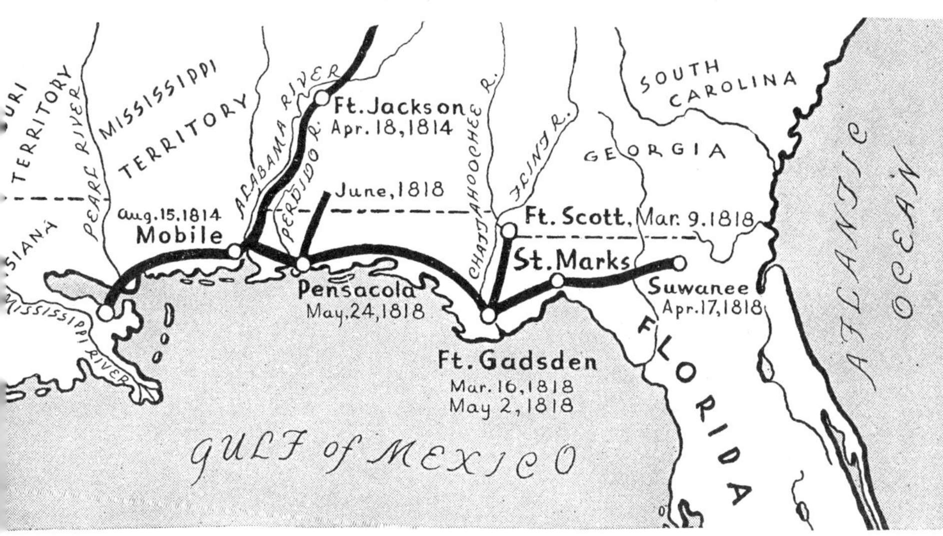

General Andrew Jackson was ordered to protect the border of Georgia. Jackson did not stop at the border but crossed into Florida. This was an invasion into foreign territory. He attacked the Indians and outlaws on their own ground. He hanged some and burned their homes. Soon all of Florida was under his control. The Spaniards were furious when they heard of Jackson's invasion. Fortunately, a peaceful way was found to settle the whole matter. Spain agreed to sell all of Florida to the United States. The map above shows the territory added by the purchase of Florida. It cost the United States $5,000,000 to settle the problem of Florida in 1819.

ANDREW JACKSON, PRESIDENT. Jackson's fame was growing greater. The ordinary people liked this daring general. They liked his great bravery, his straightforward manner, his careless dress and his rough speech. Jackson's friends felt he was just the man to be President of the United States. He was elected to that high office in 1828. Jackson's election brought about many changes. Instead of being just a rough soldier and a backwoodsman Jackson proved himself to be a statesman.

THE "SPOILS SYSTEM." Jackson had ideas of his own about running the government. He felt that "to the victors belong the spoils." The "spoils" were government jobs;

the "victors" were those who voted for him. Jackson discharged more than two thousand men who were working for the government. Then he put his own friends in their places. Jackson believed that any ordinary man was capable of taking a government job. Many of the men selected by Jackson and his friends were really not fit for the jobs they were given. Even to this day we feel the bad effects of the "spoils system."

SOUTH CAROLINA AND THE TARIFF. Jackson was very direct in his actions. During his first term as President South Carolina got in trouble with the United States government. This dispute arose over the tariff laws. A tariff is a tax on goods brought into the country. Such a tax is put on for two reasons: 1. to get money to run the government; 2. to help home manufactures.

Without such a tax people would buy the cheap goods of foreign countries. Our own factories would close and our own workers would be without jobs. So Congress passed a tariff law.

The South did not like the tariff. The people of the South were farmers. They had no factories. They wanted cheap clothes, farm implements, tools, and other goods, no matter where they were manufactured. The Southerners could not see why a farmer should be taxed to help a manufacturer. Finally, the people of South Carolina became very angry about the tariff law. They made up their minds that no tax on foreign goods would be collected in their seaports. They passed a stupid state law. The law passed by South Carolina attempted to nullify the tariff law passed by Congress. Nullify means that the law would no longer be in effect. The lawmakers of South Carolina had not thought very clearly. Only the law-making body which makes a law has the power to nullify that law. Congress had made the tariff law; only Congress could nullify it.

THE FEDERAL UNION. Jackson knew that South Carolina was doing a very dangerous thing. Every state must obey the laws of Congress, otherwise the Union would soon go to pieces. Jackson took a very dramatic way of telling what he thought. He was invited to a banquet and asked to give a toast. Jackson arose and sternly proposed this toast: "Our Federal Union: it must, and it shall be preserved." Soon after this he ordered two warships to Charleston Harbor and notified the army to be ready.

Before any real trouble happened a new tariff law was passed by Congress. It lowered the tax, little by little.

The danger to the Union passed, but only for a little while. Years later the terrible Civil War was fought to preserve "Our Federal Union."

STUDY SUMMARY

1. Terms to know. Be able to give the meaning of each term listed.

spoils system	tariff	spoils
invasion	victor	nullify

2. Dates to remember. Be able to tell one important event that took place on each of the following dates.

1819 1828

3. Places to know. Be able to locate on a wall map each place listed. Give one fact about each place as it is located.

Tennessee	North Carolina	South Carolina
Georgia	Florida	New Orleans

4. People to know. Be able to give an important fact about each group of people named.

Seminoles	pirates
government workers	run-away slaves

5. Character study. Give an example to prove that each of the following statements is true.
   1. Andrew Jackson was an earnest student.
   2. Jackson was a restless man.
   3. Andrew Jackson was a good soldier.
   4. General Jackson was a determined leader.
   5. General Jackson showed great bravery.
   6. Jackson was generous to his friends.
   7. Jackson could be stern.

ACTIVITIES

1. Name the three groups of troublemakers and explain how each made Florida a bad neighbor for the United States.
2. Make a set of brush and ink silhouettes of some dramatic moments in the life of Andrew Jackson. Be sure to show:
    1. General Jackson crossing the border into Florida.
    2. President Jackson giving the famous toast.

STUDY TEST 33—Score 10

SELECTING ENDINGS. Underscore the term which gives the correct ending to each statement. Put a period after the ending selected.

1. Andrew Jackson was born into a
   rich family comfortable family poor family
2. Florida was owned by
   Spain France Great Britain
3. The Seminoles were
   friendly troublesome kindly
4. General Jackson was ordered to protect the
   Indians border seacoast
5. Jackson's invasion of Florida made the Spaniards
   happy furious cheerful
6. The United States agreed to buy
   Georgia Tennessee Florida
7. President Jackson gave government jobs to his
   sons enemies friends
8. Jackson's plan of awarding government jobs was
   good fair bad
9. A tax on goods brought into the country is a
   tariff victor spoils
10. Andrew Jackson said that the Federal Union must be
    preserved neglected ignored

TEXAS AND MEXICO

Read to learn

1. Why American planters desired to go to Texas.
2. How bad feeling arose between the Mexicans and the Americans.
3. Why Texas revolted against Mexico.
4. How Texas became a state in the United States.
5. Why the United States and Mexico went to war.

LAND, MORE LAND. "New Land" was the motto of the American pioneers. The wilderness attracted them. Adventure was in their blood. So on they pushed, down the rivers, across the plains, over the mountains, into Oregon, into Texas, and on into California.

The Texas Country lay to the southwest of Louisiana. The planters desired new land and rich soil for their cotton crops. Planting cotton on the land year after year left the soil without much plant food. Texas belonged to the Republic of Mexico. It was a rich and almost uninhabited land. Beginning about 1820 many Americans left the United States and moved into Texas, which belonged to Mexico. Among those who went there were many slave owners from the South. The northern part of the United States was being closed to slavery by this time. The southern slave owners needed new farm land. This they could get in nearby Texas. The Government of Mexico gave to Stephen F. Austin a large tract of fertile land in Texas. Austin was a Yankee land dealer. He planned to encourage several hundred American families to settle on this land.

There were people from the Mississippi Valley who wanted to make a fresh start in life. There were very hard times in America and many families had lost their homes. Numbers of these people simply loaded a flat-boat with

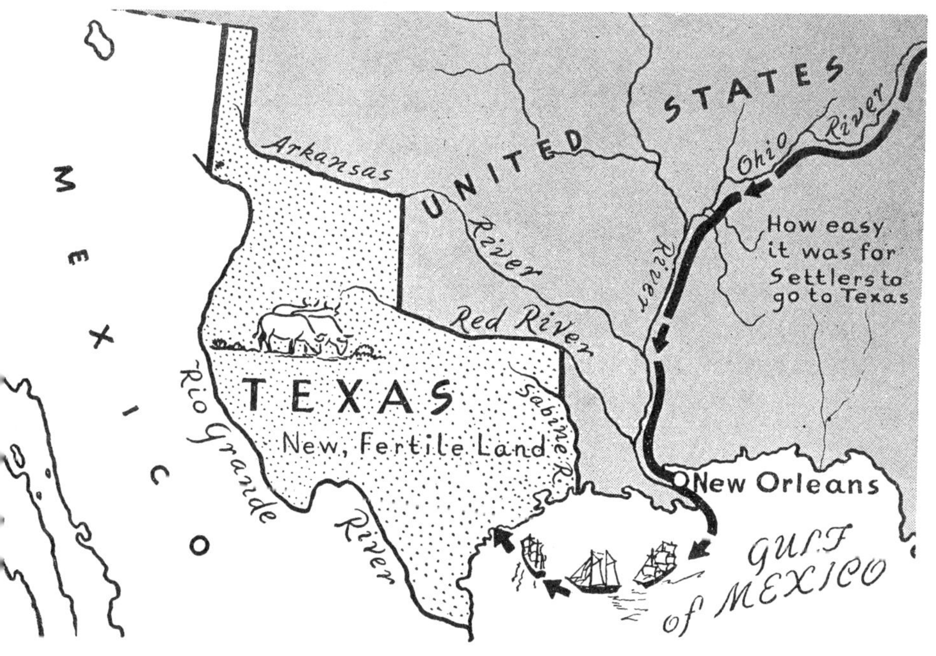

everything they owned, and floated down the Mississippi River to New Orleans. Then a journey overland, or a ship along the coast carried them into Texas.

The Americans were welcomed in Texas, which was almost an unsettled state. All Texas asked was that the settlers be respectable people and Catholics. Land was free and each family received a large estate.

More and more Americans went to Texas, but few of them were Catholics. They opened up farms and ranches. They suffered many hardships. Sometimes lack of rain would ruin their crops. Sometimes too much rain would cause the rivers to overflow. The land was flooded and the crops were destroyed. The settlers prospered in spite of all their difficulties. Soon Texas had quite a large population and its settlers were mostly American.

Friendly relations between Americans and Mexicans did not last. Not all the Americans were seeking homes in Texas. Some who went there were really adventurers who were actually looking for trouble. They were quarrelsome fellows and easily found Mexicans who were ready to fight. Bad feeling arose between the Americans and the Mexicans.

MEXICO ABOLISHES SLAVERY. This feeling became still worse when the Mexican government passed a law forbidding slavery. This was really a very good law, but it outraged the Americans. Another new order forbade the settlement of any more Americans in Texas. Texas belonged to Mexico and the Mexican government had a perfect right to make these laws. The Americans, or Texans, as they now called themselves, were angry. They wanted land and they wanted to keep their slaves. They did not like the government of Mexico, so they revolted. This means that the Texans became rebels and took up arms against the government of Mexico. Texans followed the leadership of Sam Houston.

THE ALAMO. The Mexican president was Santa Anna. He was a dictator. He had seized the Mexican government and ran it to suit himself. Santa Anna had no intention of giving up the country of Texas without a fight. At the head of an army of five thousand men he marched against the Texan rebels.

Santa Anna came upon a small force of about two hundred Texans. They had made a fort out of an old mission chapel, called the Alamo. Santa Anna's force attacked the fort. The two hundred Texans were determined to die

rather than surrender. They fought till the last man was killed. Years later an American president, Theodore Roosevelt, said that this fight at the Alamo was one of the bravest fights of which he had ever heard. After that time when Americans fought Mexicans the battle cry was "Remember the Alamo."

THE LONE STAR REPUBLIC. The Texans did not lose heart after this first defeat. Sam Houston had a fine little army under his command. He picked out a good spot for a battle near the San Jacinto River. The Mexicans felt sure that once again they could crush the Texans. They were wrong. Sam Houston's troops fell upon the Mexicans and destroyed them. Santa Anna was taken prisoner.

Texas soon declared her independence. Mexico would not acknowledge the independence of Texas. The new nation was sometimes called the "Lone Star Republic" because she had but one star on her flag. Texas remained an independent nation until 1845. Then, as many expected, this little American republic became part of the United States. This is what the Southerners had long wanted. It opened another great territory to slavery.

OUR WAR WITH MEXICO. Mexico still claimed a part of Texas. Yet Texas had become a state in the American Union. As was to be expected war broke out between the United States and Mexico. This was in 1846. James K. Polk was President of the United States. General Zachary Taylor was sent with an American army against the Mexicans. "Old Rough and Ready," as Taylor was called, won several battles.

General Winfield Scott invaded Mexico and captured Mexico City, the capital. After two years of fighting the Mexicans were defeated. General Taylor had become very popular. Later, this war hero was elected President of the United States.

The Mexican War turned out to be a splendid school for young army officers. In the picture General Scott is showing his young officers how to plan a battle by using a map. Many of the officers who fought in the Mexican War later became famous. Among these officers were Robert E. Lee and Ulysses S. Grant. They fought on opposite sides in the Civil War. They were the greatest generals of that war.

TERRITORY FROM MEXICO. Americans were proud of the way their soldiers fought in the Mexican War. The territory we gained in 1848 was a splendid one. The United States paid Mexico $15,000,000. We added a territory larger than the thirteen original states. It was a very rich territory. Study the map on page 295 and notice how the United States was growing.

Our states of Texas, New Mexico, Arizona, Nevada, Utah, part of Colorado and Wyoming, and the great state of California all once belonged to Mexico. After the Mexican War our country stretched across the continent from the Atlantic Ocean to the Pacific Ocean.

STUDY SUMMARY

1. Terms to know. Be able to give the meaning of each term listed.

   flat-boat, Alamo, Lone Star Republic, revolt

2. People to know. Be able to give an important fact about each person whose name is listed.

   Sam Houston, Zachary Taylor, James K. Polk, Winfield Scott, Robert E. Lee, Ulysses Grant, Santa Anna

3. Places to know. Be able to locate on a wall map each place listed. Give one fact about the place as it is located.

   New Orleans, Texas, Mississippi Valley, Mexico City, Oregon, California

4. Dates to remember. Be able to give an important event which took place on each of the following dates.

   1845, 1846, 1848

ACTIVITIES

1. Sketch an outline map of the United States.
   a. Shade the thirteen original states with horizontal lines.
   b. Use vertical lines to show the area added by the purchase of Louisiana Territory.
   c. Use dots to show the area added by the purchase of Florida.
   d. Fill in solid the "Lone Star State."
   e. Use diagonal lines to show the area added to the United States at the close of the Mexican War in 1848.

2. Give three reasons why American settlers moved into Texas.

3. Write a paragraph telling of the attack on the Alamo.

4. Make a table to identify the leaders in the Mexican War.

1. President of the United States during the war.	
2. President of Mexico.	
3. Led the rebels in Texas.	
4. Led the Mexican attack on the Alamo.	
5. Led the American army against the Mexicans.	
6. Led the Americans in the capture of Mexico City.	

STUDY TEST 34—Score 20

MATCHING. Before each term in Column I put the letter of the matching term in Column II.

Column I	Column II
— 1. Motto of the pioneers	A. Gen. Zachary Taylor
— 2. Almost uninhabited land	B. Santa Anna
— 3. Settlers moved into Texas from the	C. The Alamo
— 4. Forbade slavery	D. James K. Polk
— 5. Had a right to regulate Texas	E. Old Rough and Ready
— 6. Texans were led by	F. South
— 7. The Mexican president	G. Gen. Winfield Scott
— 8. Rebelled against the Mexican government	H. Mexican War
— 9. Old mission chapel used as a fort	I. Slave owners
— 10. Battle cry of the Texans	J. "New Land"
— 11. Lone Star Republic	K. Settlers in Texas
— 12. President during the Mexican War	L. Texas
— 13. Led the American army into Texas	M. Sam Houston
— 14. Added a large area to the United States	N. Republic of Texas
— 15. Led Americans in the capture of Mexico City	O. The United States
— 16. Needed new farm lands	P. Mexico
— 17. Nickname of General Taylor	Q. The Mexican War
— 18. Few were Catholics	R. Texans
— 19. Texas applied for admission as a state in	S. Mexican government
— 20. Texas was opened for slavery after	T. "Remember the Alamo"

CALIFORNIA

Read to learn

1. How California was claimed by Spain.
2. How Spanish missionaries labored among the Indians.
3. About the building of a mission.
4. How the Franciscans helped the Indians.
5. How California became a part of the United States.
6. About the discovery of gold in California.

CALIFORNIA. California is a wonderful land with a long and interesting history. Fifty years after Columbus discovered America, Juan Cabrillo discovered California. This was in 1542. Cabrillo was a Portuguese who was employed by Spain. Some years later Sir Francis Drake, the English pirate, reached California on his way around the world. Many years later England claimed part of the Pacific coast country because of Drake's visit. The cross and the Spanish flag were erected in California in 1602. The land was thus claimed for Spain.

MISSIONS OF LOWER CALIFORNIA. Spain took but little interest in California for many years. When this interest did come it was through Catholic missionaries. The great and good Jesuit, Father Eusebio Kino, started missionary work among the Indians of Lower California. The map on page 299 shows that Lower California is a peninsula. Father Kino was a great explorer and a map maker, as well as a holy priest. Many people thought Lower California was an island, but Father Kino proved it to be a peninsula which joined the mainland. He worked among the Indians of the land now called Arizona. The

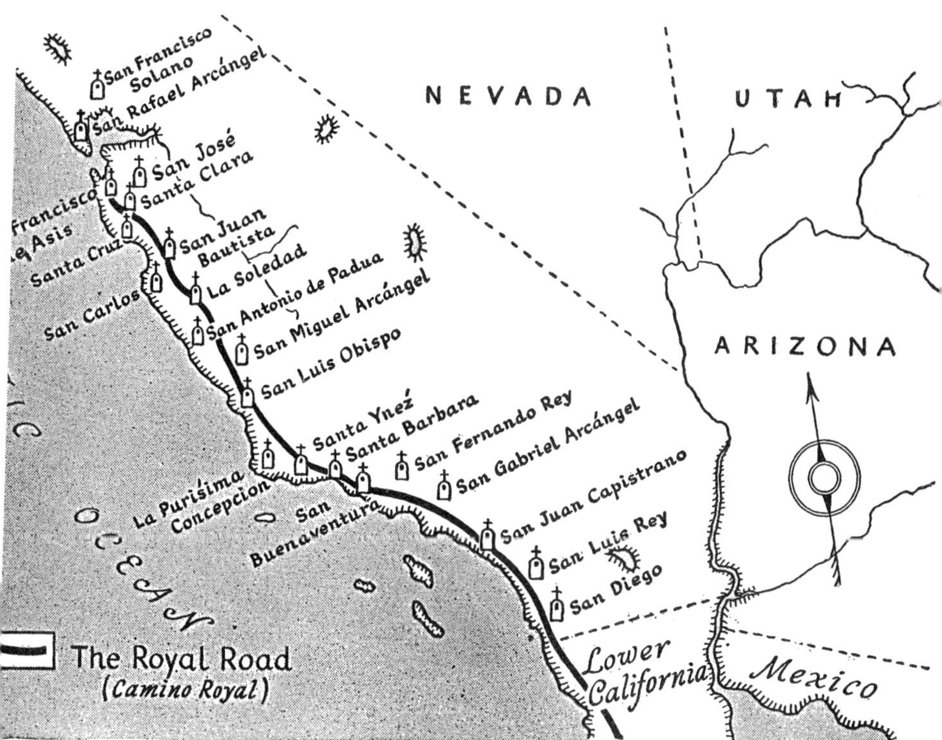

Indians showed Father Kino how to reach California from the land side. The Jesuits worked among the Indians of Lower California for almost seventy years. Suddenly the Spanish king took a dislike to the Jesuits. They were ordered to leave Spain and all the Spanish countries.

FATHER JUNIPERO SERRA. Spain was not willing to abandon California. As a Catholic nation she could not let the Indians become pagans again. Spain felt that if she neglected this land Russia would claim it. Russians were in Alaska and were pushing southward down the coast. They might soon reach Upper California. So Spain sent the Franciscan Fathers to establish missions in California. The leader of the Franciscans was Father Junipero Serra. The first mission was founded at San Diego in 1769. Year by year others were added.

Today, in California there is a magnificent motor road. It is called "The Royal Road." This was but a narrow footpath in the days of the missions. Along it the mission stations were built. There were twenty-one in all. The farthest north was that of San Francisco, on a lovely bay in mid-California. The great city that now bears the name of the mission, San Francisco, grew around the mission. Another mission was named Los Angeles in honor of Our Lady, Queen of the Angels. It is now the largest city in California.

Father Serra and the Franciscans labored hard and suffered many hardships. They won countless souls for Christ.

FOUNDING THE MISSIONS. Building up a mission was hard but interesting work. First the priests chose a good location. Then a simple little chapel was built, as a home for Our Lord. A small house for the missionaries was also built. Then the church bells, hanging perhaps from the limb of a tree, would be rung. The Indians would gather around. The priests would invite the Indians to come and live in the mission. At first the Indians were timid. They were afraid of these strange men in their brown habits. Soon the Indians came to know and to love the good priests. Then the Indians came to the missions quite willingly.

THE MISSION BUILDINGS. After a while the priests and Indians together started to build the real mission. The buildings were strongly built. Their walls were of adobe. This is a kind of hard baked clay. The roofs were covered with red tile. The buildings formed a square. The center court was always a lovely garden.

The principal building was the church. Some of these lovely mission churches are still standing. In them Indians came to attend Mass. There they heard about Our Saviour, His Mother, and the Saints. Nearby the church there was a home for the priests and a place where the sick could be treated. There was a school, and there were workrooms where the Indians could learn certain trades. Indians who

were married had little homes of their own; the other Indians lived in dormitories. A dormitory is a place where several people sleep.

A DAY AT THE MISSION. Days at the mission were busy and happy. At sunrise the mission bell called the Indians from their homes. All hastened to the church for morning prayers and Mass. Then followed breakfast and the beginning of the day's work.

Some of the Indians worked on the farm where they raised wheat, barley, corn, and beans. Some Indians were herdsmen. They took care of the cattle and the sheep. Others learned a trade and were busy tanning hides, spinning and weaving cloth, or doing carpentry work. They made wine, candles, and soap. The mission fathers trained the Indians to do many useful things.

The Franciscans brought to America fruits that had not been grown here before. From sunny Spain they brought oranges, lemons, grapes for wine, and olives for oil. These are the fruits which help to make California rich today.

WORK AND REST. The day's work was not too long nor too hard. Six or seven hours each day was enough. No work was done during the heat of the day, from eleven o'clock to two o'clock. Sundays and many Holy Days were days of rest from hard labor.

This happy and useful life at the missions continued until Mexico rebelled against Spain and became independent. Then the missions fell into ruin and decay.

JOHN CHARLES FRÉMONT

AMERICANS IN CALIFORNIA. Shortly after Americans started to go into Texas other Americans went into California. First, went a party of fur-trappers, sent out by the Rocky Mountain Fur Company. They were led by Jebediah Smith. Their idea was to find out all the secrets of the land between the Rocky Mountains and the Pacific Coast. California then belonged to Mexico and the Americans were not always welcome. This little band of Americans, footsore and weary, were well received by some of the Catholic missionaries who still remained. "Friendly gentlemen," Smith called them. After various adventures Smith worked his way, alone, up the entire length of California. He finally got back to Salt Lake.

Americans continued to go into California. Parts of that country had more Americans than Mexicans in a few years' time. Riches were there for all who would take them. The farmer found splendid soil. The rancher found grassy valleys for cattle. The trapper found that fur-bearing animals were plentiful.

A FAMOUS SCOUT. When war broke out with Mexico the United States government did not forget the Americans in California. At that time a famous scout, John Charles Frémont, was camping in that country. A scout

is a person sent to get information. The government at Washington sent a message to him. It told him to look after the Americans in California. California had now become enemy country.

Frémont was born in Savannah, Georgia. He went to college and became a surveyor. His work called him to the Middle West. There he heard a great deal about the Far West. He longed to know more about it. Frémont decided to explore the unknown western country. He climbed a high Rocky Mountain peak in Wyoming. Later, this peak was named in honor of Frémont. He went beyond the Rockies into California. There, from another high peak, he could see the blue waters of San Francisco Bay.

THE "OLD PATHFINDER." Frémont's first expedition had taken a northerly route. Now he decided to find a more southerly path to the Pacific. So the "Old Pathfinder," as the people called him, set out again. The greater the hardships the more eager he was to learn about the Far West. He had crossed the mountains and arrived in the Sacramento Valley in Central California. Here the message from the American government reached him.

THE BEAR FLAG. Word had come to the Americans in California that the United States was at war with Mexico.

The Americans decided upon a bold move. They held a meeting and declared California to be free and independent from Mexico. They raised a flag as a sign of the independence of California. This was the famous "Bear Flag." The flag was a piece of light cloth on which the figure of a bear was painted. Berry juice was used to color the bear.

Fremont soon arrived and the people of California were glad to have him as their leader. Under Frémont the Americans gave a good account of themselves. Each clash with the Mexicans found the Americans on top.

THE AMERICAN FLAG. Meanwhile the American navy and army were getting to work. Commodore John Drake Sloat had a small fleet of ships in a port of Mexico. There were English warships there also. England had her eyes on California. Sloat set sail for California and the English followed. Sloat won the race to Monterey and captured the Mexican Customs House. He raised the American flag for the first time in California. The English fleet arrived later. Sloat had his decks cleared for action but there was no trouble. The English realized that they had arrived too late.

Sloat was succeeded by Commodore R. F. Stockton who took over more territory. Then an army force arrived under Colonel Stephen Kearney. It helped complete the task of overcoming the Mexicans. California finally became American territory at the end of the Mexican War, in 1848.

THE FORTY-NINERS

THE DISCOVERY OF GOLD. No sooner had California become American than that land of sunshine turned into a land of gold. Gold! What an exciting word that is! The whole world thrills whenever gold is found. Can you imagine a man having gold discovered on his property and losing his whole fortune? Such a man was John A. Sutter.

John A. Sutter, in 1848, was one of the largest landowners in America. He was born in Baden, Germany, and from his early life had many adventures. He came to the United States and the lure of the West took him to California. Sutter received a grant of land from the Mexican government. He was a good farmer and he prospered. More acres were added to his ranches. Grain and fruit were harvested in abundance. Meat, hides, milk, and cheese were produced on his ranches.

Suddenly, all this was changed. Sutter hired a man named James W. Marshall to build a new sawmill. One day Marshall was standing by the mill-race. This was the channel that brought the rushing water to the water-wheel. Marshall noticed some shining yellow grains in the sand of the mill-race. He picked the bright grains out of the water. Could they be gold? He hardly thought so but took them to Sutter. Tests were made. "Gold!" exclaimed Sutter. He was not mistaken. Gold had really been found.

THE RUSH FOR GOLD. The news could not be kept secret. The word spread all over America, and even to Europe. Men by the thousands left their work and started for California. Everyone had the gold-fever. A few ounces of the precious metal were worth more than months of toil in the fields. The farmer left his crops, the rancher deserted his cattle. Sutter saw his fields neglected, his cattle abandoned. Squatters took his land from him and he became a poor man.

There was no easy way to reach California. Some people went across plain and mountain on horseback. Many people traveled in wagons called "prairie schooners." These were canvas-covered wagons in which settlers moved into the West. Others went by water all around South America. When the ships reached California both passengers and crews set out for the gold fields. The ships swung at anchor with no one to care for them.

Not all who set out for the gold fields reached them. But thousands did arrive. Two years after gold was discovered there were almost one hundred thousand people in California. The picture gives some idea of how San Francisco looked during the gold rush. Many who did not find gold found something better. They found fertile soil and a delightful climate. California had a large enough population to become a state by 1850.

STUDY SUMMARY

1. Terms to know. Be able to give the meaning of each term listed.

dormitories	squatters	mill-race
adobe	missions	peninsula
scout	prairie schooners	

2. Places to know. Be able to locate on a wall map each place listed. Give one fact about the place as it is located.

San Diego	Monterey	Lower California
Los Angeles	Alaska	Sacramento Valley
California	Wyoming	San Francisco

3. People to know. Be able to give an important fact about each person or group of people named.

Father Juniper Serra	Father Eusebio Kino
Juan Cabrillo	Sir Frances Drake
John Drake Sloat	John Charles Frémont
Colonel Stephen Kearney	Commodore R. F. Stockton
John A. Sutter	Franciscans
Russians	Indians
Jesuits	

4. Dates to remember. Tell one important event which took place on each of the following dates.

   1542 1602 1848

ACTIVITIES

1. Make a model of a mission. Be sure to arrange the buildings around the center court. Show the church, the school, workrooms where the trades were taught, the house where the priest lived, the Indian homes, and the dormitories.
2. List four fruits which the Franciscans brought to California.
3. Give an oral report of the explorations of John Charles Frémont.
4. Explain how the discovery of gold in California helped to people California.

STUDY TEST 35—Score 25

COMPLETION. Fill in the missing letters to correctly complete each word.

1. California was discovered by Juan C – – – – – – – –.
2. He was a Portuguese employed by S – – – –.
3. California was discovered f – – – – years after the discovery of America by Columbus.
4. California was also reached by Sir Francis Drake, the English p – – – – – –.

5. S – – – – – set up her claim to California in 1602.
6. Father Eusebio Kino began missionary work among the I – – – – – – –.
7. Father Kino proved that Lower California is a p – – – – – – – – –.
8. The Spanish king took a dislike to the J – – – – – – –.
9. Russians were already in A – – – – – –.
10. The Spanish feared that the Russians might move southward into Upper C – – – – – – – – – –.
11. Franciscan Fathers were sent to California to establish m – – – – – – – –.
12. Father Junipero Serra founded the first mission at S – – D – – – – – in 1769.
13. The Franciscan Fathers established twenty-one m – – – – – – – –.
14. The mission at San Francisco was the farthest n – – – – –.
15. The walls of the mission were made of a – – – – –.
16. Red t – – – – – were used for the roofs.
17. The Franciscans taught the Indians to love G – –.
18. Mission Fathers taught the Indians many useful t – – – – – –.
19. The Indians were taught how to make w – – – from grapes, and how to make o – – from olives.
20. John Charles Fremont was a famous s – – – – –.
21. Fremont was anxious to learn about the F – – W – – –.
22. Americans declared that California was free and independent from M – – – – – –.
23. Commodore John Drake Sloat led his little f – – – – into the harbor at Monterey.
24. The American f – – – was raised over the Customs House.
25. The discovery of g – – – in California attracted many settlers.

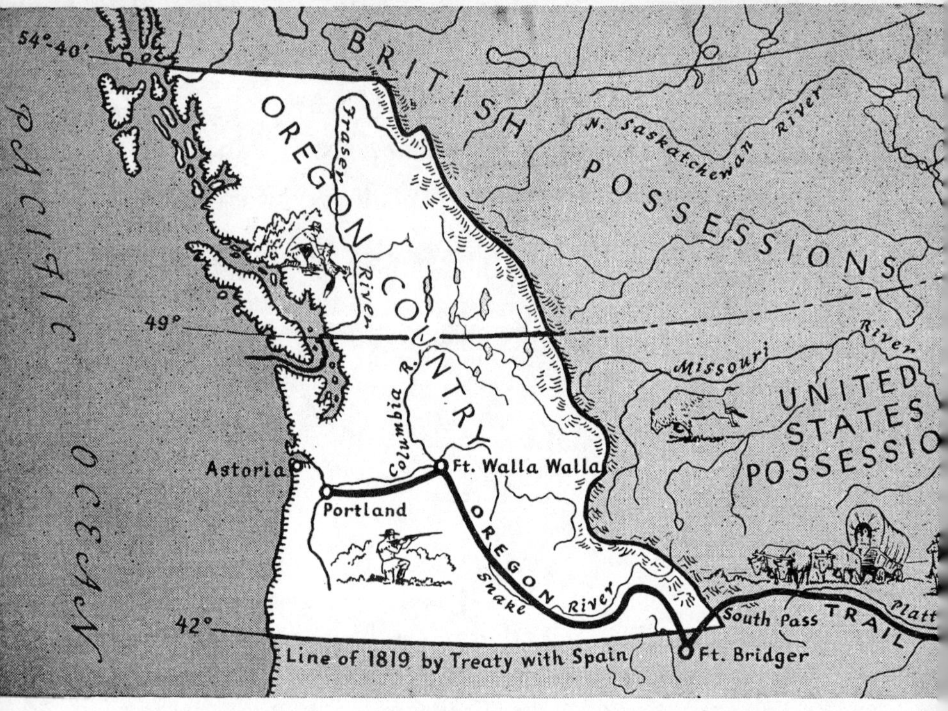

THE OREGON COUNTRY

Read to learn

1. About the Great Migration into the Oregon Country.
2. How settlers prepared for the journey over the Oregon Trail.
3. How the night camp was made.
4. How the quarrel between the English and the Americans about the Oregon Country was settled.
5. How Father Peter de Smet, the Jesuit, helped the Flatheads.
6. How Doctor John McLoughlin helped the American settlers in the Oregon Country.

THE FAR NORTHWEST. Stretching along the Pacific Coast from California to Alaska was the Oregon Country, as shown on the map. It was a rich land and much larger than our present state of Oregon.

Both England and America claimed the Oregon Country. The claims of both nations were based on discovery, exploration, and some few settlements. Neither nation had many people living in Oregon, yet both nations insisted that they owned it.

A treaty was made between the two countries. It gave both Americans and Englishmen the right to settle in Oregon. The Americans in large numbers commenced to go into the Oregon Country. The fame of the Oregon Country spread. People heard of its fertile soil and pleasant climate. Reports came of lovely valleys ready for the farmer, of fish and game in abundance, and of the fur-bearing animals for the trappers. Men got the "Oregon fever," as it was called.

THE GREAT MIGRATION. A very large band of Americans began the march to Oregon in 1843. This movement is often called the "Great Migration." A migration means a movement of people from one place to another. Independence in Missouri was the starting place of the great migration. There the pioneers in their covered wagons assembled from all parts of the country. There they had their last chance to make repairs and to get supplies. There the final plans were made. A captain was selected to head the party. A fur trader, who knew the way, was chosen as a guide to take the party over the "Oregon Trail."

THE OREGON TRAIL. It was a good thing that careful preparations had been made. These brave pioneers were facing a two-thousand-mile journey. They were to cross wide prairies and to pass around high mountains. They would be in danger from fierce and warlike Indians. It was necessary to guard against hunger and thirst, and against heat and cold.

Early on a May morning the bugle gave the signal to start. Over a thousand men, women, and children were

ready and eager to go. Some rode on horseback, some traveled in prairie schooners. The number of wagons was so great that it was decided to move in two divisions. Those owning a few cattle were to move in the "light column." Those with large herds moved in the "cow column."

THE COW COLUMN. The business of moving was difficult. The entire party, "light column" and "cow column" had to be awake before dawn. In the light of the early morning the women cooked the breakfast while the men rounded up the cattle. Everything in the wagons was lashed or fastened. The trail would be rough and bumpy. The oxen were yoked to the wagons and a bugle signal was given. The long train of wagons was on the move. "Gee, haw!" cried the drivers to keep the oxen on their path. It was no easy task to drive the oxen.

THE LONG DAY. Some of the men went ahead to act as scouts. Others swung wide on each side to protect the column. The long line of cattle followed in the rear. The wagons were heavily loaded with furniture and farm tools. Each family carried everything they owned. The brave pioneer mothers tended their fretting children. All during the hot summer days the party plodded on its weary way. The oxen were strong but they moved very slowly.

PREPARATIONS FOR THE NIGHT. Before sunset the signal to halt was given. The wagons were then placed to form a circle. The men chained the wagons together. Thus the wagons made quite a good fort. Sentinels were posted to look out for unfriendly Indians and everybody else went to work. There were no idle hands in the party. Even the boys and girls were given something to do. There were cattle to be cared for, fires to be tended and the meal to be cooked.

The families sat about the fires to eat the evening meal. Dried beef and bacon formed their simple fare except when the hunting party had good luck. Then everyone feasted on buffalo meat or prairie chicken. Hot corn cakes made at the fire were always welcome.

Even before sundown the fires and lights were put out. Shining in the darkness fires might be seen by the Indians. Soon the weary travelers were sleeping. Only the lonely sentinels kept the watch. After weeks and weeks of travel by day and rest by night, the flat prairie country was passed. Then the party plodded through the more difficult mountain trails. After six months of hardships the company finally reached Oregon. Later, other Americans followed these daring members of the "Great Migration."

THE OREGON QUESTION. The lower Oregon Country was now becoming settled with Americans. This gave the United States a good claim to it. We made an offer to England to divide Oregon but no decision was reached. Then some hotheaded Americans demanded the whole Oregon Country. "Fifty-four forty or fight" was their motto. That meant they wanted all the country north to the fifty-fourth degree of latitude. Notice on a wall map that Canada would have been cut off from the Pacific Ocean. England would fight rather than let this happen. Fortunately an agreement was reached and the Oregon Country was divided. At that time the 49° of latitude was our northern boundary east of the Rocky Mountains. The treaty of 1846 made this our northern boundary west of the mountains.

FATHER DE SMET AND DOCTOR McLOUGHLIN

TWO GREAT CHARACTERS. The story of Oregon includes the names of two great men: Father Peter de Smet, S.J., the "Apostle of the Rockies," and Doctor John McLoughlin, the "Father of Oregon."

The Flatheads of the far-off Oregon Country wanted a priest. A little band of these Indians made the long, dangerous trip to Saint Louis to ask for a "black robe." Father de Smet offered to go west to the Indians. With an Indian to guide him the good priest set out on horseback. They met with a company of American fur-traders and reached

Oregon in 1841. Father de Smet preached the Gospel to the Indians. He taught them to love Christ and to love one another. The Indians loved Father de Smet and he understood them. He spent the rest of his life with the Indians in the Oregon Country. He preached to them, taught them, and cared for them.

This is Father de Smet's beautiful description of Christmas Midnight Mass among the Indians. "The signal for rising was the firing of a pistol. This was followed by a general discharge of guns, in honor of the birth of the Infant Saviour. Then three hundred voices, from the midst of the forest, intoned the beautiful canticle 'The Almighty's Glory all Things Proclaim.' In a moment a multitude of adorers were seen on their way to the humble temple of the Lord."

DOCTOR JOHN McLOUGHLIN. The Hudson's Bay Company was the great fur-trading concern of Canada. This company was bitterly opposed to American settlements in Oregon. Settlers cut down the forests and tilled the soil. This drove away the wild fur-bearing animals.

Strange to say, the Americans in Oregon found their best friend in one who was employed by the Hudson's Bay Company. He was Doctor John McLoughlin.

John McLoughlin was born in Canada but studied medicine in Scotland. When he returned to Canada he decided not to practice as a doctor. The great wild West attracted him. He was employed by the Hudson's Bay Company, in Oregon, as a manager.

Oregon was a desolate and dangerous place when John McLoughlin arrived there. It was worth a man's life to travel about the country. People moved in large, well-armed parties to protect themselves from the Indians. Some white people had mistreated, even murdered the Indians. This made the Indians eager for revenge. Doctor McLoughlin soon changed all this. His kindly ways won the friendship of the Indians. While he was in charge of the Hudson's Bay Company the Indians stopped fighting with the whites and among themselves.

AMERICANS IN OREGON. Later, the Americans began to arrive. They were opening up a new country and frequently things went wrong. They needed help. Doctor McLoughlin was kind to the Americans. The Hudson's Bay Company sternly warned him. The English Company did not approve of his friendly relations with the Americans. McLoughlin preferred doing good to making money. He would not give up helping people, even when they were Americans. He resigned from the Hudson's Bay Company so that he could be free to help whenever help was needed.

THE FATHER OF OREGON. Doctor McLoughlin continued to help the Americans in many ways. He gave them seed for their new farms and other supplies. Much of his time was spent doctoring the sick. He brought about a better feeling between the Canadians and the Americans. He can well be called the "Father of Oregon."

STUDY SUMMARY

1. Terms to know. Be able to give the meaning of each term listed.

   migration | Oregon trail | sentinels
   "light column" | "cow column" | prairie schooners

2. People to know. Be able to give some important facts about the people named.

   Father Peter de Smet | Doctor John McLoughlin

3. Places to know. Be able on a wall map to locate each place named. Give one fact about the place as it is located.

   Independence, Missouri | Oregon Country
   Rocky Mountains | Saint Louis

4. Dates to remember. Be able to tell the important events in American history which took place in

   1843 | 1846

ACTIVITIES

1. Make a set of posters to illustrate the GREAT MIGRATION. Be sure to show:
   a. Pioneers assembling at Independence, Missouri.
   b. Movement of the "light column" and of the "cow column."
   c. The halt before sunset.
   d. Sentinels on night watch.
   e. Getting ready in the morning.

   Use the posters for oral reports.
2. Make a list of the things which had to be guarded against before the migration began.
3. Explain the meaning of "Fifty-four forty or fight."
4. Write two paragraphs on the subject of SELF-SACRIFICING LIVES. Have one paragraph tell about Father de Smet and the other paragraph about Doctor McLoughlin.

STUDY TEST 36—Score 30

FILL IN OUTLINE. Use only terms listed below.

1. The Oregon Country extended from .... to ....
2. Oregon Country was claimed by both .... and ....
3. Both nations based their claims on ...., ..., and ....
4. A treaty gave equal rights to settle to .... and to ....
5. People heard of the Oregon Country and its fertile ...., pleasant ...., lovely ...., and abundant ...., and ....
6. Pioneers moved on .... and in ....
7. The settlers had to guard against ...., ..., ... and warlike ....
8. The wagons were heavily loaded with ...., and farm ....
9. The Oregon Trail was .... miles long.
10. The journey took about .... months.
11. A compromise made .... degrees of latitude our northern boundary in Oregon.
12. The Apostle of the Rockies was ....
13. The Father of Oregon was ....
14. Father de Smet spent his life in the service of God for the ....
15. Doctor John McLoughlin was self-sacrificing in helping the Indians and the ....

fish	thirst	climate	United States
game	Americans	Indians	settlement
heat	English	furniture	horseback
2000	valleys	hunger	exploration
cold	discovery	Indians	John McLoughlin
49	England	Americans	prairie schooners
soil	Alaska	California	tools
six			Father de Smet

INVENTIONS TO SAVE LABOR

Read to learn

1. Why times were so bad in the South.
2. How the invention of the cotton gin brought prosperity to the South.
3. How the cotton gin caused an increase in slavery.
4. About the invention of the reaper.
5. How the invention of the sewing machine helped the clothing industry.

ELI WHITNEY

Can you imagine a pair of cotton stockings being "fit for a queen"? That was so in Queen Elizabeth's day. Cotton was rare and expensive in those days. Even after cotton began to be cultivated in America it continued to be costly. Let us follow the story of the man who changed all this. His name was Eli Whitney and he was born in Massachusetts. When Eli was young, almost the only thing he knew about cotton was that it was expensive.

A NAIL MAKER. Whitney was a boy at the time of the Revolutionary War. While still quite young he helped to support his family by making nails. He made good nails and he easily sold them all. He had a motto, "Whatever is worth doing, is worth doing well." When he went to Yale College he lived up to this motto. He became known as a good student.

After college Eli Whitney went to the South, traveling by boat. A passenger on the boat was Mrs. Nathanael Greene. She was the widow of General Nathanael Greene,

who fought so well in the Revolution. When they arrived in Georgia, Mrs. Greene introduced young Eli Whitney to her friends. Whitney in this way met some of the leading men in the South.

THE POOR CONDITION OF THE SOUTH. Mrs. Greene gave a party and invited young Whitney. All the men at the party were talking about the bad condition of the South.

Everyone agreed that cotton was hardly worth growing. Whitney could not understand that. He knew that many people in the world would be glad to get cotton. So they explained the whole problem to Whitney.

THE COTTON PROBLEM. Cotton was grown very easily and very cheaply in the South. There was no problem about that. The trouble was with the cotton seed. Hidden in each fluffy cotton boll, as it grows on the bush, are dozens of seeds. Before the cotton lint can be used the seeds must be removed. The work of removing the seeds was very slow. Every seed in a boll of cotton had to be removed by hand. This was slow and tedious work. It took a slave a whole day to clean about one pound of cotton. If this work could only be done by machine! Then the South would become rich indeed.

THE COTTON GIN. Whitney went into the fields and for the first time saw cotton bolls. He decided to invent a machine to clean the seeds from the cotton. Eli Whitney shut himself up in a workshop. First, he even had to make the tools he needed. For three months he worked patiently. He had many disappointments. At the end of three months he turned out a real cotton cleaning machine. This machine was invented in 1793. Eli Whitney's machine could remove in a day the seeds from many hundreds of pounds of cotton. The machine was called the "cotton gin," that is "cotton engine."

The South was delighted with Whitney's invention. Thousands of acres of land were planted in cotton. New fields were quickly covered with snow white bolls. Cotton cloth became cheaper and everybody wanted cottons. The Southern planters were becoming very wealthy growing the cotton to supply the mills. Prosperity had come to the South, but at a terrible price.

This price was the spread of slavery. Slavery had begun to die out before the invention of the cotton gin. This machine made cotton "King." Thousands of slaves were needed to work on the cotton plantations.

Whitney did not grow rich on his invention. Many men used the cotton gin without paying him anything for his

invention. His first machine was even stolen and copied. However, the state of Georgia granted him a sum of money as a reward for the invention of the cotton gin.

Later, Whitney got rich by making guns for the government. Whitney was perhaps the first person in the United States to introduce mass production. Each one of his men worked at making a certain part of a gun. These parts were all interchangeable; that is the parts were made exactly alike so that any one of them would fit any gun. In that way the parts could be quickly assembled or put together, and the gun was ready to use. The modern automobile is made along the same plan.

CYRUS McCORMICK

THE STAFF OF LIFE. There is an old and a wise saying that, "bread is the staff of life." It is one of the most important of our foods. Bread is made from flour and flour is made from wheat. Wheat is easy to grow, but in the old days, it was difficult to reap, or cut. A little over a hundred years ago there lived a Virginia farmer named Robert McCormick. Each year when McCormick's wheat was ripe he had it cut with a long curved knife, called a scythe. A scythe can cut only a few stalks of wheat at a time. The work was hard and the result was only a small amount of grain. Robert McCormick wished he had some sort of a big cutting machine. Then he could reap a whole wheat field in a short time.

THE PROMISE OF A REAPER. Thinking about a wheat cutting machine led McCormick to start thinking of how to make one. It took some time but at last he built a reaper that he thought would do the work. He called together his neighbors and friends. Sad to say, the machine was not a success. Robert McCormick was discouraged and did not try to make another reaper.

THE McCORMICK REAPER, 1834. Robert McCormick had a son named Cyrus. Cyrus began tinkering with his father's machine. Then he put that machine aside and started to build one on his own plan. He worked at the machine for three years. Then success came. Cyrus McCormick turned out a machine that would cut the grain evenly. Best of all very little grain was wasted. It was nine years before a single reaper was sold. Then better times came. Farmers began to buy the McCormick reaper. Other reaping machines had been invented about that time. The farmers liked the McCormick reaper best.

Cyrus McCormick was more than an inventor, he was a keen business man. He looked around for a good place to build his machines. He felt that the level prairies of the West would, in time, become the great wheat growing sections of America. So McCormick moved to Chicago, in 1847. At that time Chicago was only a small city. McCormick expected his business to grow with Chicago and that is exactly what happened.

The McCormick reaper did its part in helping to make America great and rich. We became the greatest wheat-growing country in the world. This could not have happened without a harvesting machine such as Cyrus McCormick invented.

ELIAS HOWE

THE SEWING MACHINE. This is the story of another "Yankee Inventor." It is the story of another long struggle to win success in the making of a sewing machine. The sewing machine is another labor-saving device, as were the cotton gin and the reaper. They helped the planter and the farmer. The sewing machine was of greatest help to the women in the home and to the workers in the factory. Its inventor was Elias Howe.

Elias Howe was born in Massachusetts. His father was the town miller. The farmers brought their wheat to his mill to be ground into flour. Young Howe had only a few terms in school. He had to go to work. His first job was with his father in the mill. Soon he left home and went to work in the city of Lowell, Massachusetts. Even in those days Lowell had a number of textile factories or mills.

A NEEDED MACHINE. The South sent cotton to Lowell to be spun and woven into cloth. The mills were making plenty of cloth. There was no trouble about making the cloth. The trouble was to sew the cloth into clothing. Every stitch of this sewing had to be done by hand. Howe had the idea that there should be a machine to do the sewing. It would be a most important link in the chain of making clothing.

Elias Howe began to work on a sewing machine. His tools were poor and the work was slow. He had a little money and could only work on the new machine now and then. At times Howe almost starved, but he would not give up. At last he made a machine that would really sew. He was granted a patent on the sewing machine in 1845. A patent is an official paper granted by the government. It protects an inventor. A patent gives an inventor the sole right to manufacture and to sell the article invented.

A MISUNDERSTOOD INVENTION. Howe had a sewing machine and a government patent, but this did not help him much. No one would lend him money to make sewing machines which he could sell to other people. The hard-headed business men of Boston would have nothing to do with Howe's machine. Elias Howe then went to England, but no one there would take a chance on his invention. To make matters worse some people began to claim that Howe was not the real inventor of the sewing machine. Howe went to law and proved his rights. Then came a change in his fortunes. Quite suddenly people seemed to see the enormous value of the sewing machine. A factory was built to make them. Almost everyone wanted a sewing machine. Sewing machines were used in the home and in the factory. They could sew cloth and canvas and all sorts of materials. Soon an improved machine could stitch even leather. Then cheap boots and shoes could be made.

The first sewing machines were run by hand. Then Isaac Singer made a sewing machine with a foot pedal. Modern sewing machines are usually run by electricity.

STUDY SUMMARY

1. Terms to know. Be able to give the meaning of each term listed.

   assembled — scythe — mass production
   cotton gin — patent — interchangeable parts
   Yankee inventor — reap — labor-saving devices

2. People to know. Be able to tell some interesting fact about each person whose name is listed.

   Cyrus McCormick — Mrs. Nathanael Greene
   Eli Whitney — Robert McCormick
   Elias Howe

3. Places to know. Be able to locate on a wall map each place listed. Give one fact about the place as it is located.

   Chicago — Boston — Lowell

4. Dates to remember. Be able to tell one important event about an invention in connection with the following dates.

   1793 — 1834 — 1845

ACTIVITIES

1. Make a table and fill in the terms and the dates.

SOME YANKEE INVENTIONS			
Name	Invention	Date	Industry helped
1.			
2.			
3.			

2. Explain how each of the following inventions helped the development of some particular industry.

   a. cotton gin b. reaper c. sewing machine

STUDY TEST 37—Score 20

IDENTIFICATION. After each statement which you identify with Eli Whitney, or the invention of the cotton gin, put W; after each statement which you identify with Cyrus McCormick, or the invention of the reaper, put McC; and after each statement which you identify with Elias Howe, or the sewing machine, put H.

1. He knew that cotton was expensive. —
2. He planned to make guns by mass production. —
3. He worked for three years on his invention. —
4. His invention was a great help to the South. —
5. He studied the machine made by his father. —
6. He worked for his father in a grain mill. —
7. He invented a machine to cut grain. —
8. His invention caused an increase of slavery. —
9. Georgia rewarded him for his invention. —
10. He did not sell a machine for nine years. —
11. He invented the cotton gin. —
12. His invention helped to make the United States a great wheat growing country. —
13. He invented the sewing machine. —
14. His tools were poor and he had little money but he never gave up. —
15. His invention was very helpful in the home. —
16. He was a good business man as well as a clever inventor. —
17. He met some leading cotton planters. —
18. He selected Chicago as the center for the manufacturing of his machine. —
19. His invention was a great help to the clothing industry. —
20. "Whatever is worth doing, is worth doing well," was his motto. —

UNIT VIII: INVENTIONS AND DISCOVERIES

MAKING IT EASIER TO TRAVEL

Read to learn

1. How people traveled in the early days in America.
2. About the invention of the steamboat.
3. How the steamboat helped transportation.
4. About the building of the Erie Canal.
5. How the Erie Canal helped the country.

TRAVEL IN OLDEN DAYS. Everybody likes to travel. Today, it is easy to go from one part of our country to another. There was a time when travel was not only difficult but it was slow and dangerous.

Suppose you had lived in the time of George Washington. How would you have enjoyed taking a trip on "the flying machine"? This flying machine was considered to be the last word in speed. It was really a stagecoach. It made the ninety mile trip from New York to Philadelphia in three days. Was that speedy? It took the flying machine seventy-two hours to go ninety miles. The rate of travel was about one and a quarter miles in an hour. The average walking rate is about a mile in fifteen minutes.

TRAVEL AND COMMUNICATION

TRAVEL BY WATER. The most common means of travel in the early days was by water. There were three reasons why this was so.

1. Few of the settlements were very far inland. Most of the settlements were easily reached from the sea.
2. There were many navigable streams. These became the natural routes between settlements.
3. Between the rivers often there were lowlands. These were used as portages. Places between waterways where goods and boats may be carried to another stream are called portages.

Few bridges had been built in the early days. Boats, called ferries, were often used to carry people and goods across streams. Shallow streams were often crossed by fording. When the horses or oxen swam or walked through the shallow water it was called fording the stream. A stream could not be easily forded if the water was high.

Later, toll bridges were built. A small fee or toll was collected for the privilege of crossing the bridge.

TRAVEL BY LAND. The early settlers had so many important things to do that they gave little attention to road building.

Horses were used for riding and as pack animals. The pack horse was useful to carry goods along the trails that led through the mountains.

Sleighs and sleds were commonly used in New England and in the northern part of the Middle Colonies. It was far easier to carry goods over the frozen ground than it was to haul goods over muddy roads.

The stagecoach was a means of passenger travel. A carriage or coach mounted on wheels was called a stagecoach. Often the stage was drawn by four or more strong horses. Not every man could be a stagecoach driver because:

1. A driver needed skill to drive so many horses and to keep them pulling together.
2. The driver must be an honest man. He was trusted with the care of passengers, mail, and packages.
3. He needed to be a quick thinker for ever so many things might happen on a journey. He needed to know how to decide what was best to do at all times. He needed to be ready to act quickly.
4. He needed tact because he had to know just how to deal with the Indians. There was always the danger that savage Indians might surround the stagecoach at some lonely place.

Early roads often followed Indian trails. The roads were dusty in dry weather and muddy whenever rain fell.

As travel became more popular and more necessary there arose the need for better roads. There was but little money to spend for materials or for labor to build better roads. This problem was solved by cutting sturdy trees. The strong logs were placed close together across the road. The wheels of the wagons and the stagecoaches could not sink so easily in such a road. These log roads were called corduroy roads. Corduroy is a kind of a cloth with ridges. This was a good name for the log roads. Travel on a corduroy road was far better than travel on a dirt road but it was rather rough riding.

Later, better and smoother roads were built. Sand, gravel, and crushed stone were used to make a hard, smooth road. These roads cost more to build than a corduroy road. The colonist solved this problem by charging a tax or a toll for riders and vehicles using the road.

These toll roads came to be called pikes. Often they were called turnpikes. A rider or a wagon that was not willing,

or not able to pay the toll would have to turn back when they reached the tollgate.

The people of New England and of the Middle Colonies gave more attention to building roads than did the people of the South. Southern planters were content because it was pleasant to ride horseback along a trail. Nearly every plantation had its own wharf. Here goods could be loaded and unloaded. So the Southern planter was not as dependent upon roads as were the colonists of New England or of the Middle Colonies.

THE CUMBERLAND ROAD. The greatest of the old roads was the Cumberland Road. It was also called the National Road. This road was built by the United States government in 1811. It first ran from Cumberland, Maryland, across the mountains to Wheeling, Virginia. Later,

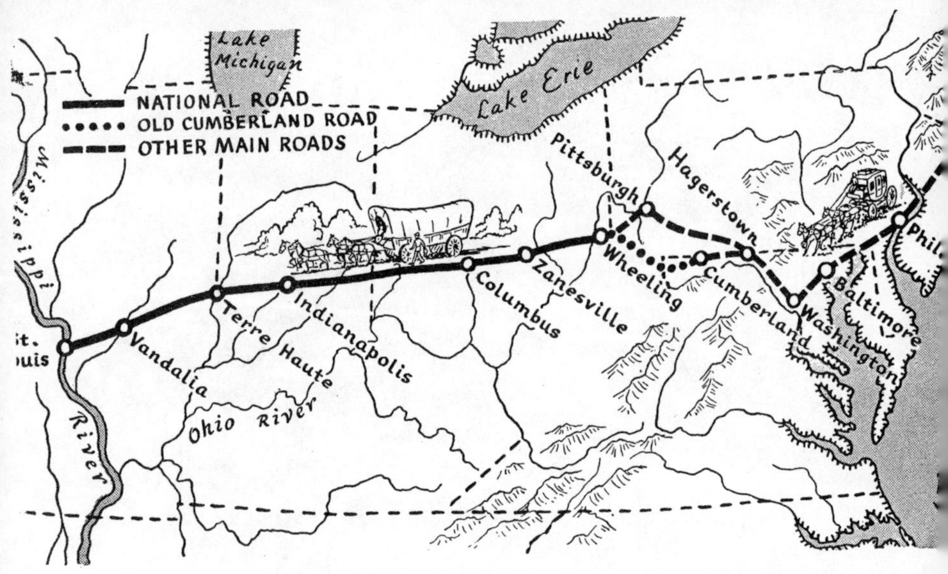

this road was built westward as is shown on the map. The National Road reached to the Mississippi River.

This road was an easy path for settlers moving into the West. The road was often crowded with emigrant trains of covered wagons and straggling cattle. Groups of wagons moving into another part of the country were called emigrant trains.

Stagecoaches carried passengers and mail over the Cumberland Road.

Heavy freight was carried in large canvas-covered wagons. These were called Conestoga wagons. They were large and strongly built. These wagons hauled from one ton to two tons of freight. The Conestoga wagons were pulled by four or six strong horses. Bells of various tunes jingled pleasantly as the teams traveled over the road.

All travel in the early days was slow, difficult, uncomfortable, and expensive. Whenever it was possible people traveled by sailboats.

ROBERT FULTON

HOW PEOPLE TRAVELED. There had been very little change in the way people traveled. Men had used the same modes of travel for thousands of years. They traveled on foot, were drawn by animals, or sailed over the water.

The steamboat marked the first big change in the manner of water travel. Other great improvements followed one another rapidly. Within a hundred years after 1807 man's ways of traveling were completely changed.

The man who helped to change men's ideas of travel was Robert Fulton. He invented the steamboat. John Fitch and others built steamboats, but Fulton built the kind of a steamboat that came into general use.

THE *CLERMONT*. After years of planning Robert Fulton had a boat built by a New York ship builder. Then he advertised the fact that his boat would make its first trip in August, 1807. It was to steam up the Hudson River from New York to Albany. When the day came, a crowd gathered to see the strange craft. Fulton named his steamboat the *Clermont*. This was the name of Robert Livingston's lovely estate on the Hudson. The crowd called the steamboat "Fulton's Folly." They were sure that it would never be able to move from the dock.

A SUCCESSFUL STEAMBOAT. The signal was given and the paddle wheels began to turn. The *Clermont* moved ahead. Then the paddle wheels stopped and the *Clermont* drifted astern. The crowd roared with laughter at the silly craft as it tossed on the stream. They did not laugh long. The damage was repaired and once again the paddle wheels churned the water. Steadily up the river moved the *Clermont*. She caused as much amazement as had Hudson's *Half Moon* nearly two hundred years before. The steamer's tall stack gave out a column of black smoke. Sparks flew high in the air. Now and then there was a burst of flame. People thought the boat would blow up, but to their astonishment the trip to Albany was safely made. The *Clermont* began to make regular trips. It took

the *Clermont* less than a day and a half to go the one hundred and fifty miles. Its rate was between three and four miles an hour. Today, we would consider this very, very slow travel. People were delighted with the *Clermont* when it made the journey between Albany and New York in a day and a half. The stage-coach journey took about a week. Transportation was growing speedy!

PROGRESS OF THE STEAMBOAT. Steamboats soon began to take the place of sailing vessels. Like all new inventions some people fought against them. The captains of the sailing boats on the Hudson saw that they would lose their passenger and freight trade. Sometimes these captains tried to run their boats into the *Clermont*. They could not stop the progress of steam-driven boats and ships. The steamboat was soon in use on many rivers and lakes. Engines were put into sea-going ships as well. First they used sails to help the engines. The steamship *Great Western* crossed the Atlantic Ocean in 1838. It used only steam power.

It would be impossible to tell how much the invention of the steamboat added to the wealth of our country.

THE ERIE CANAL

FULTON'S CANAL SCHEMES. Another one of Fulton's ideas had to do with canals. Goods could be carried easier and cheaper by water than overland in Fulton's time. The United States has many rivers and lakes which form splendid water routes. Unfortunately, these waterways did not always connect with one another. There were often stretches of land between them. Fulton felt that it would not be too hard to cut canals and connect the waterways. Canals would pay for themselves and help the country. The rich products of the western farms could be brought to the cities on the coast at small cost. The things the farmer needed could be sent to him cheaply from the eastern cities. Many other people thought as Robert Fulton did about canals.

DE WITT CLINTON. De Witt Clinton was interested in a canal in his own state of New York. Lake Erie is on the western side of New York. The map at the top of the page shows how Lake Erie connects with Lake Ontario. Together the Great Lakes form a magnificent waterway into the heart of the United States.

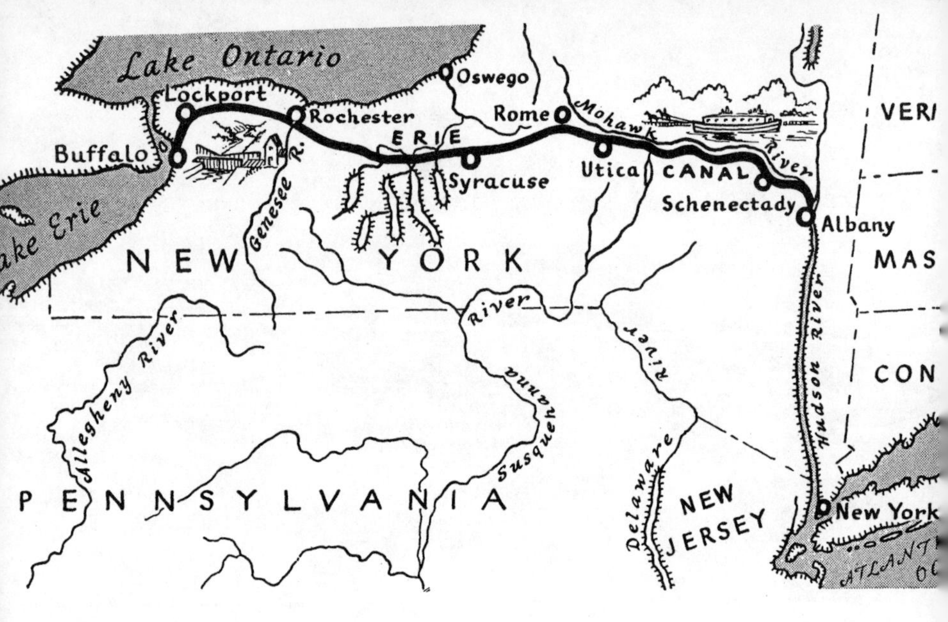

Running down along the eastern side of New York is the deep, wide Hudson River. At Albany, the Mohawk River flows into the Hudson River. This tributary of the Hudson River has its source near Lake Erie. Between Lake Erie and the Hudson River the land is nearly level. There are no mountains to cross. De Witt Clinton felt very strongly that a canal should be built to connect the Mohawk and Hudson rivers with Lake Erie. This would provide a water route from the far end of the Great Lakes to the Atlantic Ocean. It would make New York City a great port.

CLINTON'S DITCH. The plan was very simple; to carry it out was very difficult. Well over three hundred miles of canal had to be dug. The water in Lake Erie is on a higher level than the water in the Hudson River. A canal with many locks would have to be built. A lock is an enclosure between two gates in a canal, or a stream. Boats are lowered or raised from one water level to another by the use of locks. Locks were expensive to build. The canal planned by Clinton would cost millions of dollars. Nevertheless, De Witt Clinton talked about the canal constantly. He tried to get the United States Government to build it. Statesmen in Washington said that this was New York's job as the canal would be entirely within that state and the state would be benefited.

Clinton was a politician and was finally elected governor of New York. Then he succeeded in getting New York State to build the canal. It took eight years to build the Erie Canal. It cost $8,000,000 to construct this waterway. The Erie Canal was opened in 1825.

THE MARRIAGE OF THE WATERS. When the work was finished there was a gay ceremony. Governor De Witt Clinton and a party of guests journeyed to Buffalo. That city was at the Lake Erie end of the canal. There the party went on board a gayly decorated canalboat. The boat was drawn by tow horses which walked along a towpath on the banks of the canal. The horses pulled or towed the boat by means of strong ropes attached to the boat. People all along the way cheered the boat. At Albany, the boat left the Erie Canal and floated down the Hudson River to New York Harbor. Here a cask of water, taken from Lake Erie, was poured into the Atlantic Ocean. This ceremony was called the "Marriage of the Waters."

THE EFFECT OF THE CANAL. New York City became America's largest and richest city partly because of the Erie Canal. The vast trade of the Central States might have been forced to go down the Mississippi River to reach the sea if the Erie Canal had not been built.

The Erie Canal also helped the West. That region found an easy market in the East for its produce. This brought more and more settlers to the fertile prairie lands. Along the length of the canal busy cities such as Buffalo, Rochester, Syracuse, and Utica grew and prospered.

About one hundred years after it was built the Erie Canal was rebuilt. It is now known as the New York State Barge Canal. A barge is a large flat-bottomed boat used for carrying freight on rivers and canals.

The success of the Erie Canal caused a wave of canal building. Pennsylvania and Maryland joined in the building of the Chesapeake and Ohio Canal. This canal was dug to connect the Ohio River with the Chesapeake Bay.

Many shorter canals were built throughout the Central States. The coming of the railroad caused a decline in canal building.

STUDY SUMMARY

---

1. Terms to know. Be able to give the meaning of each term listed.

National Road	barge	Marriage of the Waters
turnpike	locks	emigrant train
Clermont	toll	Conestoga wagons
	tow	

2. People to know. Be able to give an important fact about each person whose name is listed.

James Watt	De Witt Clinton
Robert Fulton	John Fitch

3. Places to know. Be able to locate on a wall map each place listed. Be able to tell one fact about the place as it is located. Be sure to trace rivers from their source to their mouths when locating them on a map.

Erie Canal	Syracuse	New York State Barge Canal
Cumberland	Rochester	Chesapeake Bay
Wheeling	Utica	Hudson River
New York City	Buffalo	Mohawk River
Lake Erie	Albany	Ohio River

4. Dates to remember. Be able to tell one important event which took place on each of the following dates.

1807 1825 1838

ACTIVITIES

1. Sketch a map of the United States east of the Mississippi River.
   a. Locate and name the following places.

Hudson River	Buffalo
Mohawk River	Albany
New York City	Rochester
Lake Erie	Syracuse

   b. Draw in and color blue the Erie Canal.
2. Write a paragraph telling about TRAVEL ON A TURNPIKE.
3. Make a set of sketches showing TRAVEL LONG AGO. Be sure to illustrate:
   a. A turnpike and its toll gate.
   b. An emigrant train on the Cumberland Road.
   c. Traveling in a stagecoach.
   d. Travel by sailboat.

STUDY TEST 38—Score 15

CONTRASTS. Fill in the word to correctly complete each contrast sentence. Add a period to complete the sentence.

1. A stagecoach trip from Philadelphia to New York took three ....
   The same ninety mile journey by railroad now takes only a few ....

2. Before the days of Robert Fulton travel by water was in .... boats.

3. Henry Hudson, in 1609, sailed up the Hudson River in the *Half Moon* which was a .... boat.
   Robert Fulton, in 1807, sailed up the Hudson River in the *Clermont* which was a .... boat.

4. The stagecoach journey between Albany and New York took about a ....
   The *Clermont* made the 150-mile trip between Albany and New York in a .... and a half.

5. The *Clermont* made its first successful trip on the Hudson River in the year ....
   The *Great Western* was the first steamship to cross the Atlantic. It made the trip in ....

6. De Witt Clinton tried to get the .... government to build the Erie Canal.
   The Erie Canal was finally built by the government of .... State.

7. The opening of the Erie Canal helped the .... to buy produce from the West more cheaply.
   The opening of the Erie Canal helped the .... to get their produce to market more easily.
   The trade of the Central States was no longer forced to use the .... River.

UNIT VIII: INVENTIONS AND DISCOVERIES

THE RAILROAD AND THE TELEGRAPH

Read to learn

1. About the early railroads.
2. How Samuel Morse invented the telegraph.
3. About the invention of the cable.

THE COMING OF THE IRON HORSE

HORSE-CAR ON RAILS. The first cars on American railroads were horse-cars. They were simply the old stage-coaches mounted on rails. These coaches were pulled by horses. The first rails were made of wood with thin strips of iron nailed to the top of the rails.

The horse-car railroad did not last long, except in cities. A steam locomotive had been invented. John Stephenson, an Englishman, was the first to put an engine and a steam boiler on wheels. His locomotive ran on rails and pulled a train of cars. A machine that moves under its own power

Courtesy of New York Central Railroad.

is called a locomotive. Soon some of Stephenson's locomotives were brought to America. Later, Americans began to build locomotives.

EARLY TRAINS. A trip on one of these old trains was very interesting but hardly comfortable. Passengers who could not pay much rode on flat-cars. These were platforms mounted on wheels. The passengers sat on rude pine benches. The richer people rode in coaches, much like the old stagecoaches. The locomotives were small and could not move faster than fifteen miles an hour. Even at that the people were often terrified at such great speed.

RAILROADS AND PROSPERITY. Perhaps the railroad has done more than any other invention to make our country rich. At first, only a few wise people realized how important railroads would be. Charles Carroll, the cousin of the great Archbishop Carroll, firmly believed in railroads. As a very old man he turned the first sod in the building of the Baltimore and Ohio Railroad. "This act," he said, "is the most important of my life, next to the signing of the Declaration of Independence." He realized that the railroad was to make many changes in American life.

THE TELEGRAPH

SAMUEL F. B. MORSE. The telegraph is useful to us in many ways. Messages between businessmen or between friends are sent by telegraph. News is sent by telegraph to the newspapers. Railroad trains could hardly run unless the telegraph brought the message to clear tracks. All this seems very natural to us. It is hard for us to understand why the inventor of the telegraph had to struggle so long to prove what a useful thing it was. This inventor was Samuel F. B. Morse.

WINNING AID FROM CONGRESS. After years of hard work Morse had his telegraph in fair working order. Then he asked the aid of Congress. Morse set up his telegraph and showed it to members of Congress. They were interested but looked on the telegraph more as a toy than as anything of importance. Congress would give no money for a telegraph.

A few years later Morse again went before Congress. His telegraph was now in fine working order. He asked for thirty thousand dollars to build a line from Washington to Baltimore. The House of Representatives voted to give the money. Then the bill had to pass the Senate. The final

day of the session came and the Senate had not acted. All day Morse waited and hoped. Failure meant ruin for him. At last he was told that nothing would be done. With a heavy heart Morse went home. He awakened the next morning and was told that all was well. In the last minutes of the session the Senate had voted to give Morse the necessary money to build the telegraph line.

THE FIRST MESSAGE. It took a year to build the first telegraph line, which was forty miles long. The telegraph was first used in 1844. Then Morse set up his instrument in the Supreme Court in Washington. He flashed the message to Baltimore, "What hath God wrought!" Morse had done a wonderful thing; all his sufferings were forgotten. Today, his little line of 40 miles has grown into a network of about 2,400,000 miles of telegraph lines in the United States alone.

CYRUS W. FIELD AND THE ATLANTIC CABLE. It would be very useful to be able to telegraph to Europe. News and messages took a long time to cross the ocean by ship. Cyrus W. Field had the idea of laying a telegraph line, or a cable, under the Atlantic Ocean. His first cable was laid in the year 1858. It soon broke, but others were put down. Now cables carry messages across the Atlantic, the Pacific, and the Indian oceans.

STUDY SUMMARY

1. Terms to know. Be able to give the meaning of each term listed.

   miniature, flat-car, locomotive, cable, telegraph

2. People to know. Be able to tell an important fact about each person whose name is listed.

   John Stephenson, Samuel Morse, Charles Carroll, Cyrus Field

3. Places to know. Be able to locate on a wall map each place listed. Give one important fact about the place as it is located.

   Baltimore, Atlantic Ocean, Washington, D. C.

4. Dates to remember. Be able to name the invention which you identify with each of the following dates.

   1844, 1858

ACTIVITIES

1. List several ways in which the telegraph is daily used to help business, travel, etc.
2. Make a table filling in the facts and dates.

INVENTIONS			
Inventor	Invention	Date	Where first used
1.			
2.			
3.			

3. Give an oral report on Samuel Morse's struggle to complete his invention.
4. Prove that Samuel Morse and Cyrus Field were men who were not easily discouraged.

STUDY TEST 39—Score 15

Brief answers. Each question is to be answered with a word, a name, or a date.

1. What material was used to make the first rails? ....
2. Was a trip in the old horse cars comfortable? ......
3. Who invented the steam locomotive? ....
4. What is a machine called which moves under its own power? ....
5. Where were the first successful steam locomotives made? ....
6. What were platforms mounted on wheels called? ....
7. Who invented the telegraph? ....
8. Between what cities was the first telegraph built? ....
9. In the .... in Washington, Morse set up his instrument to flash the first message.
10. Who gave Morse the money to build the telegraph? ....
11. How long did it take to build the first telegraph line of forty miles? ....
12. Give the date of the invention of the telegraph.
13. Who invented the cable? ....
14. What year was the Atlantic cable opened? ....
15. Name the three oceans which have cables. ....

THE SOUTH AND SLAVERY

Read to learn

1. How conditions in the South favored slavery.
2. How slavery threatened the peace of the nation.
3. About John C. Calhoun's ideas on the question of states' rights.
4. What the Missouri Compromise was.
5. About the great service rendered by Henry Clay.

THE GREAT PROBLEM OF SLAVERY. The United States had become a great nation by 1860. There were over 31,000,000 people living here. Thousands of miles of railroad had been built. There were steamships on every important river and on the Great Lakes. Cotton was "King" in the South. Factories, in the North, by the hundreds were making articles to wear and for the home. The fields of the West were covered with corn and wheat. Every ship sailing to America was filled with sturdy immigrants. The Irish and Germans came in large numbers. This was all very fine but there was a great danger which was threatening the very life of the Union. This danger was the slavery question. Slavery was like an open sore that would not heal.

Slavery was an old problem. It began in 1619 when a Dutch ship brought a cargo of Negroes to the Jamestown settlement. These poor people had been captured in Africa. Then they were taken ashore and sold to the Virginia planters as slaves. The right of slaves as human beings was not respected. They belonged to their masters as much as a horse, or a cow, or a piece of land.

SLAVERY, NORTH AND SOUTH. Even in the North in the early days few people objected very strongly to slavery. Some New England shipowners made fortunes

Photo from "Dixie," a Chronicles of America Photoplay.
© Yale University Press. By permission.

selling slaves to the Southerners. The people of New England did not need slave labor. New England farms were small. They were worked by the people who lived on them. Again, the climate was too cold for Negroes, who came from the hot parts of Africa. Slavery, therefore, was not profitable in the North. This is one reason why it died out there. Another reason was that there were people in the North who really hated slavery. They realized that it was unjust to deny the slaves their liberty.

Conditions in the South favored slavery. The climate was warm. The plantations were large and cheap labor was needed. More and more slaves were needed after the invention of the cotton gin. On large plantations slaves lived in cabins like those in the picture.

As time went on there grew up a sharp difference between North and South on the question of slavery. The North commenced to think that it was wicked to keep human beings in slavery. The South bitterly resented this viewpoint of the North. Southerners insisted that slavery was necessary.

The slavery question was often hotly debated in Congress. There were great orators and statesmen on both sides of the slavery question. Feeling often ran high. John C. Calhoun, Henry Clay, and Daniel Webster were forceful leaders of this time. Great speeches were made both for and against slavery.

JOHN C. CALHOUN

CALHOUN IN CONGRESS. John C. Calhoun was a lawyer from South Carolina who entered politics and was elected to Congress. He served as Vice President of the United States under President Andrew Jackson. Later he resigned from that office and was elected to the Senate.

Calhoun had become a states' rights man. That is he placed the rights of a state above the rights of the United States. Congress had passed a high tariff law. John C. Calhoun's home state of South Carolina did not like this tariff. South Carolina passed a law attempting to undo the law of Congress. That is, South Carolina attempted to nullify a law passed by Congress. This idea was seriously wrong. Only the body which makes a law can later declare that law null or not in force. Calhoun approved of the action of his state. He said, "I am a states' rights man." You will remember what President Andrew Jackson did when South Carolina passed the Nullification Act. President Jackson would not permit any state to nullify a law of Congress. Calhoun and many Southerners continued to believe in states' rights.

CALHOUN'S IDEAS ON SLAVERY. Calhoun could see only the slave owner's side. He believed that slavery was necessary in the South. There were some Southerners who thought slavery was bad. They put up with it because they

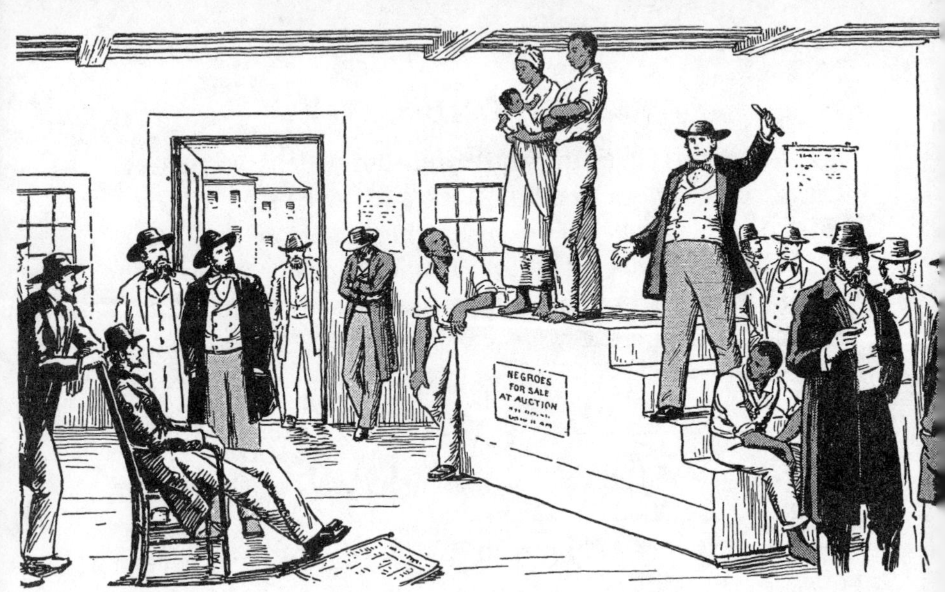

could see no way to get rid of it. There were other Southerners who upheld slavery because it was profitable. John C. Calhoun went further. In a speech in Congress Calhoun declared, "Slavery is a good, a positive good."

Calhoun held the extreme view of the South in favor of slavery. There were also extreme views in the North against slavery. Between these two opposites there were men like Henry Clay. His lifework was to preserve the Union and to keep peace between the sections of the country. He was a peace-loving man.

HENRY CLAY

VIRGINIAN AND KENTUCKIAN. Virginia and Kentucky both claimed Henry Clay as their own. Clay was born in a part of Virginia called the "Slashes." The Slashes was a lowland, almost a swamp, overgrown with Slash Pine. It was very poor land. Henry Clay was one of seven children. His father died when Clay was very young. Mrs. Clay, Henry's mother, had had a comfortable home but the "Slashes" section was running down. People were moving to better parts of Virginia or to Kentucky. Henry Clay decided to move also.

CLAY IN KENTUCKY. Clay built up a good law practice in Kentucky. People liked him. He took an interest in public matters and often spoke on the problems of the day. The greatest of these problems was slavery. Henry Clay thought and talked much about slavery. He believed that the slaves should be freed, but he felt this could not be done all at one time. At different times Clay freed some of his own slaves.

Henry Clay became a United States Senator from Kentucky. He remained in Congress practically all the rest of his life. Three times Clay was a candidate for President, but he was never elected. No doubt the stand he took on slavery hurt his chances for election. Henry Clay believed in compromise; that is, he tried to please both sides.

THE GREAT PACIFICATOR. Some of the Presidents of Clay's time are almost forgotten. Although Henry Clay failed to be elected President, he will always be remembered. He is known in history as the "Great Pacificator." That means that for many years he did more than any other man to keep peace between the North and the South.

THE MISSOURI COMPROMISE. Henry Clay brought about the first of the great compromise laws in 1820. This was the "Missouri Compromise." Under this law an imaginary line was drawn dividing the country into two sections. Slavery was forbidden north of this line but permitted south of the line. There was peace then for a time. It is well to remember these two facts about the Missouri Compromise:

1. Missouri was admitted to the Union as a slave state.
2. The rest of the land in Louisiana Territory, north of the Missouri line was to be forever free.

The slavery question was not settled. It kept coming up again and again. Every time a new territory was opened to settlement there was another dispute. People from the South wanted to bring their slaves into the new land. Settlers from the North wanted to keep the new territory free. Slavery was not permitted in free territory. Feeling between the North and South was becoming more bitter.

THE COMPROMISE OF 1850. There was a furious outburst of bad feeling in 1850. Each section wanted to control the great territory taken from Mexico. Henry Clay, now an old man, once more offered a compromise plan. Again Clay tried to please both sides. Some points in his plan pleased the North, others favored the South. However, neither side seemed willing to give in. Clay believed that his plan must pass to keep peace between the North and the South. He felt it his duty to see that it did pass. He was a powerful orator. He felt that if he could only speak before the Senate his last compromise would be accepted and peace would be restored.

Henry Clay was in very poor health. He was in no condition to stand the strain of making so important a speech. His love for his country made him forget that he was ill. He entered the Senate chamber and walked slowly and feebly to his place. He knew that this was to be his last great effort for his country. He must not fail!

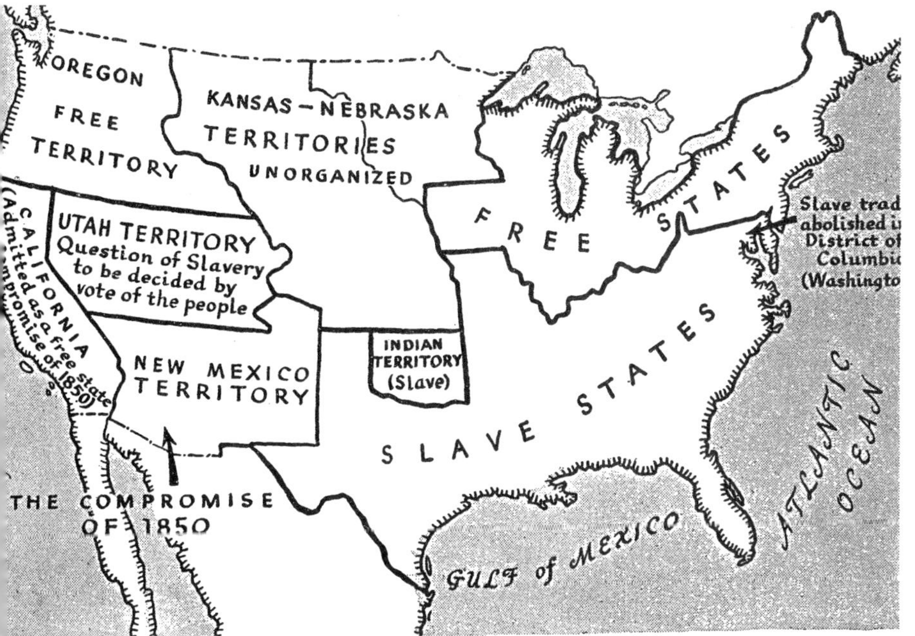

The Senate floor and galleries were crowded. People came long distances to hear the great orator speak. Clay spoke with his old eloquence. He compelled men to listen and then act. Once again he won the day. The Compromise of 1850, Clay's bill, became a law. The chief facts to remember about the Compromise of 1850 are:

1. California came into the Union as a free state.
2. The rest of the land taken from Mexico was divided into two territories. The people in these territories were to decide for themselves whether to come into the Union as slave or as free states. The territories could not apply for admission into the Union until they had a population of a certain size.
3. The new law about runaway slaves was intended to prevent Northerners from helping slaves to escape to Canada.

The peace brought by the Compromise of 1850 lasted but a short time. Henry Clay died in 1852, an old man, worn out by his efforts in behalf of his country. He did not live to see the tragedy of the Civil War. Slavery was one of causes of this war. The question of states' rights really was the direct cause of the Civil War.

STUDY SUMMARY

1. Terms to know. Be able to give the meaning of each term listed.

   states' rights   Slashes   slavery   compromise

2. People to know. Be able to tell some interesting facts about each person named.

   John C. Calhoun   Henry Clay   Daniel Webster

3. Places to know. Be able on a wall map to locate each place named. Give an important fact about the place as it is located.

   Kentucky   California
   Missouri   South Carolina

4. Dates to remember. Be able to give one important event which took place on each date named.

   1619   1820   1850

ACTIVITIES

1. Make a contrast study by filling in all the facts you can under each heading.

   A. Slavery was not profitable in the North because:

   1. . . . .   3. . . . .
   2. . . . .   4. . . . .

   B. Slavery was very profitable in the South because:

   1. . . . .   3. . . . .
   2. . . . .   4. . . . .

2. Write two sentences to explain the meaning of the term states' rights.
3. Explain how Henry Clay earned the title of the "Great Pacificator."
4. Make a poster showing Henry Clay pleading before Congress for the Compromise Bill of 1850.

STUDY TEST 40—Score 20

EITHER—OR. Underscore the term or the date which answers the question.

1. Was the question of slavery an old or a new problem in the United States by 1860?
2. Was slavery begun here in 1619 or in 1763?
3. Did slaves have no rights or some rights?
4. Did Southern or New England shipowners make fortunes in the slave trade?
5. Were farms in New England large or small?
6. Was the climate of New England too cool or too hot for the Negro slaves?
7. Was slavery more profitable in the South or in the North?
8. Were more or fewer slaves needed in the South after the invention of the cotton gin?
9. Did the North begin to think that slavery was necessary or that it was wicked?
10. Did John C. Calhoun defend or oppose slavery?
11. Was a high or a low tariff passed by Congress?
12. Was South Carolina pleased or displeased with the new tariff?
13. Did Calhoun approve or disapprove the high tariff law?
14. Has Congress or a state the right to nullify a law passed by Congress?
15. Did Calhoun believe that the nation or the state had the higher rights?
16. Did Henry Clay believe that the slaves should be held in slavery or that they should be freed?
17. Was slavery forbidden or encouraged in the North after the passage of the Missouri Compromise?
18. Was slavery forbidden or permitted in the South after the Missouri Compromise was passed?
19. Was Henry Clay a poor or a good orator?
20. Did the peace brought by the Compromise of 1850 last a long time or a short time?

THE NORTH AND SLAVERY

Read to learn

1. How Daniel Webster defended the Union.
2. About the trouble in Kansas and Nebraska.
3. How civil war arose in Kansas.
4. Why Northerners hated the Fugitive Slave Law.
5. About the Dred Scott Decision.
6. How a new political party came into power.

DANIEL WEBSTER

A NORTHERN LEADER. John C. Calhoun spoke for the South. Henry Clay spoke for both North and South. Daniel Webster spoke for the North and for the Union. Daniel Webster and John C. Calhoun were born in the same year, 1782. Daniel Webster was next to the youngest of ten children. He was the son of a New Hampshire judge who was also a farmer. Daniel Webster studied law. Later he entered politics.

WEBSTER AND THE UNION. The greatest work of Daniel Webster's life was his defense of the American Union. Times were changing. Some people were saying that the states had the right to nullify, or undo, the laws of Congress. Others went so far as to say that a state could withdraw from the Union if it so wished. These people, like John C. Calhoun, believed in what is called states' rights. Daniel Webster began to see that the Union itself was in danger. He saw the danger of allowing any state to put its own interests before the interests of the entire country.

Perhaps Webster's greatest speech was his reply to Senator Robert Y. Hayne, of South Carolina, in 1830. The debate was on the question of states' rights. A discussion in which arguments on both sides of a question are heard is called a debate. The opponents of the Union seemed to be having it all their own way. Senator Hayne closed his argument with a most masterly speech defending the rights of the states.

At last, Daniel Webster rose to defend the Union. It was a never-to-be-forgotten picture as he made his reply to Hayne. Webster was a fine looking man. His voice was powerful yet musical. His arguments were impressive. The crowded Senate chamber listened with great attention. Argument followed argument and then came the dramatic finish. Webster rose to his greatest height as his powerful voice rang out, "Liberty and Union, now and forever, one and inseparable."

The effect of this speech was felt throughout the entire country. Thousands of copies of it were printed and distributed. It was read with great eagerness. Those who supported the Union found in Webster's speech greater strength. Many who disagreed, began to think they might be wrong.

Late in life, Webster joined Henry Clay in one more earnest appeal for the Union. Their pleadings were so successful that Henry Clay's Compromise Bill of 1850 was passed. Two years later both Clay and Webster died. They had fought for a long time to preserve the Union. Their words in its defense will never be forgotten. The time was fast coming when words would fail. The Union would live and slavery would fall, not by words, but by the sword.

TROUBLE WAS BREWING

THE FAILURE OF COMPROMISE. The Missouri Compromise of 1820 had fixed a certain line on the map north of which there was to be no slavery. The Compromise of 1850 had not changed this line. A few years later the new territories of Kansas and Nebraska were being rapidly settled. They were north of the Missouri Compromise line. The South wanted to bring slaves into these territories. This caused intense excitement.

THE KANSAS-NEBRASKA BILL. A bill passed by Congress allowed the people of these territories to decide whether they should be slave or free states. This bill was called the Kansas-Nebraska Bill. It gave the South a chance to change the Missouri Compromise line. This line had lasted for thirty-four years. Any change in the boundary between the slave and the free states or territories would anger the North.

CIVIL WAR IN KANSAS. There were many settlers in Kansas who had come from New England. They had gone to Kansas to build their homes. They wanted Kansas to become a free state. At the same time other settlers had arrived from the South. Some brought their slaves with

them. These settlers wanted Kansas to be a slave state. Soon the people of New England and the southern slave owners were quarreling. Kansas got the name of "Bleeding Kansas" and people said, "There is civil war in Kansas."

THE DRED SCOTT DECISION. The North was thoroughly indignant. It objected to the efforts of the South to win Kansas for slavery. Then another law was passed which was horrible in the eyes of the North. This was the Fugitive Slave Law. Northerners had been helping slaves to escape from their masters. These run-away slaves were called fugitives. Under the new law the government could send its officers right into the free states and arrest these slaves. The fugitives would be returned to their owners.

Worst of all was the Dred Scott Decision. Dred Scott was a slave who had been taken into free territory. He claimed that this act of his master had made him free. The Supreme Court of the United States in 1857 decided otherwise. The ruling of the Supreme Court on a question is a fixed opinion. That is why it is called a decision. The Supreme Court decided that, under the Constitution, slaves were not "persons" but "property." As property they could be taken into any part of the Union, at their owner's will. The North was not only furious but it was alarmed.

THE REPUBLICAN PARTY. These troublesome times had their effect on political parties. There were disputes and disagreements within the old parties. A new political party was formed in the North in 1854. It was called the Republican Party. Its plans were to stop the spread of slavery. It did not oppose slavery as it already existed in the old South. It did insist that all new states entering the Union should be free. The South would not accept these new political ideas.

The Republican Party soon grew strong. The Dred Scott Decision brought thousands to the banner of the Republican Party. A critical time was at hand. A President was to be elected in 1860. The Republicans nominated Abraham Lincoln of Illinois. The South was excited. Its leaders warned the nation not to elect the Republican candidate. Abraham Lincoln, the Republican, was elected President of the United States.

STUDY SUMMARY

---

1. Terms to know. Be able to give the meaning of each term listed.

states' rights	Fugitive Slave Law
debate	Dred Scott Decision
decision	Kansas-Nebraska Bill

2. People to know. Be able to tell some interesting fact about each person named.

Daniel Webster	Robert Y. Hayne
Abraham Lincoln	John C. Calhoun
Henry Clay	

3. Places to know. Be able to locate on a map each place listed. Tell one fact about the place as it is located.

Kansas	Nebraska	New Hampshire
Missouri		South Carolina

4. Dates to remember. Be able to tell what important event in American history took place on each date listed.

   1830 1854 1857 1860

ACTIVITIES

1. A diagram. Make a set of four steps to show the events leading up to the break between the North and the South. Above each step name the event, below the step put the date.

EVENTS LEADING TO THE BREAK BETWEEN NORTH AND SOUTH

2. Explain how the conflict, about Kansas entering the Union, slave or free, arose.
3. Write an essay on THE DRED SCOTT DECISION. Be sure to tell:
   a. Who Dred Scott was.
   b. The Fugitive Slave Law.
   c. What the Supreme Court decided.
   d. What the North thought about the Dred Scott Decision.

STUDY TEST 41—Score 20

SELECT ENDINGS. Underscore the term which gives the correct ending to each sentence. Put a period after the term selected. Re-read the sentence.

1. Daniel Webster became a very successful
   doctor lawyer farmer
2. John C. Calhoun believed the highest power to be the
   state Congress Senate

3. Henry Clay liked to settle a dispute by a
   war / quarrel / compromise
4. The question of states' rights was defended by
   Ralph Hayne / Daniel Webster / Henry Clay
5. Daniel Webster, in a brilliant speech, defended the
   Union / states / South
6. Both Webster and Clay fought to preserve the
   North / Union / West
7. Slavery was forbidden north of a certain line by the
   Kansas-Nebraska Bill / Missouri Compromise
8. The Fugitive Slave Law was displeasing to the
   West / South / North
9. A ruling by the Supreme Court is called a
   decision / law / rule
10. Dred Scott was a
    master / politician / slave
11. The Supreme Court ruled that slaves were
    persons / property / free men
12. The Dred Scott Decision made the Northerners very
    happy / joyful / angry
13. A new political party was formed in the
    South / West / North
14. The Republican Party planned to stop the spread of
    slavery / education / politics
15. The Republican Party insisted that all new states should come into the union
    slave / free
16. The ideas of the Republican Party were pleasing to
    Northerners / Southerners
17. The Republican Party did not oppose slavery in the
    new states / South / North
18. Before long the Republican Party was growing
    weak / feeble / strong
19. The Republican Party in 1860 nominated
    Daniel Webster / Henry Clay / Abraham Lincoln
20. The election of Abraham Lincoln did not please the
    West / South / North

UNIT IX: SLAVERY AND THE UNION

ABRAHAM LINCOLN

Read to learn

1. How Lincoln educated himself.
2. How hard work helped Abraham Lincoln.
3. About the Lincoln-Douglas debates.
4. How the Civil War began.

A SON OF KENTUCKY. Everyone knows that Lincoln's Birthday is on February 12th. Abraham Lincoln was born in 1809. His birthplace was a miserable log cabin on a poor Kentucky farm.

EDUCATION. Abraham Lincoln spent less than one year in school. The school was a very poor one. Young Abe had to walk through four miles of forest to reach the school. After his year at school Lincoln tried to educate himself. Paper was very scarce so Lincoln did his sums on the back of a wooden shovel. He used a burnt stick as a pencil. No one helped him with his work. He had to figure everything out for himself. He made up his mind to learn to write and to speak well. He wanted to be sure that people would understand whatever he said as he meant it. Lincoln trained himself to write and to speak honestly and simply.

LINCOLN'S WORK. As a young man Abraham Lincoln worked very hard. His father needed help to support the family and young Abe did what he could. He earned money by splitting rails for fences. That is why he was given the nickname, "the rail splitter." He did not stop at any kind of hard work. Before he was twenty-one years old Lincoln had grown to be six feet four inches in height. Hard work had given him a strong body with powerful muscles.

As he grew older Lincoln took up a number of different jobs. At times he worked as a mill hand; for a while he was a clerk in the village store; he served as postmaster and worked as a surveyor. No matter what his job was Lincoln made friends. People liked him. That was because he was kind and honest. He always tried to be pleasant.

LINCOLN IN POLITICS. Abraham Lincoln went into politics, and politics changed his whole life. He had those qualities that a good politician needs. A person who is skilled in the science and the art of government is called a politician. Lincoln was a plain, but a forceful speaker. He could make ordinary people understand difficult questions. He was honest and people trusted him, so they voted for him whenever he was a candidate. Lincoln did not like slavery.

THE LINCOLN-DOUGLAS DEBATES. Stephen A. Douglas was a United States Senator from Illinois. He was called the "Little Giant." His body was small but his mind was powerful. He was very popular, too, and had great hopes of one day being elected President of the United States. Douglas was a Democrat and many Democrats favored slavery. In 1858 Douglas again was a candidate for the United States Senate.

The Republican Party chose Lincoln as the candidate against Douglas. Lincoln went about the state opposing Douglas. Several times the two men met on the same platform in debate. These debates interested thousands of people. Men traveled from distant places to hear the speakers. Lincoln had one great advantage in the argument. He knew exactly where he stood on the slavery question. Lincoln said: "A house divided against itself cannot stand. I believe that this government cannot endure permanently half slave and half free. It will become all one thing, or all the other." Douglas had to try to please all the Democrats. That meant the Democrats of the North who disliked slavery and the Democrats of the South who favored slavery. Lincoln only had to please one group. All the Republicans opposed slavery.

THE PRESIDENCY. Lincoln lost the election for Senator but he won the interest of the whole country. His clear, strong arguments against slavery made a great impression. Many Northerners began to realize that Abraham Lincoln was the leader the country needed.

The Republicans in 1860 nominated Lincoln for President. The Democrats were hopelessly divided. The Northern Democrats nominated Lincoln's old opponent, Stephen A. Douglas. The Southern Democrats nominated another man. The excitement was intense. The South openly declared that it would not accept Lincoln as President even if he were elected. The South would leave the Union rather than have him for President. The votes were counted and Abraham Lincoln was elected.

SECESSION. At once the Southern leaders declared that the time had come for the Southern states to leave the United States and form a separate nation. This was called secession. A month after the election of Lincoln, South Carolina declared that it was no longer a part of the United States. Within a short time ten other southern states had seceded from the Union. The map shows the

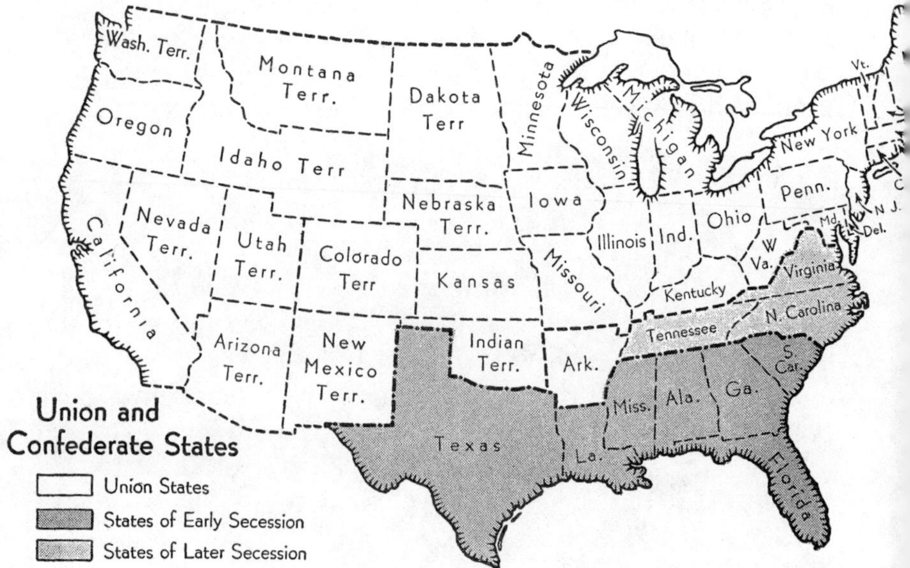

states which seceded. They formed a new union, which they called the Confederate States of America. They selected Richmond, Virginia, as their capital. Jefferson Davis was elected their first President. He was the only President that the Confederacy ever had.

THE CIVIL WAR. President Lincoln declared that no state had the right to leave the Union. He denied that there was a new nation in the South. Nevertheless, the Confederate States began to act as an independent nation. They took over all the United States property within the borders of the Confederacy. One piece of United States property was Fort Sumter. Fort Sumter was on an island near Charleston, South Carolina. Its commander was Major Robert Anderson, of the United States Army. A Confederate General called upon Anderson to surrender the fort. The demand was refused. Then at 4:30 in the morning of April 12th, 1861, the Confederates fired the first shot of the Civil War. Fort Sumter was forced to surrender. The terrible Civil War had begun.

It was fortunate indeed that during these times Abraham Lincoln was our President. He labored four long years of the war. He guided the country, working and praying, that the Union might be saved.

STUDY SUMMARY

1. Terms to know. Be able to tell the meaning of each term listed.

secession	"the rail splitter"
politician	debate

2. People to know. Be able to tell some interesting fact about each person named.

Abraham Lincoln	Major Robert Anderson
Stephen A. Douglas	Jefferson Davis

3. Places to know. Be able to locate on a wall map each place listed. Tell one fact about the place as it is located.

Kentucky	Indiana	Illinois
Richmond	Fort Sumter	Charleston

4. Dates to remember. Be able to tell the most important event in American history which took place on each of the following dates.

1860	1861

5. Character study. Prove that Abraham Lincoln had the following good character traits.
    1. He was very ambitious.
    2. He was a hard worker.
    3. He was honest.
    4. He had a friendly manner.
    5. He was very firm in his opinions.

ACTIVITIES

1. Write a BIOGRAPHY OF ABRAHAM LINCOLN. Use the following outline to help you.
    A. When and where born.
    B. The family.
    C. The early life of Abraham Lincoln.
        1. Moving into Indiana.
        2. Helping the family.

D. Education.
   1. Kind of school attended.
   2. How he helped to educate himself.
   3. Books he liked to read.
E. Kinds of work young Lincoln did.
F. Lincoln, the politician.
   1. Qualities that made Lincoln a good politician.
   2. His attitude on slavery.
   3. His ability as a debater.
   4. His attitude on the rights of the states to leave the Union.
G. Lincoln, the leader during the Civil War.
   1. The attack on Fort Sumter.
   2. How Lincoln helped to save the Union.

2. Discuss Lincoln's ideas about slavery.

STUDY TEST 42—Score 15

ASSOCIATION. Put L after each term which you associate with Abraham Lincoln; put D after each term you associate with Stephen A. Douglas.

1. Hated slavery. —
2. Called the "Little Giant." —
3. Served as Senator from Illinois. —
4. Had a small body but a brilliant mind. —
5. Was a Republican. —
6. Lost the election for Senator. —
7. Presented strong arguments against slavery. —
8. Had only one year's education in a school. —
9. Hoped some day to be elected President. —
10. Republicans nominated him for President. —
11. Democrats nominated him for President. —
12. South did not favor his election. —
13. Declared that no state had the right to leave the Union. —
14. Was a very strong Democrat. —
15. Served as President during the Civil War. —

© Yale University Press. By permission.
Photo from "Dixie," a Chronicles of America Photoplay.

UNIT IX: SLAVERY AND THE UNION

CIVIL WAR LEADERS

Read to learn

1. How experience prepared Jefferson Davis to be the leader of the South.
2. About Robert E. Lee's army record.
3. The serious decision Lee had to make.
4. About the military career of Ulysses S. Grant.

JEFFERSON DAVIS

CONTRAST WITH LINCOLN. Jefferson Davis was the President of the Confederate States of America. Davis and Lincoln make an interesting study. Both were born in Kentucky; they were about the same age; but they were different in many ways. Lincoln's boyhood had been passed amid the rudest surroundings. Almost every advantage had been denied him. Most of his knowledge was gained by hard knocks. His hands had been hardened by toil.

Davis came from a fairly well-to-do family. His boyhood was spent on a small plantation. Here Davis had seen slavery. The very comforts that he enjoyed came from the toil of his father's slaves. It was hard for Davis to believe that slavery was wrong.

DAVIS'S CAREER. Jefferson Davis had received a good education. He went to college and later entered the United States Military Academy at West Point. Davis made a good soldier. He fought with great bravery in the Mexican War. The army suited Davis in wartime, but he left it when peace came. He chose to enter politics. He was elected to the Senate of the United States. He also served as Secretary of War. His experience in the government service was a fine training for Davis. His career as a soldier and as a statesman seemed to fit him to lead the South. When Jefferson Davis arrived to take up the presidency of the Confederacy an onlooker remarked, "The man and the hour have met."

ROBERT E. LEE

A LEADER OF MEN. Robert E. Lee was one of America's greatest soldiers. That might be expected, for he was the son of another fine soldier, "Light Horse Harry" Lee, of the Revolution. The Lees were one of Virginia's finest families, so Robert Edward Lee was brought up in a good home. The chief fact about his boyhood was the kindness and attention he showed his mother, who was an invalid. Young Lee went to a good school and then he entered West Point, where he received his military training.

AN ARMY MAN. Lee's record at West Point was an excellent one. He worked hard at his lessons and won the respect of his teachers. The cadets liked him, too. Cadets are students in military schools. Among them were men he would meet later in life; one of the cadets was Jefferson

Davis. After four years of study and work Lee graduated from West Point. He ranked second in his class. His record was excellent. There was not a single demerit against his record when he was graduated.

Robert E. Lee took up the life of an army officer after he graduated from West Point. For some years this was not very exciting; then came the Mexican War. Lee fought bravely and well, first as a scout, then as an engineer. General Scott said he was "the greatest living soldier in America," and that he had performed "the greatest feat of physical and moral courage performed by any individual." This was great praise for the young soldier.

A few more years and Lee was called upon to make the hardest decision of his life. The Civil War was breaking.

HIS STATE OR HIS COUNTRY. Lee did not believe in slavery. He said that slavery was an "evil in any country." Furthermore, Lee loved the Army. He had just been made a Colonel of Cavalry. He had a splendid chance of being placed at the head of the whole Union Army. Now the Union seemed to be breaking. Lee had to make a choice. Which would it be, his state or his country? "How," he asked, "can I draw my sword upon Virginia, my native state?" So Robert E. Lee left the United States Army when

Virginia left the Union. He felt strongly that it was his duty to serve his state. Duty was an important thing in his life. Listen to his words: "Do your duty in all things. You cannot do more—you should never wish to do less." The Confederate States were sure to make a great fight, with such a man commanding their forces.

ULYSSES SIMPSON GRANT

A BOY OF OHIO. Ulysses Simpson Grant was the general who finally defeated the South. Hiram Ulysses Grant as he was christened, was born at Point Pleasant, Ohio. His father was a tanner. He prepared hides for shoemakers, harness makers, and those who use leather. Grant's father made enough money to give the boy a fair education. Young Grant did not like the tanning business. He much preferred to cultivate a small patch of ground and to ride a horse.

IN THE ARMY. When he was seventeen young Grant received an appointment to West Point. He also received a new name. His real name, Hiram Ulysses Grant, had unfortunate initials, H.U.G. The boy knew he would be "Hug" to the other cadets at West Point. But, strangely enough the name written in his appointment papers was Ulysses Simpson Grant. Grant did not object. He was glad to use Simpson, which was his mother's name. He was also delighted to get rid of an ugly nickname. So he became U. S. Grant.

Grant did not particularly like the idea of being a soldier. His principal interest in going to West Point was that he would pass through Philadelphia and New York City on the way. He was only fair at his studies except in mathematics and engineering. He hated drilling, he never seemed to be able to keep in step. No one equalled him

as a rider. If only horsemanship had counted Grant would have been first in his class. As it was, after four years he graduated twenty-first in a class of thirty-nine.

The next ten years Grant spent in the Army. The Mexican War was fought and Lieutenant Grant served well. He did well because it was his duty, not because he liked it. As a matter of fact this great soldier never did like war. Years later, Grant remarked to the German leader, Bismarck, "The truth is I am more of a farmer than a soldier. I never went into the army without regret and never retired without pleasure."

There is a great lesson for us in Grant's life. He never gave up just because he did not like his job. He went right ahead and won.

After the Mexican War, Grant married and settled down to army life. Then he resigned from the army. He took up farming, storekeeping and tried to sell real estate. He was a dismal failure at each of the jobs he tried.

COLONEL U. S. GRANT. It was 1861, and the North faced the South on the battlefield. The "call to arms" found Grant at the lowest point in his career. He was without money and without friends. The single thing that he could boast of was his training as a soldier.

Grant offered his services to the United States Army but no attention was paid to him. Finally, the governor of Illinois made him colonel of a regiment. A large group of soldiers is called a regiment. Grant took charge but could not appear with his regiment in public. The reason was that a colonel had to buy his own horse and uniform and Grant had no money. It was some time before he could borrow enough to fit himself out. Finally Grant became an officer in the Union Army.

"UNCONDITIONAL SURRENDER" GRANT. Grant was not long in showing he could handle troops. In command of a small army he attacked Fort Donelson in Tennessee. The fort was well defended by the Confederates, but Grant's attack was skillful. The Confederate commander saw he was beaten and tried to make easy terms of surrender. Grant's answer was to the point. "No terms except unconditional and immediate surrender can be accepted. I propose to move immediately upon your works." The fort was surrendered as well as the army that defended it.

This victory earned Grant a fine reputation. It also earned him a new name, "Unconditional Surrender Grant."

Grant was now a Major General of Volunteers. He made some mistakes. That is why people thought he was just a blundering leader. He kept on fighting. A protest was raised for Grant's removal. Lincoln refused to consider that. He said, "I can't spare this man, he fights."

VICKSBURG. Grant repaid Lincoln's trust by a great victory. Early in the Civil War the North saw that it must control the Mississippi River. The country west of that river was "the bread basket of the South." Large food supplies came from that district.

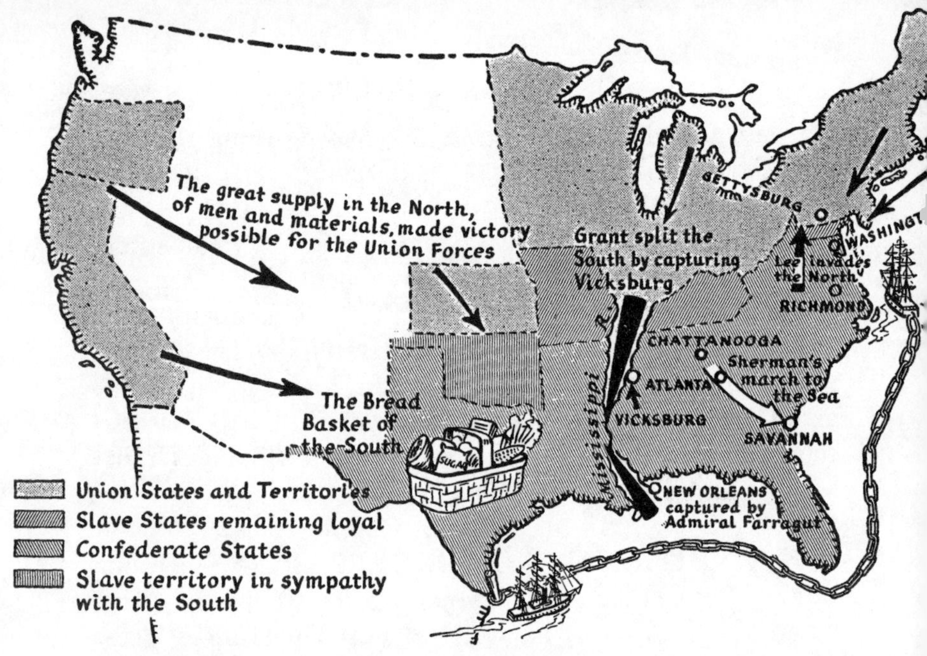

The South had built a great fortress at Vicksburg on the Mississippi River. General Grant was sent to capture it. It was a difficult job that was well carried out. On July 4th, 1863, Vicksburg surrendered.

Other victories came to Grant. Soon he was in command of the whole West. In the meantime Lincoln had tried one general after another in the East. One after another had failed him. Grant was called to Washington. Lincoln gave Grant command of the Union Army.

STUDY SUMMARY

---

1. Terms to know. Be able to give the meaning of each term listed.
   cadet regiment
2. People to know. Be able to give some interesting facts about the people whose names are listed.
   Jefferson Davis Ulysses S. Grant Robert E. Lee
3. Places to know. Be able to locate each on a wall map. Tell one fact about the place as it is located.
   Fort Donelson Vicksburg

4. Date to remember. Be able to give an important event which took place on July 4, 1863.

ACTIVITIES

1. Make a table on Civil War Leaders.

CIVIL WAR LEADERS		
	Grant	Lee
Where educated		
Rank when graduated		
War in which he fought		
Position in Civil War		
Position at close of Civil War		

2. Explain why it was so difficult for Lee to decide which army to enter.

STUDY TEST 43—Score 20

TRUE—FALSE. Put T after each true statement; put F after each false statement.

1. Jefferson Davis and Abraham Lincoln were both born in Kentucky. —
2. Robert E. Lee was one of America's greatest military leaders. —

3. Jefferson Davis did not believe that slavery was wrong. —
4. Robert Lee, Ulysses Grant, and Jefferson Davis had all been trained at West Point. —
5. The first president of the Confederacy was Jefferson Davis. —
6. Virginia never withdrew from the Union. —
7. Ulysses Grant, Robert Lee, and Jefferson Davis all fought in the American Army during the Mexican War. —
8. Robert E. Lee believed that slavery was an evil. —
9. The Confederate States chose Lee to lead their army against the Union. —
10. A colonel in the Union Army had to buy his uniform and his horse. —
11. General Grant fought to save the Union. —
12. General Grant fought in the Confederate Army. —
13. The Confederate general at Fort Donelson was forced to surrender to General Grant. —
14. Abraham Lincoln placed great trust in General Grant's ability to lead the Union Army to victory. —
15. Vicksburg, on the Mississippi River, was a Confederate stronghold. —
16. The capture of Vicksburg by the Union forces was an easy task. —
17. The Confederate forces surrendered Vicksburg on July 4, 1863. —
18. The North desired to control the Mississippi River. —
19. Some people thought that Grant was a poor leader. —
20. General Grant was given command of the entire Union Army. —

UNIT IX: SLAVERY AND THE UNION

SAVING THE UNION

Read to learn

1. The advantages which the North had.
2. Why the North needed to capture Richmond.
3. How the South was blockaded.
4. About the fight between the *Monitor* and the *Merrimac*.
5. How Abraham Lincoln freed the slaves.
6. About the surrender of Lee.

THE BLUE AND THE GRAY. The Civil War was one of the saddest and bravest in history. Thousands of fine young men were killed, more thousands were wounded. The question of slavery was forgotten for the time. The "boys in blue" fought bravely to save the Union, which to them was sacred. They were called the "boys in blue" because of the color of the uniforms they wore. The "boys in gray" fought just as bravely for the Confederacy, which to them was just as sacred.

At first sight it seemed that the North had a much better chance to win the war and to win easily. There were about twenty-two million people in the North. There were but nine million people in the South and four million of these were slaves. The North had much greater wealth. It had factories, and machinery for making guns and cannon and

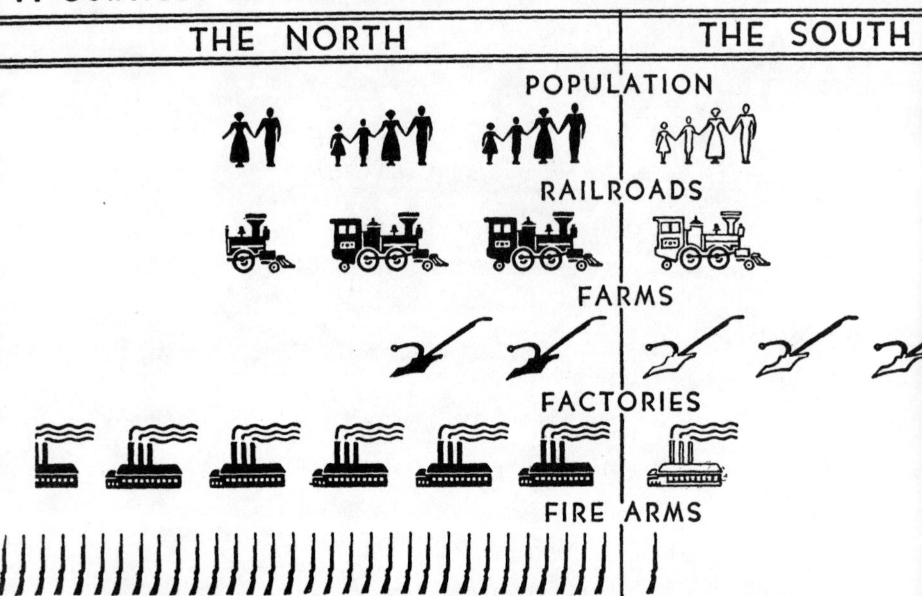

supplies for its army. It could build all the ships that were needed to carry soldiers and supplies.

The South had few of these things. It had great plantations instead of factories. The South relied on selling its cotton. There were no important shipyards in the South.

NORTHERN FAILURES. The North started out confident that it could end the war quickly. The first thing was to capture Richmond, the capital of the Confederacy. It took four long bitter years of fighting before Richmond was captured by the Union Army.

The first battle of the Civil War was Bull Run. The blue-clad warriors of the North were brave but the Southerners had better generals. The Union Army was badly beaten at Bull Run. Lincoln called for more Union troops. A great army was organized. It was called the Army of the Potomac. General George B. McClellan was put in command. Battles were lost and battles were won, but Richmond was not taken by the Union Army. This was very bad for the South. The South could not stand a long war. One of the Southern generals very truly remarked that, "the South to win had to win quickly."

THE BLOCKADE. While the armies struggled on land the North made splendid use of its navy. The South sold great quantities of cotton in Europe, particularly in England. If this trade could be stopped the South would have no money to carry on the war. Lincoln called on the Union Navy to blockade all Southern seaports. There were three thousand miles of coast to guard. The North had to build over four hundred ships, but finally the blockade was tight. No cotton could leave the South. No clothing, guns, medicines, or other necessary things could be brought into the South. The South was badly crippled.

THE *MONITOR* AND *MERRIMAC*. The blockade was slowly strangling the South. Something must be done. At Norfolk, in Virginia, there was an old warship called the *Merrimac*. The Confederates had a brilliant idea. They would cut the *Merrimac* down almost to water level. Then they would build a small iron fort on her decks. They would fit her with an iron prow or ram. The wooden ships of the Union Navy would stand no chance against this Confederate fighting machine.

The North too, had built an iron-clad. It was called the *Monitor*. This ship had two large guns inside a turret built of iron. This turret was a squat round tower. It could be turned around so the guns could fire in any direction. The Monitor floated so low in the water that the Confederates called her "a cheesebox on a raft."

A DRAWN BATTLE. The two iron-clads met in battle. Neither could sink the other. It was a drawn battle, that is, neither of the ships was really the victor. But the South could not build many iron-clads. The North had materials for all that were needed. The North was in a position to keep up the blockade for a very long time.

THE EMANCIPATION PROCLAMATION

LINCOLN'S BRAVE ACTION. The war had been going on for nearly two years. The South was fighting grimly and well. The final outcome was by no means certain. At this difficult time Lincoln thought of doing a most courageous thing. He planned the Emancipation Proclamation. Emancipation means setting free from slavery. A proclamation was a formal notice to the people. Lincoln's proclamation was a formal notice declaring that "all slaves in the states in rebellion shall be forever free." Freeing these

slaves had a great effect. It gave satisfaction to those people all over the world who hated slavery.

THE TIDE OF WAR TURNS

THE TURNING POINT OF THE WAR. The Emancipation Proclamation did not itself free the slaves. Only victorious armies could do that. These victories commenced to come. In Virginia the Union armies had met with some serious setbacks. Nevertheless the fighting had been mostly on Southern soil. Now, General Lee made up his mind to carry the fight to the North. He led his army into Pennsylvania in the early summer of 1863. Lee dared to dream that he might lead his army to Baltimore or Philadelphia, even on to New York.

The North had had trouble with its commanding generals. They had been changed often. The situation was critical. At this point General George Meade was called on to take command and give battle to the great Lee.

The two armies faced one another near the town of Gettsyburg, in Pennsylvania, on July 1, 1863. The armies

Picture courtesy of B. F. Williamson.

fought furiously for two days. The South had the advantage; the North was on the defensive. That is they had to defend themselves against the Confederate Army.

JULY 3, 1863. All during the morning of the third day the battle raged. General Lee decided to risk all on one great attack. He ordered General Pickett to charge the Union breastworks. It was one of the boldest attacks in history. With their officers in front, the boys in gray swept across the battlefield at Gettysburg. They moved through a sweeping rain of shot and shell. The Confederate Army was defeated. That was the high tide of the Confederacy. Lee led his shattered army back into Virginia. Next day General Grant sent word of the capture of Vicksburg. The South had received two terrible blows.

GRANT'S HAMMERING CAMPAIGN. Lee's army held off Union victory for two years more. Before that time had passed Lincoln found the man who would finally win. General U. S. Grant was moved in from the West and placed in command of all the Union armies. Grant's plan to win the war was simple. He had twice as many men as Lee. He began a "hammering campaign." He would give the enemy no rest. He said, "I propose to fight it out on this line if it takes all summer." So it did, and all winter, too. It was a long, hard campaign.

THE END. The South was nearly exhausted. General William T. Sherman had captured Atlanta. Next Richmond fell. Lee was now in full retreat with a small and half starved army. Then General Philip Sheridan placed his cavalry squarely in Lee's path. Lee knew it would be folly to fight any longer. He asked Grant for terms of surrender.

The surrender took place at Appomattox Court House, in Virginia. It was April 9th, 1865. Lee held his head high in defeat. Dressed in a fine new uniform of Confederate gray, General Lee went to meet General Grant. A beau-

Photo from "Dixie," a Chronicles of America Photoplay.

tiful sword in a gilded scabbard hung at Lee's side. Grant was dressed like a private soldier. Only his shoulder straps showed his high rank. He seemed sad over the downfall of the Confederate Army led by General Lee. Grant realized that the enemy had fought long and bravely.

HORSES FOR SPRING PLOWING. Lee gave no sign of the feelings that must have filled his heart. The generals spoke of old times when they had fought in the Mexican War. They chatted for a time; then Lee politely mentioned the purpose of the meeting. Grant drew up a table and wrote out the terms of surrender.

Grant's terms were generous. The officers were allowed to keep their swords and their horses. At Lee's request a soldier who owned a horse or a mule might also keep it. Grant said this might be done, "To help in the spring plowing." The two men parted. Lee mounted his beloved horse, and rode away. The Civil War was really at an end.

The Union had been saved and the slavery question was settled and so was the question of states' rights.

RESULTS OF THE CIVIL WAR. There were three very definite results of the Civil War.

1. The Union was saved.
2. A state had no right to secede. This question was forever settled.
3. The question of slavery was settled. Slavery was forever abolished in the United States by the XIIIth amendment to the Constitution in 1866.

STUDY SUMMARY

---

1. Terms to know. Be able to give the meaning of each term listed.

   iron-clad — blockade — emancipation proclamation — turret

2. People to know. Be able to tell some interesting fact about each person named.

Ulysses S. Grant	William T. Sherman	George Meade
Robert E. Lee	George B. McClellan	Philip Sheridan

3. Places to know. Be able to locate on a map each place listed. Tell one fact about the place as it is located.

Richmond	Baltimore	Gettysburg
Bull Run	Atlanta	Norfolk

4. Dates to remember. Be able to tell the most important event in American history which took place on each of the following dates.

   July 3, 1863 — April 9, 1865

ACTIVITIES

1. Make a sketch map of the United States.
   a. Locate and name each of the following places.

Richmond	Vicksburg	Gettysburg
Baltimore	Charleston	Norfolk
Bull Run	Atlanta	

   b. Draw a line under the name of the Capital of the Confederacy.
   c. Sketch ships to represent how the South was blockaded by hundreds of Northern ships.
   d. Below the map or on a separate paper write one sentence about each place located on the map. Be sure to tell why the place was important in the Civil War.
2. Make a poster to show the surrender of General Lee.

STUDY TEST 44—Score 25

COMPLETION. Fill in the word which will correctly end each sentence.

1. The boys in blue fought to save the . . . .
2. The boys in gray fought for the . . . .
3. There were 22 million people in the . . . .
4. There were only 9 million people in the . . . .
5. There was much greater wealth in the . . . .
6. All the ships they needed could be built by the . . . .
7. There were great plantations in the . . . .
8. The great money crop of the South was . . . .
9. It took the Union Army four years to capture . . . .

10. The first battle of the Civil War was fought at ....

11. General George B. McClellan was placed in command of the Army of the ....

12. President Lincoln ordered all southern ports ....

13. The blockade prevented the South from selling ....

14. No guns, powder or supplies could enter the South while the North kept up the ....

15. Emancipation is the setting free from ....

16. A proclamation is a public or official ....

17. The Emancipation Proclamation freed the slaves in the states in ....

18. General Lee decided to carry the war into the ....

19. Most of the fighting had taken place in the ....

20. The Confederate Army faced the Union Army on July 1, 1863, at ....

21. Vicksburg and Gettysburg were great victories for the ....

22. General Sherman had captured ....

23. Lee asked Grant to name the terms of ....

24. The Confederate Army surrendered at Appomattox Court House, ...

25. The victory of the Northern Army in the Civil War saved the ....

UNIT IX: SLAVERY AND THE UNION

THE SOUTH AFTER THE CIVIL WAR

Read to learn

1. How the South suffered after the Civil War.
2. The plan of Congress for the reconstruction of the South.
3. How evil men from the North took an unfair advantage of the South.
4. How President Hayes helped the South.

A WASTED LAND. Confederate soldiers returning home after the Civil War saw things to bring tears to their eyes. Often a soldier found that his house had been burned to the ground. Fruit trees were cut down. Fields were destroyed and his cattle had been driven away. These misfortunes were bad enough but he had still other worries. What was the United States Government going to do to him? How would Congress treat the Southern states that had tried to leave the Union? These were questions that caused great worry.

RECONSTRUCTION. President Abraham Lincoln realized how terribly the South had suffered. He had a plan to help restore the South. The South had to be reconstructed. This means that the Southern states had to be reorganized as parts of the United States. Lincoln's plan is called the Presidential Plan for Reconstruction. We can easily learn how Lincoln wanted to handle Reconstruction. We have only to read one of his great speeches. This speech was made when he was inaugurated as President for the second time.

> "With malice toward none, with charity for all, with firmness in the right as God gives us to see the right, let us strive on to finish the work we are in, to bind up the nation's wounds, to care for him who shall have borne the battle and for his widow and his orphan, to do all which may achieve and cherish a just and lasting peace, among ourselves and with all nations."

DEATH OF LINCOLN. Before he could carry out his plan Lincoln was murdered. The President was sitting in a box at the theater, on Good Friday, of 1865. Behind him

crept a desperate man, a man maddened by the defeat of the South. He shot Abraham Lincoln and the great President died the next morning. Vice-President Andrew Johnson succeeded Lincoln as President.

THE PUNISHMENT OF THE SOUTH. President Andrew Johnson meant well. It was too bad that he quarrelled with some of the members of Congress. There were men in Congress who had a plan of their own for the South. It was a cruel plan. Unfortunately, these men had their way and the so called Plan of Congress went into effect. This really hindered rather than helped the South.

According to the Plan of Congress many of the best white people in the South were not allowed to vote or to hold office. On the other hand, the Negro ex-slaves were allowed to vote. Evil men from the North and the South saw that this was their chance to gain power. They planned to fool the Negroes into electing them to office. The evil men from the North were called "carpet baggers" because everything they owned could be carried in a small carpet bag. The dishonest Southerners were called "scalawags" by their neighbors. "Carpet baggers" and "Scalawags" were dishonest men. They raised the taxes very high to get the money. Much of this public money they took for themselves. Thousands of Southern people were ruined by these evil men. The South suffered for twenty years from this kind of evil doing.

THE END OF RECONSTRUCTION. Ulysses S. Grant was elected President of the United States. He served from 1869 to 1877. He listened to the politicians who hated the South and so the South continued to suffer.

After Grant came President Rutherford B. Hayes. Hayes ordered the last of the United States troops to leave the South. The South must now take a hold and begin to reconstruct itself. Southern leaders began to take an interest, once again, in not only local but in national politics. The Southern states began to manage their own affairs. It took the South a long time to recover from the Civil War and the terrible years of Reconstruction.

STUDY SUMMARY

1. Terms to know. Be able to give the meaning of each term listed.
   reconstruction | scalawags | carpet baggers
2. People to know. Be able to tell some interesting facts about each person named.
   Ulysses S. Grant | Abraham Lincoln
   Rutherford B. Hayes | Andrew Johnson

ACTIVITIES

1. Make a list of things which were disappointments to Confederate soldiers when they returned from the war.
2. Explain how Lincoln's speech at his second inaugural proved that he had a kind and a charitable attitude toward the South.
3. Explain why the Plan of Congress for Reconstruction was unfair to both whites and Negroes.

STUDY TEST 45—Score 15

YES—NO. Answer each question with either YES or NO.

1. Was the South in a bad state after the Civil War? _____
2. Did Lincoln realize how badly the South had suffered? _____
3. Did the Southern states have to be reorganized as parts of the United States? _____
4. Was Abraham Lincoln able to carry out his plan for reconstruction? _____
5. Did Abraham Lincoln desire a just and a lasting peace? _____
6. Was Abraham Lincoln ill a long time before he died? _____
7. Did President Andrew Johnson get along well with Congress? _____
8. Under the Plan of Congress for Reconstruction were ex-slaves allowed to vote? _____
9. Were some white people denied the right to vote or to hold office under the Plan of Congress? _____
10. Were the carpet baggers dishonest men? _____
11. Did the scalawags help the South to recover after the Civil War? _____
12. Did the carpet baggers and the scalawags lower the taxes in the South? _____
13. Was the South prosperous while Ulysses S. Grant was President? _____
14. Did President Hayes order the United States troops to leave the South? _____
15. Did it take the South a long time to recover from the Civil War and from the evils of Reconstruction? _____

UNIT X: BUILDING THE WEST

THE INDIANS

Read to learn

1. About the West after the Civil War.
2. Why the government set aside Indian Reservations.
3. How the end of the Indian Wars helped the settlement of the West.

THE UNSETTLED WEST. The great Civil War was over. The United States was once more a united nation. The land east of the Mississippi had been divided into states. There were villages, cities, and thriving farms in these states. This was not the case west of the Mississippi River. Here in the West was a vast amount of almost vacant land. Only a few states had been organized in this region. The rest of the western country was divided into territories. A territory was a region under a temporary government. The officers of the territories are appointed by the President. These territories were waiting for people to come to settle in them. As soon as their population became large enough they, too, would become states. They would be admitted to the Union and then they would elect their own officers.

The West did not long remain unsettled. People started to go there in large numbers. Settlers came from Europe and from the southern and the eastern sections of our own country. After the Civil War more and more people came to America from Europe. These people were known as immigrants. Migrate means to move. Immigrate means to move into. Some of these immigrants stayed in the cities of the East. Others sought homes in the West. The Old World was sending us some of its best people. Native-born Americans, too, were looking for new homes and new riches in the West. Many Southerners who had lost everything in the Civil War were attracted to the West.

THE WESTERN COUNTRY. What sort of a country did the new comers find in the West? They found a country that could be made very rich. There were grassy plains for the cattleman and fertile lands for the farmer. There were gold and silver veins waiting for the miner. They found a land that was mostly unexplored, difficult to

travel through, and dangerous to live in. Much of the vast territory was dangerous because of warlike Indians.

THE BUFFALO. The buffalo is a kind of a wild cattle. At one time there were countless thousands of these animals on our western plains. Indians depended upon them entirely. Buffalo meat was good to eat. Buffalo skins, with their long shaggy hair, kept the Indian warm. The Indian used buffalo hides in making his tent, or wigwam.

As the white man came to the western plains the buffalo were driven off or killed. They were easy to kill. Have you ever heard of a scout named "Buffalo Bill"? He was given that nickname because in a year and a half he killed 4,000 buffalo. The Indians were enraged by the slaughter of the buffalo. They hated the whites more than ever. A series of Indian Wars, which lasted for over twenty years started.

INDIAN RESERVATIONS. The United States Government had been trying for a long time to get the Indians to live on reservations. A reservation was a large tract of land set aside by the government for Indian use only. The government put an agent in charge of the Indians on the reservation. Schools were built, and food, blankets, and medicine were provided.

The Indian agents were not always honest. The Indians were cheated and often they were cruelly treated. This added to the Indians' hatred of the white men.

CUSTER'S LAST STAND. After twenty years or more of fighting most of the Indians had been forced to live on reservations. The most troublesome of those left were a tribe called the Sioux. The Sioux were stubborn. They refused to go to their reservations. Chief Sitting Bull and Chief Crazy Horse led the Sioux. United States troops were ordered to see that the Indians obeyed. Our best Indian fighter, General George A. Custer, was in command of part of these troops. The Sioux were well armed and they

were wild with rage. They surrounded Custer and his 225 soldiers. The whites were outnumbered ten to one. They could not escape, they would not surrender. They fought till the last man was killed.

Another year's fighting and the Sioux were tamed. The Indians in the North were all on their reservations by 1877. There was trouble for a few years more in Arizona. Geronimo, an Apache chief, was finally captured. This ended the Indian Wars.

Now the white man could settle the Far West in peace. He no longer need be afraid that the Indians would drive off his cattle, burn his ranch home, or kill his family.

STUDY SUMMARY

---

1. Terms to know. Be able to give the meaning of each term listed.

territory	immigrant	war-path
migrate	reservation	buffalo
wigwam	immigrate	

2. People to know. Be able to tell an important fact about each person named.

General George Custer	Chief Crazy Horse
Chief Sitting Bull	Buffalo Bill

3. Date to remember. Be able to tell why 1877 is an important date in a study of the American Indians.

ACTIVITIES

1. Make a list of the things in the West which attracted settlers.
2. Tell the story of CUSTER'S LAST STAND.

STUDY TEST 46—Score 10

EITHER—OR. Underscore the term which answers the question.

1. Was the West settled or unsettled when the Civil War ended?
2. Were the territories under regular or temporary government?
3. Were the officers in the territories elected or appointed?
4. Was most of the West unexplored or was it an explored region?
5. Did the Indian Wars in the West last twenty or fifty years?
6. Is a reservation set aside for the use of Indians or for the use of white men?
7. Were the Indians willing, or were they forced, to live on the reservations?
8. Were the Sioux a peaceful or a warlike tribe?
9. Did General Custer or the Indians win the battle?
10. Was it 1877 or 1867 before the Indians were all living on their reservations?

HOW SETTLERS REACHED THE WEST

Read to learn

1. The three routes to the West used by settlers.
2. How freight was carried into the West.
3. How the pony express served the people.
4. Why the pony express lasted only two years.
5. How the United States government helped in the building of railroads.

THE WESTERN TRAILS. Americans had been going in great numbers to the Pacific coast long before the Civil War. They traveled across the Great Plains, and over or around high mountains.

There were three principal ways of reaching the west coast:

1. The Santa Fe Trail was the oldest. It started from the town of Independence in Missouri. This trail ran to the old town of Santa Fe, in the present state of New Mexico. In 1849 the gold rush to California started. So the Santa Fe trail was pushed on to Los Angeles as is shown on the map.

2. Then there was the Southern Overland Trail. It started from either St. Louis, or Memphis, and it ran far south across Texas, New Mexico, and Arizona. It entered California along the Gila River.

3. The Oregon Trail was the most traveled. It, too, started westward at the Missouri River. When it came to Great Salt Lake it divided. One branch went northwest to Oregon. The other kept westward to California. Trace these trails on the map.

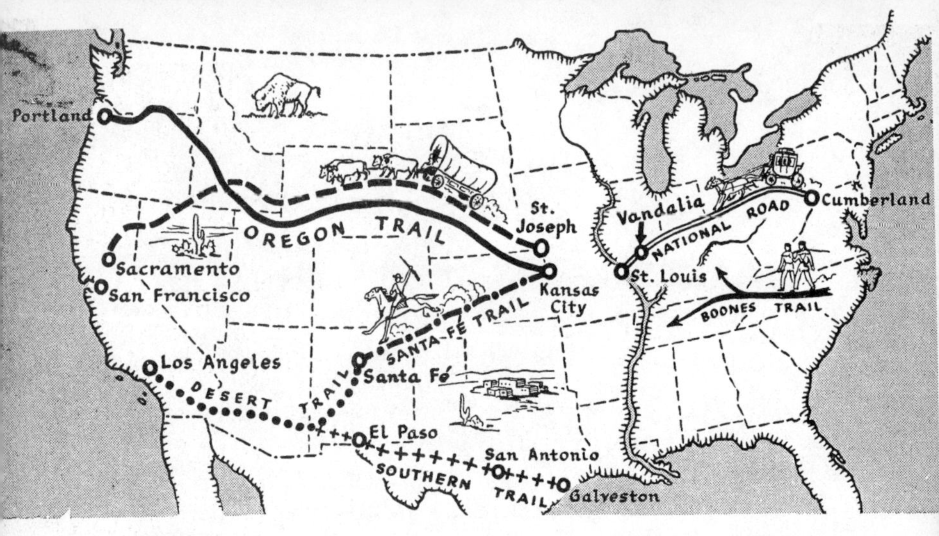

These trails were not laid out by highway engineers. Often the trail was one that had once been used by the Indians. Fur trappers coming into a region frequently followed the Indian trails. Then came the emigrants' wagon trains or the mail coach making a rutted road over the old trail. Today, some of the fine concrete highways follow these old routes into the West.

CARRYING GOODS, PASSENGERS, AND MAIL

FREIGHT TRAINS. As the population grew on the Pacific coast more and more supplies were needed. Some of these were sent by ship but much goods was sent westward by overland freight train. The "freight trains" of these early days were not railroad trains. They were made up of many covered wagons, each drawn by ten or twelve oxen. Twenty or twenty-five wagons made up a freight train. The wagons carried articles which were manufactured in the East. Shovels, hoes, picks, scythes, hammers, saws, nails, guns, pistols, powder, tobacco, blankets, and dozens of other items, were carried into the West. These were stored in the body of the wagon under its canvas cover. The Indians had to be very strong to attack a freight train.

THE WESTERN STAGE. Passengers going to the West traveled by stage-coaches. Just before the Civil War the United States government determined to provide the people of California with regular mail service. A line of stage-coaches was planned. This line would carry both passengers and mail.

The stages traveled day and night, stops being made to water the horses or to change teams. The stages were like those in the East except that they were less comfortable. They were probably of stronger build for the stages had to travel over a rough trail. Sending mail by stage-coach was very slow. A quicker system of carrying mail was tried. This was the pony express.

THE PONY EXPRESS. Mail sent by stage-coach from St. Louis to San Francisco took twenty-five days. Mail sent about the same distance by pony express took only ten days. There was a good reason why the pony express was able to save so much time.

The pony express was speedy because the horses used were very fast. These horses carried only about ten pounds of mail; for this reason letters had to be written on thin paper. The pony express riders, like the jockeys of today, were small, light men. A man who weighed more than one hundred and thirty-five pounds could not get a job as a pony express rider.

THE ROUTE OF THE PONY EXPRESS. The pony express route extended from St. Joseph, Missouri, to Sacramento, California. Each rider had his special part of the route, riding westward one day and returning eastward the next. Each horse was ridden at top speed for about fifteen or twenty miles. Then a lightning change to another horse and the rider was off again. Each rider had a route of fifty or sixty miles. At the end of his particular route the express rider handed the bag of mail to the next rider who continued the journey. It was like a long relay race.

LETTERS BY PONY EXPRESS. Letters sent by pony express cost the sender five dollars in gold. The price was really necessary because of the large number of riders and the many swift horses that were needed for this work. The pony express was started in 1860. It only lasted two years because by that time the telegraph had been extended to California. Telegraph messages could be sent instantly. The pony express was no longer needed.

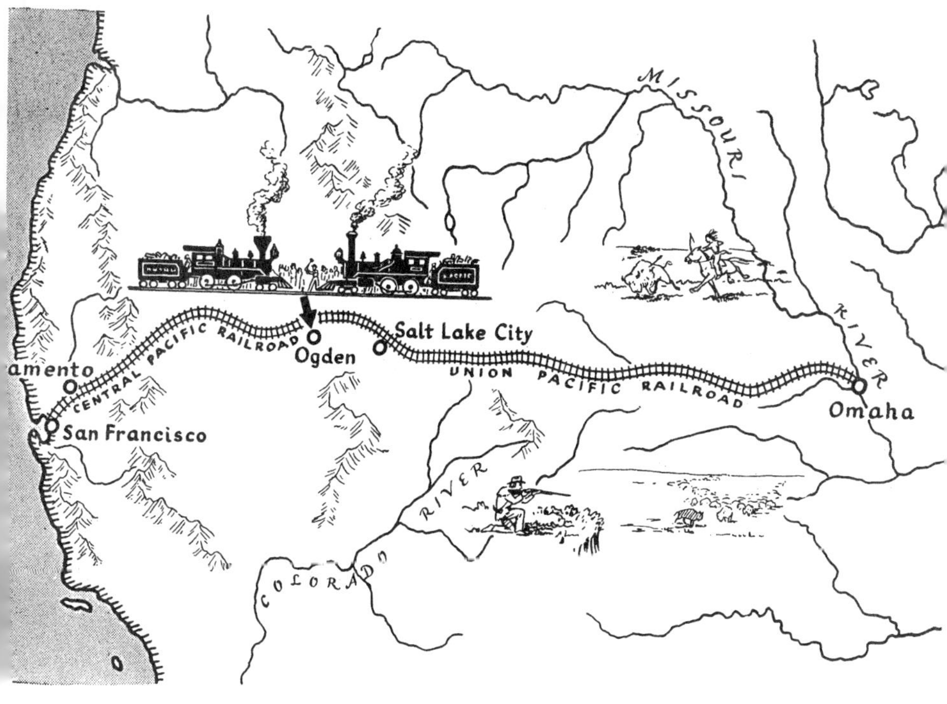

RAILROADS

THE FIRST RAILROAD ACROSS THE COUNTRY. Everyone knew that a railroad ought to connect the Pacific coast with the East. Many difficulties stood in the way of building such a railroad across our country.

Huge sums of money would be needed to build a railroad across the country. Money was hard to get for such a purpose. There would not be very much business for the railroad because so few people lived west of the Missouri River. To make money, railroads must carry freight and passengers. People who had money to spare would not invest it in building a railroad in a part of the country where few people lived. Consequently, it was necessary for the United States Government to help. The government did not have any too much money but it had plenty of land. So the government agreed to give the railroad companies a certain amount of land for every mile of railroad built. The companies could sell the land and thus get money.

UNION PACIFIC AND CENTRAL PACIFIC. Two companies were formed to build the railroad. One, called the Central Pacific, agreed to begin work in California and build toward the east. The other road, called the Union Pacific, began at Omaha, in Nebraska, and extended westward. The two roads were to meet in the Far West.

The building of the railroad was thrilling work. The Central Pacific, starting eastward from California had special difficulties to overcome. The rails and other equipment had to be brought to California by boat, around Cape Horn. This railroad had to cross mountains and bridge deep gorges. It was built mostly by Chinese laborers who were called coolies. They worked hard for very low wages.

The builders of the railroad for the Union Pacific also had their troubles. These workers were mostly Irish. Many of them had fought in the Civil War. Now they had to face dangers of a different sort. There was very little water on the Great Plains. Wood for camp fires was scarce. The workers were always in danger from Indian attacks. The Indians seemed to understand that the railroad was going to take from them the last of their hunting grounds.

THE FINISH OF A GREAT WORK. In spite of all sorts of obstacles the building progressed. The men worked with such spirit that each day they tried to outdo what they had done the day before. At last, on May 10, 1869, the eastern line met the western line near Ogden, Utah. It was a day for great rejoicing. A great crowd of people came to see the last spike driven into place. This spike was made of gold from California. A silver sledge hammer drove the spike into a beautifully polished railroad tie. The blows of the hammer were recorded by the telegraph so that the entire country could know that now the East and West were united by a railroad.

Celebrations were held in many cities throughout the country. In Chicago a parade was organized. Church services were held. The old Liberty Bell, which had rung out the news of the signing of the Declaration of Independence, now announced that East was linked to West by rails of steel. This railroad is often called the Transcontinental Railroad. Trans means across. Transcontinental is a good name for a railroad which goes across the continent. The map on page 403 shows the first transcontinental railroad.

STUDY SUMMARY

1. Terms to know. Be able to tell the meaning of each term listed.

   freight train — transcontinental
   pony express — coolies

2. Places to know. Be able to locate on a wall map each place listed. Tell one important fact about the place as it is located.

Cape Horn	Arizona	Independence
Sacramento	Texas	Santa Fe
St. Joseph	Oregon	New Mexico
St. Louis	Ogden	San Francisco
California	Omaha	Great Salt Lake

3. Dates to remember. Be able to tell the important event which took place on each date listed.

   1849 — 1860 — 1869

ACTIVITIES

1. Make a sketch map of the United States.
   a. Use red to show the three principal trails to the West. Name the trails.
   b. Locate and name the following places.

Independence	Memphis
St. Louis	Great Salt Lake
Los Angeles	Ogden

   c. Use blue to show the route of the pony express.
   d. Use green to show the route of the first transcontinental railroad.
2. List the three dangers the railroad builders met.

STUDY TEST 47—Part I—Score 10

TIME ORDER. Number each group of facts in the order of their happening.

Group A.

( ) Gold discovered in California
( ) Transcontinental railroad completed
( ) Pony express

Group B.

( ) Indian trail
( ) Concrete highway
( ) Fur trappers' path
( ) Road for stage coaches

Group C.

( ) Mail carried on railroad
( ) Mail carried by stage-coach
( ) Mail carried by pony express

STUDY TEST 47—Part II—Score 20

SELECT ENDING. Underscore the term which gives the correct ending to the sentence.

1. The Santa Fe Trail was the
   oldest trail   newest trail
2. The gold rush took place in
   Arizona   California
3. The most traveled trail was the
   Oregon Trail   Santa Fe Trail
4. The Oregon Trail divided at
   St. Louis   Great Salt Lake
5. Freight trains were pulled by
   horses   oxen

6. The pony express was
   speedy — slow

7. The pony express was started in
   1860 — 1850

8. Letters sent by pony express cost
   $1.00 — $5.00

9. The pony express lost importance with the use of the
   cable — telegraph

10. Land for the railroads was given by the
    Indians — government

11. Railroads sold land to get
    money — farms

12. The Central Pacific Railroad began in
    Oregon — California

13. The Union Pacific Railroad began at
    Omaha — St. Louis

14. The rails were carried around
    Cape Horn — Cape of Good Hope

15. Laborers on the Central Pacific were mostly
    Germans — Chinese

16. Laborers on the Union Pacific were mostly
    Irish — Italian

17. There was very little water on the
    Great Plains — Pacific slope

18. Wood on the Great Plains was very
    scarce — plentiful

19. The railroads met at
    Omaha — Ogden

20. Across the continent is called
    Continental — transcontinental

UNIT X: BUILDING THE WEST

SETTLING MOUNTAIN AND PLAIN

Read to learn

1. Why miners were attracted to the West.
2. How the Great Plains came to be settled.
3. The profit in cattle raising on the Great Plains.
4. About the coming of farmers to the Great Plains.
5. How the Homestead Act helped the settlement of the Great Plains.
6. About the opening of Oklahoma.

LOOKING FOR GOLD. There was gold in California. Could it not be found in other places? The Rocky Mountains seemed a likely place. There might be gold in the hills. Gold was discovered near Pike's Peak, in Colorado in 1859. Soon the news that there was gold in Colorado reached the East. Thousands of eager young men set out for that state hoping to "strike it rich." Their destination was not easy to reach. Many a hardship had to be met but they were not afraid for their spirits were high. Their slogan was a brave one, "Pike's Peak or Bust."

THE MINING POPULATION. After the Civil War there were many soldiers who had nothing to do. Many of these men moved to the region of the gold and silver mines. Conditions in the southern states were very bad. Wherever the armies had fought the land was destroyed and much property was ruined. Many Southern men believed that the life of the miner was the only life left for them to follow. They were willing to search for gold.

The discovery of gold and silver brought miners into what is now the state of Nevada. Other discoveries of gold and silver were made in Idaho and Montana. Soon the Rocky Mountains region had a fair-sized population. It was composed almost entirely of miners.

THE MINING TOWN. The mining town of the West was a very poor place for a home. The main street was a narrow muddy road with a few unpainted buildings on either side. Here were to be seen the post office, general store, and a hotel. The hotel was usually small with only two or three rooms.

The "diggings" were just outside the town. When a miner arrived he became a prospector. That is, he searched around until he found a place where he thought there was gold ore. Then he drove a stake in the ground with his name on it. That was called staking out his claim. It gave him a right to any gold that he might find within the claim he had staked. If he did strike gold, he was fortunate, and

he continued to work on his claim until the gold "petered out." Then he prospected again in some other likely spot.

ROCKY MOUNTAIN STATES. The search for gold and silver in the Rocky Mountain region helped develop the country. A government of some sort was needed, so the United States organized this region into territories. Later these territories became the states of Colorado, Nevada, Idaho, and Montana.

FIRST WHITE PEOPLE OF THE PLAINS

THE GREAT PLAINS. Thousands of emigrants had crossed the high grassy plains east of the Rocky Mountains. They had not lingered on the Great Plains, to settle. There was too little water and too few trees. It took a later generation to find out how to farm that land. Before that could take place the cattleman and his cowboys took possession of these plains.

HABITS OF EATING. Americans have always liked to eat meat. In colonial times people ate game, deer meat which is called venison, squirrel, rabbit, opossum, and the flesh of other small animals. The people also raised hogs for meat. The pork was salted so that it would keep for a long time. Sheep provided mutton. Beef, which we relish, was not eaten then as often as it is now. Cows were raised for milk rather than killed for flesh.

After the Civil War people began to change their manner of living. They began to move into cities. People were going from the farm to the factory. The farmer could raise hogs and cattle for his own meat supply. This would not be of much help to people who lived in the cities. Providing meat for city people to eat was a big problem. This problem was solved by the cattlemen of the West and by their cowboys.

THE WILD CATTLE OF TEXAS. There were large herds of cattle in Texas. These animals were the descendants of cattle which the Spaniards had introduced three hundred years earlier. These cattle were known as "long-horned cattle" because of the great spread of their horns.

When the Americans moved to Texas they found the wild cattle there. Soon quite a business was built of selling cattle, to the people who lived in the southern states.

During the Civil War the cattlemen lost their market in the South. After the Civil War was over the herds of cattle in Texas were larger than ever. At the same time the people living in the cities of the East were demanding more and more beef. Cattle for beef were becoming valuable. The railroads were reaching out into the "cow country." Therefore, cattle raising in Texas and also in the north in Colorado, Wyoming, and Montana, became an important way of making money.

UNFENCED PRAIRIES. The prairies of the West had thousands of acres of land covered with rich grass. The prairies became the great "cow country" of America. There were no fences and the cattle wandered over the prairies eating the rich grass and getting fat. Then came the round-up and the drive to the railroad.

THE ROUND-UP. Twice a year, in the spring and in the fall, each cattle owner gathered all his cattle at his own ranch. This gathering together of the cattle was called the round-up. Every cattle owner could tell his own cattle because they were marked by a special brand. Branding was done with a hot iron which burned away a part of the hair on the hide. This left a mark, or brand, which lasted as long as the animal lived. The young calves which had not yet been branded followed their mothers. So that the calves might not get lost or stolen they, too, were branded.

THE COW TOWNS. When the cattle had reached the proper weight they were driven to the cow towns of Kansas. Fine cities like Wichita and Atchison had their start as cow towns. These cow towns were convenient shipping points. Here the cattle were placed in cattle yards and then shipped by train to the slaughter houses of Kansas City or Chicago.

THE LIFE OF THE COWBOY. The cowboy's life was hard whether at home on the ranch, or in the saddle away on a cattle drive. There were no fences and the cattle could roam great distances. Often the cattle got lost. It was then the cowboy's task to find the stray animals. Sometimes a herd became frightened and began to run wild. This was called a stampede. Only great daring and skillful riding by the cowboys could bring the herd under control. Cattle thieves, called "cattle rustlers," often caused the cowboys great trouble.

The great "cow country" was at its best for about twenty years. Then came the farmer and his barbed wire fence. The days of unfenced pastures hundreds of miles wide were over.

PEOPLE WHO CAME TO THE FARMS

NEW FARMS. The railroad had been the friend of the cattleman. It carried his beef cattle to market. Now the railroad was to spell the doom of the open cattle range. A large group of settlers came by rail to the West. They came to raise crops instead of cattle. The barbed wire fence commenced to enclose the prairie. The cattle kings were indignant. They hated the "nesters" as they called the farmers. There were quarrels, between the cattlemen and the farmers. Wire fences were cut, homes were burned, but in the end the farmers won.

WHEAT. Wheat might be called the pioneering crop of America. Wheat was moved westward with the frontier.

Wheat was grown principally in the northern and middle colonies in the early days. When the Erie Canal was opened up, wheat commenced to be raised with profit in Ohio. The railroads reached Chicago in the fifties of the last century. Then wheat was raised in Indiana, Illinois,

and even across the Mississippi into Missouri. Wheat was now ready to take over the great cow country of the western plains. Wheat was moving with the frontier.

THE HOMESTEAD ACT, 1862. Cheap land was what the wheat farmer needed. Congress helped him get that land by a new law. This was called the Homestead Act. Under this act a settler could get 160 acres of free land. All he had to do was to live on the land and cultivate it for three years. The dream of the small farmer was to own his own farm.

Nevertheless the farmers going to the Great Plains had many difficulties to overcome. Wood was scarce as there were few trees. So the farmer's first home was often built of sod. Water, too, was often lacking. Farmers depended upon wells and ditches for water. Wolves and coyotes sometimes destroyed the livestock. At times a plague of grasshoppers laid waste the fields. There were times when a cyclone madly whirled across the land. A cyclone is a bad storm with strong winds. The winter blizzard took its toll in the north. The prairie fire caused horror in the summer. In spite of all the difficulties the farms extended. The tough prairie sod was turned over. The profitable crop of wheat was raised and marketed.

THE SETTLEMENT OF OKLAHOMA. The last great stretch of free land was located in Oklahoma. This land had been set aside as an Indian reservation. There was much more land than the Indians really needed. So the United States bought the land from the Indians. This land was to be thrown open to those who would make homes there. President Benjamin Harrison set April 22, 1889, as the day for the opening of the Oklahoma Territory. Thousands of Americans came from distant places to get their share of this rich free land.

THE BUGLE BLOWS. Guards were stationed at the border so that no one could steal on ahead. As noon approached about 50,000 people waited along the border. They were all set to jump ahead when the signal was given. A United States officer rode to a mound where he could be seen and heard. Exactly at twelve o'clock he raised his bugle, sounded a call, and dropped a flag. The race was on! Some settlers rode swift horses; others drove carriages, or urged slow oxen forward. Some of the land seekers had nothing but their own legs to carry them on. That night there were tent cities at Guthrie and at Oklahoma City. Within a year 250,000 people had moved into Oklahoma and more were coming. In 1907 Oklahoma became the 46th

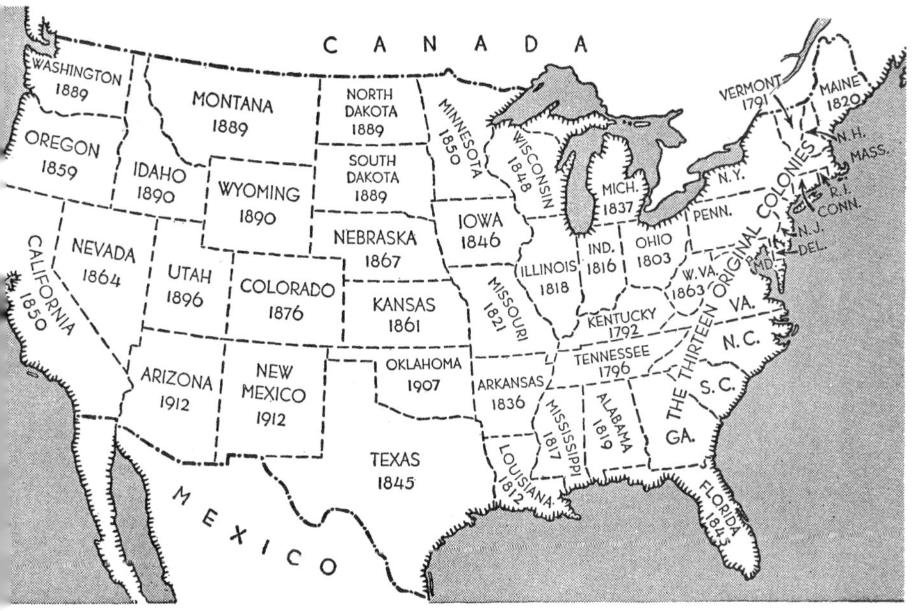

state of the United States. Five years later the 47th and 48th States entered the Union when Arizona and New Mexico were admitted. Since 1912 the United States has had 48 states. That is why our flag has 48 stars.

The miner, the cattleman and the farmer, had completed the settlement of the West. There was no longer any frontier in America.

ALASKA. It is true that the frontier had passed from the main part of the United States. We had acquired a new frontier in far-off Alaska.

Alaska is the most northern and western part of North America. Only the narrow Bering Strait separates Alaska from the Russian part of Asia. The Russians had crossed Bering Strait and had taken possession of Alaska. Only a few adventurers went there to hunt the seal for its fur. The Russian government paid little attention to Alaska.

The Russians offered to sell Alaska to the United States for $7,200,000, in 1867. Our Secretary of State, William H. Seward, because of the fur seals that were found there, wanted to buy Alaska. People laughed at Seward. They thought of Alaska as a worthless ice-bound land fit only

for a few Eskimos. They called it "Seward's ice-box." Our Senate hesitated, but finally took Seward's advice and bought Alaska in 1867.

It was some time before our country paid much attention to its new purchase. Finally, it was given a government as a territory. Gold was found there and many people rushed to the fields. Coal and other valuable minerals were discovered. People found Alaska was far from a barren country. It has turned out to be a very valuable possession. Its greatest value lies in its furs, fish, and forests.

STUDY SUMMARY

---

1. Terms to know. Be able to tell the meaning of each term listed.

cow country	stampede	long-horned cattle
prospector	branding	round-up
ore	claim	"petered out"
venison	cyclone	cattle rustlers

2. People to know. Be able to tell one fact about each person named.

Benjamin Harrison	William H. Seward

3. Places to know. Be able to locate on a wall map each place listed. Give a fact about the place as it is located.

Chicago	Rocky Mountains	Oklahoma City
Nevada	Kansas City	Guthrie
Montana	Pike's Peak	California
Idaho	Atchison	Alaska
Witchita	Oklahoma	Colorado

4. Dates to remember. Be able to tell some important event in the settling of the West that took place on each date listed.

1859	1862	1867	1912

ACTIVITIES

1. Make a sketch map of the United States. Show by shading the different wheat areas.
   a. Use horizontal lines to show that in colonial days wheat was grown in the northern and middle colonies.
   b. Use vertical lines to show the Ohio Valley where wheat became an important crop after the opening of the Erie Canal.
   c. Use diagonal lines to show Indiana, Illinois, and Missouri where wheat was the important crop after the coming of the railroad.
   d. Use vertical lines over horizontal lines to shade the present Wheat Belt.
   e. Below the map write a paragraph telling about wheat as a frontier crop.
2. List some of the difficulties a pioneer farmer had to overcome in the West.
3. Make a poster to illustrate the OPENING UP OF OKLAHOMA, THE LAST FREE LAND.

STUDY TEST 48—Score 30

CHECKING. Check the items which correctly belong under each heading.

1. Gold was discovered in: Check 6.

... California	... Montana
... Oregon	... Nevada
... Colorado	... Idaho
... Alaska	... Oklahoma

2. Meats used by colonists. Check 7.

... beef	... lamb
... game	... opossum
... venison	... pork
... calf's liver	... dried beef
... squirrel	... mutton
... rabbit	... lamb

3. How settlers entered Oklahoma. Check 4.

... horseback	... carriage
... bicycles	... trucks
... walking	... oxen carts

4. Difficulties farmers in the West had to overcome. Check 7.

... miners	... grasshoppers
... lack of wood	... blizzards
... wolves and coyotes	... prairie fires
... heavy rainfall	... lack of water
... cyclones	... no markets for crops

5. Last 3 states admitted to the Union. Check 3.

... California	... Arizona
... Oklahoma	... Oregon
... Idaho	... New Mexico

6. Products of greatest wealth in Alaska. Check 3.

... cattle	... wheat
... gold	... fish
... furs	... forests

COAL, IRON, AND OIL

Read to learn

1. How the invention of the steam engine encouraged coal mining.
2. Why the English iron masters objected to the home-made iron products made by the colonist.
3. Why the demand for steel increased.
4. How the canning of foods came to be a great business.
5. About the services rendered by Luther Burbank.
6. How petroleum came to be so useful a product.

CHANGING CONDITIONS. Even after the Civil War people lived very differently from the way in which we live today. Things that are common to us were unknown to our grandfathers. Great changes were to take place. Buildings were not very tall before steel was used in building. People did not have many different kinds of foods before foods were canned. Homes and streets were poorly lighted before the electric light was invented. How did people travel about before the automobile and airplane? Many changes have taken place in the daily life of Americans during the last century.

First, let us study about the things we get from the earth, the minerals. Then we can learn about the things that grow in the earth, our foods. At the same time we will learn the history of how man has used these things in his industries and through his inventions.

COAL

COAL. Father James Marquette, S.J., noticed coal in the Mississippi Valley. A few years later the Franciscan, Father Louis Hennepin, wrote of a "cole mine" near the Illinois River. About 1750, a small soft coal mine was

Courtesy of Exide Battery Co.

opened near Richmond, Virginia. This soft coal was used principally by blacksmiths. It was called "Richmond coal."

The use of coal was slow in spreading. People would not use coal in their stoves. Who was going to try to burn black stones? The steam engine was not known at that time. What little industry existed was moved by water power, particularly in New England.

Then came the invention of the steam engine. The steam engine made possible the factory. Soon more power was needed than could be supplied by waterfalls. Steam power was used and coal was burned to make the steam.

The coal mining industry in America rapidly increased. Two different kinds of coal had been discovered. There was a hard coal called anthracite. It was found only in a small part of Pennsylvania. There was a soft coal called bituminous. It was found in large fields in several parts of the country. States like West Virginia and Illinois have immense fields of bituminous, or soft coal. It is also found in the Rocky Mountains district. The United States has by far the greatest amount of coal of any country in the world. Coal mining has become one of our chief industries.

Besides its use as a fuel, coal has many other uses. It may be heated and turned into various kinds of gas. Hundreds of the most useful chemicals, dyes and medicines are obtained from these gases.

IRON AND STEEL

TWIN GIANTS. Iron and steel are the two giants that have made possible our modern way of living. Today, we look about us and see the big ships and heavy auto trucks, great bridges and tall buildings, and a thousand other things made of steel. America has built up some of the greatest steel mills and factories in the world. If we look back to colonial days we recall that the only iron works were small forges and tiny foundries.

Ship building was one of the first industries to need things made of iron. Nails, bolts, anchors, and chains were needed. Cannon and shot were also needed. Iron works commenced to supply the New England shipbuilders. The ore from which the iron was made was found in bogs and swamps. Before the Revolution iron making was well started. Valley Forge, so famous in the Revolution, received its name from an iron forge.

The English iron masters objected to the home-made American product. They wanted to supply the colonies with all their ironware. Parliament passed a law limiting American iron manufacture. Parliament acted too late. The iron works had fortunately been established. The

American Revolution could hardly have succeeded had it not been for these thriving foundries and forges.

When America became a nation the iron industry continued to expand. Cincinnati, Ohio, and Pittsburgh, Pennsylvania, were early iron centers.

STEEL. Steel is iron that has been hardened and made stronger. As modern industry and invention advanced the demand for steel became greater. The value of steel had been known for many centuries. Steel was difficult to make. When a simpler and better method of making it was found the use of steel spread far and wide. The men who helped to find this method were William Kelly in the United States and Henry Bessemer in England.

SKYSCRAPERS. One of the most interesting uses of steel is in building skyscrapers, as very tall buildings are called. Before the days of cheap steel, buildings could be built only as high as their stone or brick walls could support them. This was seldom more than eight or ten stories high.

About 1888, Chicago builders commenced to put up buildings with steel skeletons. In this way very high buildings could be built. American skyscrapers in time became famous throughout the world.

STEEL AND FOOD

FOOD IN CANS. It is possible to roll or press steel into very thin sheets. Large and small cans could be made from this sheet steel. The oil industry needed metal cans or containers of many sizes. This demand was met by factories where metal cans were manufactured.

From the earliest times in American homes it has been the custom for the women and girls to make preserves and jellies. At the end of the fruit season berries, peaches, apples, pears and other fruits were cooked and then sealed in jars. These preserves of fruit or pickled food were rarely sold and were not shipped great distances.

American business men began to think of using cans for foods. Then the food could be kept a long time, shipped great distances, and yet remain fresh. A way was found to make food cans cheaply and well. The sheet steel was plated with tin, so that it would not rust. The cans were tightly sealed so that no air could enter. Not only fruits and vegetables but fish and meats were canned. Then the canned goods business grew very important.

LUTHER BURBANK

BETTER FRUITS AND FAIRER FLOWERS. What we have learned about canning fruits and vegetables brings to mind the name of Luther Burbank. That is because Burbank was able to do an astonishing thing. He was actually able to give us new and better fruits and vegetables. Besides giving us better things to eat he was also able to give us more beautiful flowers to admire.

LUTHER BURBANK'S BOYHOOD. Luther Burbank was born in Lancaster, Massachusetts, in 1849. He was the tenth child. The place where he grew up was very beautiful. Tall elm trees lined the streets of the village where he lived. The country nearby had green meadows through which ran singing brooks. Luther Burbank's toys were flowers. He tells us himself how much he loved them. His boyhood was very happy. He had about him the things that he loved most, the trees, flowers, springs, and the small wild animals.

BURBANK'S EARLY STRUGGLES. Luther Burbank's days in school were happy but he could not remain there very long. He went to work for an uncle in a wood-working factory. Here Burbank earned fifty cents a day and spent the entire fifty cents for board. As he had to pay board on Sunday but did not work that day Burbank's week's wages netted a loss of fifty cents. The dust of the factory injured his health, this made matters worse.

BURBANK'S SEVENTEEN ACRES. Luther Burbank left the factory and took up gardening. He began to learn a great deal about seeds and plants. Burbank had his first success when he grew an excellent potato. It is now called the Burbank potato and grows all over the world. Burbank made little money in spite of the success of the Burbank potato. He decided to move to California.

BURBANK IN CALIFORNIA. Luther Burbank arrived in California owning only the clothes on his back, a few books, and his precious seeds. He settled in Santa Rosa, a place named in honor of Saint Rose of Lima. His first year's work in California as a seedman netted him $15.20. His second year brought him $84.00. The young man kept on trying to succeed.

Burbank carried on many experiments with the trees and the flowers of California. He grafted one tree on another. That is he took the bud of one fruit and joined it to the stem of another plant. The result would be a new and better kind of tree. Another way Burbank worked was to choose the finest fruit on a tree and plant its seeds. Other excellent trees grew from these seeds. Again the best fruit would be selected and its seeds planted. This

was done many times over until a much improved fruit or flower was obtained. Burbank would also watch his growings things and choose any unusual form that might appear. Burbank was able to help Nature to give us better plants and better trees.

BURBANK'S WISH. Among Burbank's greatest successes is the walnut tree which he called Paradox. The Shasta Daisy with its large gay flowers which brighten many gardens is one of Burbank's finest plants. A cactus without thorns is another. Before his death, people from all parts of the world visited him. Luther Burbank once said: "I shall be content if because of me there shall be better fruits and fairer flowers." His wish came true.

THE PETROLEUM INDUSTRY

PETROLEUM. Petroleum is an oil which comes from the ground. The word petroleum is taken from two Latin words which mean rock oil. From this oil we get an amazing number of important products. Petroleum makes a splendid fuel. Railway locomotives, steamships, and many kinds of steam plants use oil as fuel. Then again, when petroleum is refined it gives gasoline. The oil when it comes from the well is called crude oil. Certain impurities are taken out of it; it is then said to be refined. You do not need to be told that gasoline gives power to run automobiles, airplanes, and gas engines of all sorts. There are numberless useful products made from petroleum.

Photo by Ewing Galloway.

THE DISCOVERY OF OIL. The first mention of petroleum in America was made by a Franciscan priest. In 1632, Father d'Allion visited what were called the oil springs in New York. Later on, people in Pennsylvania came to know about oil. They often saw small ponds where the oil had oozed out of the earth. Some thought it would be useful as medicine but no one seems to have realized its full value. Slowly people began to find out that this oil could be burned in lamps to give a good light. More oil was needed. A number of rich men wanted to go in the oil business. They sent E. L. Drake to Pennsylvania. Drake was to search out a place where he saw signs of oil. He was then to bore a deep hole in the ground. This was called drilling an oil well. The picture shows Drake at his first well which was drilled at Titusville, Pennsylvania, in 1859. It produced a good supply of oil. Many uses for this sort of oil were soon found. During the Civil War it was found to be good to make machinery run smoothly. It seemed as though oil's greatest usefulness had been discovered when a way was found to refine oil to make kerosene. This refined oil, or kerosene, could be used for lamps. So a better way to light homes had been found.

OLD WAYS OF LIGHTING IN HOMES. Until the drilling of oil wells, most people depended upon candles or whale oil lamps to light their homes. Candles gave an exceedingly poor light. Lamps burning whale oil were not much better than candles. Besides, whale oil was fairly expensive because the supply of whales was growing smaller. Captains of whaling ships had to sail farther and farther from New England ports in search of whales. So the kerosene lamp became very popular. It was also discovered that kerosene could be used as fuel for heating and for cooking.

DEMAND FOR OIL. As the demand for oil increased many wells were sunk in Pennsylvania and elsewhere. There was a big demand for oil and those who had it to sell became rich. Men rushed to the oil fields as they had rushed to the gold fields. People even came to call oil "liquid gold."

ROCKEFELLER'S CAREER. John D. Rockefeller was among the first to realize that great wealth could be made in the oil business. When he died he was one of the richest men in the world. Rockefeller was from a farm in New York. When he was still a small child his family moved to Cleveland.

During the Civil War Rockefeller went into the provision business. He sold meat, flour, and foods to the army. He made money in this venture but his greatest profits were yet to come. It was the oil business that made Rockefeller a millionaire many times over.

ROCKEFELLER AND OIL. With a man named Andrews, Rockefeller commenced to deal in oil. The firm of Rockefeller and Andrews bought the crude oil as it came from the wells and refined it in their own oil refinery. Rockefeller made so much money this way that he was able to buy out his competitors. Those he could not buy out he forced out. Soon he controlled all the oil refineries of Cleveland. Rockefeller was not satisfied. In 1882 he controlled almost all the oil refinery business of the country. His oil business was called the Standard Oil Company.

OIL IN AMERICA. The oil business started in Pennsylvania but today that state produces only a small part of what is used. The millions of automobiles in our country use a tremendous amount of gasoline. Oil was searched for and found in California, in Texas, in Oklahoma, and in other parts of America. Thousands of men are engaged drilling wells, refining, and selling oil. Great pipe lines carry the oil long distances from the wells to the refineries.

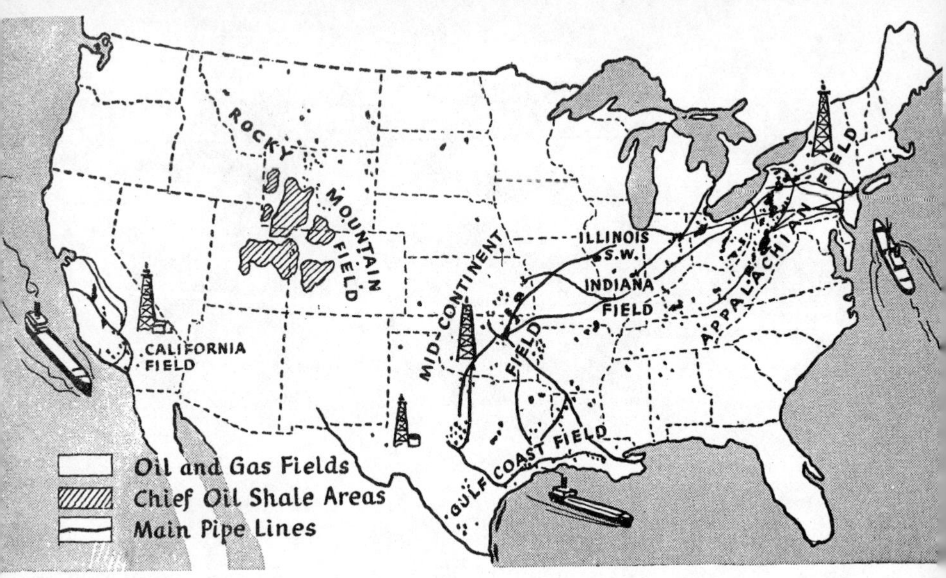

The map shows our largest oil areas and the most important pipe lines. Tank ships and tank cars are also used to carry this important product.

STUDY SUMMARY

1. Terms to know. Be able to tell the meaning of each term listed.

crude oil	petroleum	kerosene
anthracite	companies	bituminous
skyscraper	trusts	corporations
grafted		drilling

2. People to know. Be able to give one important fact about each person named.

Father James Marquette	Henry Bessemer
Father Louis Hennepin	John D. Rockefeller
Luther Burbank	William Kelly

3. Places to know. Be able to locate on a wall map each place listed. Be able to give one important fact as the place is located.

Richmond	Valley Forge
Chicago	West Virginia
Pittsburgh	Pennsylvania
Illinois	Cincinnati

ACTIVITIES

1. Make a list of at least five uses of coal.
2. Discuss in class how steel has changed the manner of living in America.
3. Make a table. Try to make each list as long as you can.

CANNED FOODS				
Fruits	Vegetables	Meats	Fish	Other Foods

4. Sketch a map of the United States. Shade the 4 states most important in producing petroleum. Shade a darker tone the state where the oil business was begun.

STUDY TEST 49—Score 30

COMPLETION OUTLINE. Fill in each missing letter to correctly complete the outline.

A. COAL

1. Anthracite is h — — — coal.
2. Bituminous is s — — — coal.
3. Coal is a good f — — —
4. Coal was burned to make s — — — —
5. Anthracite coal is mined in P — — — — — — — — — — — —
6. Coal is burned to make g — —
7. Other useful products obtained from coal are:
   Chemicals
   D — — —
   M — — — — — — — —

B. IRON AND STEEL

1. Ship builders needed many things made of i – – –
2. Ships needed iron

   n – – – –　　　　a – – – – – –

   b – – – –　　　　c – – – – –

3. Limited American iron manufacturing – – – – – – – – – –
4. Skyscrapers are buildings whose frames are made of s – – – –

C. STEEL AND FOOD

1. Cans are made from sheet s – – – –
2. Advantages of canned goods:
   a. keep a long t – – –
   b. can be shipped a long d – – – – – – – –
   c. foods keep f – – – –
3. Sheet metal is plated with t – – to make cans

D. OIL AND THE PETROLEUM INDUSTRY

1. The word petroleum means rock o – –
2. Petroleum is an excellent f – – –
3. When the oil comes from the ground it is c – – – – oil
4. Crude oil is refined to get g – – – – – – – –
5. Gasoline gives power to run:

   a – – – – – – – – – – –

   a – – – – – – – –

   e – – – – – – –

6. Kerosene is used to burn in l – – – –
7. Kerosene came to be used for lighting, h – – – – – – and c – – – – – – –

ELECTRICAL INVENTIONS

Read to learn

1. About the many uses of electricity.
2. Our debt to Thomas Edison.
3. How Alexander Bell came to invent the telephone.
4. About the invention of the radio.

THE HARNESSING OF ELECTRICITY. What is electricity? Nobody knows. The best we can say is that it is a natural force or energy. While we cannot tell exactly what it is, we have come to use it in thousands of different ways. Electricity is one of mankind's most useful servants. Samuel Morse used electricity to send messages with his telegraph. Alexander Bell invented the telephone by which we can talk with people in near and in distant places. The telephone depends upon electricity. Thomas Edison showed us how to use electricity to light our homes and our streets. Many of the wonderful things electricity does are connected with the name of Thomas A. Edison.

THOMAS ALVA EDISON

AN AMBITIOUS BOY. Thomas Alva Edison was born in Milan, Ohio, during the time of the Mexican War. He was a little lad when his family moved to Michigan. Edison's boyhood was over when he was twelve for then he had to go to work. His first job was that of a train-boy on a branch of the Grand Trunk Railway.

A train-boy has much free time on his hands. Young Thomas A. Edison used his spare time well. It gave him a chance to get an education by study and reading. Edison read all the good books he could get. Then he put into use the knowledge he gained from these books.

Young Edison edited and printed a small newspaper which he called the *Grand Trunk Herald*. A corner of the baggage car served as a printing shop and an editorial room. This little paper was bought by over three hundred railroad men who worked for the Grand Trunk Railroad.

EDISON'S FIRST EXPERIMENTS. Edison was also interested in chemistry. He even set up a little laboratory in another part of the baggage car. One day when Edison was experimenting the car swayed, and his chemicals fell upon the floor. A stick of phosphorus, the chemical used for making matches, struck the floor and burst into flame. Soon the car took fire. The conductor was enraged when he saw what had happened. Edison, with all his precious equipment, was thrown off the train at the next station.

EDISON AS TELEGRAPH OPERATOR. A brave act of Edison's gave him the chance he needed to get on in life. One day when the train was at a station in Michigan, Edison saw the station master's little boy playing on the tracks. The little fellow did not see a train approaching. It was almost upon him when Edison leaped upon the track just in time to snatch the child from certain death.

The boy's father was so grateful that he could not

speak. He wanted to do something for Edison. He offered to teach him how to use a telegraph instrument. Edison accepted his offer.

Edison learned telegraphy quickly and was a good operator by the time he was sixteen. Telegraphy is the sending and receiving of messages by telegraph. Thomas Edison was deeply interested in the telegraph instrument itself. He began to look for ways in which it might be improved. After much study he invented the telegraph repeater. Other inventions followed. Edison had an inventive mind and he kept his mind working.

EDISON'S LABORATORY. Edison sold one of his inventions for forty thousand dollars. This money made it possible for him to buy a laboratory. His laboratory grew in size and usefulness. Here Edison gathered around him skilled workmen and inventors, who spent their time in making improvements on old devices or in inventing new ones. Edison's best known inventions were the phonograph and the electric light bulb. Among his other inventions were devices for driving street cars and automobiles by the use of electricity.

EDISON INVENTIONS

ELECTRICITY IN MODERN LIFE. Modern life depends greatly on the electric motor. All kinds of machinery can be run by electric motors. Long trains of cars are pulled by giant electric motors. Small electric motors run sewing machines. The electric motor is of great benefit to us in everyday life. Hardly a day goes by but a new use is found for electricity. Without it airplanes and motor cars could not run. Our streets and homes would lose their brilliant lights. The telegraph, the telephone, the radio, would stop. It would indeed be an inconvenient and an uncomfortable world to live in if we did not know how to use electricity.

ALEXANDER GRAHAM BELL

THE INVENTOR OF THE TELEPHONE. Alexander Graham Bell is looked upon as the inventor of the telephone. Bell and Edison were born in the same year, 1847. Bell, however, was not born in America but in Scotland, where he received an excellent education. Alexander Graham Bell also studied music. After a college course he became a teacher. He did not teach ordinary boys and girls. He taught those who could not speak well. He helped his father, who was a speech teacher, to correct speech defects. He also taught those whose hearing was not good. Thus Bell became interested in the human voice.

BELL'S TELEPHONE. Our voice consists of sounds made by the vibrations of our vocal cords. Bell began to wonder whether these vibrations could be made to travel over a wire by the aid of electricity. He was on the right track but there were many difficulties to overcome. One day while experimenting Bell burned himself. He called into the telephone, "Mr. Watson, come here. I need you." In a moment Watson rushed into the room. The telephone had sent its first message!

THE CENTENNIAL EXPOSITION. Bell finished his telephone in time to show it at the Centennial Exposition in Philadelphia, in 1876. This was the one hundredth anniversary of the signing of the Declaration of Independence. All sorts of articles were on display at the Exposition and visitors came by the thousands to see them. Learned men acted as judges passing upon the value, or the usefulness of the different articles. Prizes were awarded.

THE TELEPHONE AT THE EXPOSITION. Bell's telephone had a place at the Exposition. It was in the section given to the department of education. People hardly noticed the telephone. The judges who passed upon the different articles looked over Bell's telephone but did not seem to be very much interested. Fortunately, there was

a great visitor present who saved the day for Bell. The Emperor of Brazil, Dom Pedro, had met Professor Bell in Boston. Bell asked him to try the telephone, and he did. The Emperor's astonishment was great. "It talks!" he exclaimed. Then the telephone was given some of the attention it deserved.

At first people were slow to appreciate the value of the telephone. As time went on its importance began to be realized. Today, we depend upon the telephone so much in business and in social life that we think we could hardly get along without telephone service.

WILLIAM MARCONI

THE WIRELESS. The telephone is a wonderful invention but the wireless, or radio, is even more wonderful. The telephone sends or transmits sounds by means of wires. The radio transmits sounds through the air.

The radio is an invention of an Italian, William Marconi. Marconi attended the University of Bologna in Italy. Here he learned that it might be possible to send signals through the air. He was only sixteen when he began work on his plan for sending messages without wires. By the

time Marconi was twenty-one years old he had succeeded in sending messages through the air without wires to a point one mile distant.

Improvements were made which added to the usefulness of Marconi's invention. Soon it became possible to send messages for many thousands of miles through the air.

THE RADIO. American inventors have done many things to increase the usefulness of the wireless. The radio has been of great service and gives pleasure to millions of people. The people shown in the picture are enjoying a radio broadcast.

TELEVISION. Inventors got the idea that it might be possible to send pictures by electrical signals in a manner similar to the sending of messages. Years of experimentation have resulted in some measure of success. Today, inventors are laboring to perfect a practical manner of reproducing images. Then a person in a distant place may see or visualize a scene as it is happening. This science or art is called television. It means the seeing of things from far off. The time may not be very far away when in our homes, by means of electrical equipment, we may be able to see scenes that are happening in distant places. Keep your mind and your eyes open for developments in the field of television.

STUDY SUMMARY

1. Terms to know. Be able to tell the meaning of each term listed.

   electricity transmit television
   laboratory telegraphy

2. People to know. Be able to give some interesting facts about each person named.

   Alexander Bell William Marconi
   Samuel Morse Thomas Edison

ACTIVITIES

1. Make a table and fill in all the items you can.

EVERYDAY USES OF ELECTRICITY			
In the home	In the school	In the street	In buildings

2. Make a list of the inventors you have studied about. After the name of each inventor name the invention he made.

3. Use these words correctly in sentences.

   a. inventor inventing invented invention
   b. telegraph telegraphy telegrapher
   c. electric electricity electrician

STUDY TEST 50—Score 15

CHOOSING SUBJECTS. Fill in the correct subject for each sentence. Use only subjects listed below the exercise. One subject will be used twice. (2)

1. .... knows just what electricity is.
2. .... is a natural force.
3. .... invented the telephone.
4. .... was a great electrician.
5. .... is the sending and the receiving of telegraph messages.
6. .... were invented by Thomas Edison.
7. ...., a pleasure instrument was also invented by Thomas Edison.
8. .... is very important to operate machines.
9. .... invented the phonograph.
10. .... interested Alexander Bell.
11. .... is the sound made by vibrations on the vocal cords.
12. .... was greatly interested in Bell's invention.
13. .... sends sound by means of wires.
14. .... sends sounds through the air.
15. .... invented the radio.

Thomas Edison (2)	The Emperor of Brazil
The radio	William Marconi
Voice	The telephone
Nobody	The human voice
Electric light bulbs	The electric motor
The phonograph	Electricity
Telegraphy	Alexander G. Bell

TRANSPORTATION BECOMES A KEY INDUSTRY

Read to learn

1. How railroads helped the growth of our country.
2. Why better roads became a necessity of the twentieth century.
3. How aviation has advanced in the twentieth century.

EARLY RAILROADS. Do you know the rate of speed the train goes that passes nearest to your home? You have already learned about the first railroad, the Baltimore and Ohio Railroad. It began to carry passengers and freight in 1830. The famous Tom Thumb engine on this railroad made the rate of fifteen miles an hour. This was thought to be speedy in those days.

The early railroads were crude compared with the rails, roadbeds, engines, and cars used today.

IMPROVEMENTS IN RAILROADS. Times change. Shops were built where better and larger locomotives were made. It became no longer necessary to use horses on rainy days or on curved roads. The locomotive was now doing a full time job of pulling passenger and freight trains. Rails were improved. Steel rails took the place of the old wooden beams which were covered with a strip of iron. Roadbeds were more carefully graded. More gravel was used in making the roadbed better. Large coaches

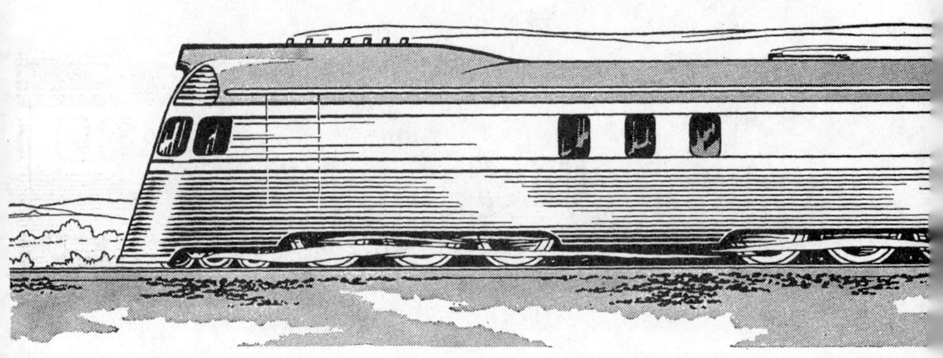

were built to replace the passenger cars. Men began to think of distance in hours of travel rather than in miles. This was indeed progress.

GOVERNMENT HELP. The story of the building of the first transcontinental railroad in 1869 is told on page 403. The help given by the United States government made possible the building of the railroads spanning the continent. The United States government aided the railroad builders in many ways.

1. The government gave the railroad companies land grants along the right of way of the railroad.
2. The government allowed the railroad companies to use timber and stone from the government lands.
3. The government loaned large sums of money to encourage railroad building.

Branches of railways pushed out to reach every place where passengers and freight might be carried to meet the main line. A network of railroads criss-crossed over the land in every direction.

Today, there are over two hundred and forty thousand miles of railroad in the United States. The map of railroads in the United States shows some interesting facts:

1. Most of our railroads are east of the Mississippi River and north of the Ohio River. This northeastern part of our country is where most of our population lives. This is the part of our country where most of the mills and factories are.

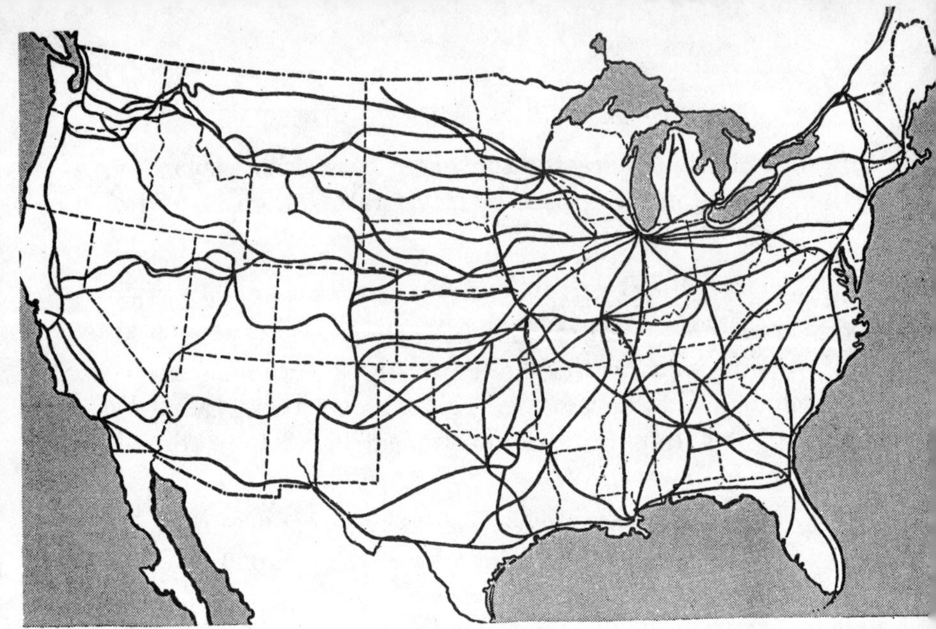

2. Most of our railroads have an east-west direction.
3. There are few railroads in the West.
4. Many railroads meet in Chicago.

HOW RAILROADS HAVE HELPED OUR COUNTRY. It is hard to realize the many ways in which railroads have helped our country.

1. Settlers moved into the cheap lands offered by the government along the right of way of the railroads.
2. Vast farms growing wheat and corn made possible cheaper grain and flour in the East.
3. Cattle ranches increased because now there was a good way to send the cattle to market. Cheaper meat was the result.
4. Small towns came into being along the railroad. These became important trading centers for the farm communities.
5. Mines and forests were opened up now that there was a better way of getting ore and timber to market.
6. Mills and factories in the East became more prosperous because they were now able to buy the raw materials they needed. They had a market in the West for the articles they made.

7. Best of all, the railroad helped to more closely unite the parts of our country.

For many years railroads did not have to worry about competition. Railroads almost put canals out of business. Then came the use of the automobile and the building of good roads. The automobile and the auto-bus began to cut heavily into the passenger business. Auto-trucks began to haul large quantities of freight. Railroads felt a decline in business.

Railroads could not afford to let the automobile, the auto-bus and the auto-trucks take all their business. The railroads had to improve in order to attract business. Better roadbeds, stream-lined trains, electric engines, and better rates have all helped the railroads to recover some of their business. The automobile, the auto-bus, and the auto-truck are the greatest rivals of the railroads.

THE HORSELESS AGE

THE HORSE IN AMERICAN HISTORY. The Spaniards first brought the horse to America. Since that time the patient animal has played a very important part in our history. The horse was a good friend to the early settlers. He pulled the plows over their fields, he hauled the crops, and carried his owner from place to place. He served the patriots throughout the Revolution. Later, the pony express carried mail to the distant part of our country. The horse served both the Blue and the Gray in the Civil War. After the war the horse took a great part in carrying on the business of the country. All the trucking and hauling in the cities was done by horse. On the farms, large and small, the horse plowed, reaped, and hauled. The time was coming when machines would take the place of the horse.

THE FIRST AUTOMOBILES. The first automobiles were so queer-looking that few people believed that such machines could ever take the place of horses. The machines were clumsy and they ran so badly that boys used to run after them shouting, "Get a horse!" This was good advice because when the automobile broke down, as it very often did, a horse had to pull it home. The first problem in building an automobile was to get an engine that would be small but powerful. It was not until after 1890 that the first of the modern automobiles was built. One inventor, Ransom E. Olds, invented a three-wheeled carriage with an engine to make it move. Charles Duryea built an automobile with four wheels. Henry Ford, another inventor, built a somewhat better machine in 1893.

The gasoline engine was the principal thing that made the automobile successful. The manufacturing of automobiles and auto-trucks is now one of our greatest industries. This is largely due to the improvements that have been made in motors, tires, brakes and indeed in all parts of the auto.

QUANTITY PRODUCTION. The early automobiles were very expensive. A low-priced car was much to be desired. The low-priced cars were finally made possible through quantity production. That means making a great

many cars and selling each car for a small profit. Henry Ford deserves much credit for planning a low priced car. "I will build a car for the multitude," said Henry Ford.

MODERN CARS AND MODERN ROADS

NEED FOR BETTER ROADS. Year after year the automobile was made better and cheaper. Year after year the number of automobiles, buses, and auto-trucks increased. This increased use of motor transportation made necessary better roads. Roads cost the people of the United States over two billion dollars each year. This is a very great sum of money. States and counties also build roads.

Some roads are macadam. These roads use broken or crushed stone. Such roads are higher in the center so that rain will drain off easily. Roads are sometimes made of asphalt. This is a hard substance somewhat like tar. Asphalt, spread over a crushed stone roadbed, makes a very good road.

Excellent roads are made of concrete. The concrete road is made by pouring cement over crushed stone. Steel rods

are sometimes set in the concrete. This gives the road greater strength. Then a layer of liquid cement is spread to give the road a smooth surface.

Part of the license fee charged for automobiles goes into a fund to keep the roads in good condition.

CHARLES GOODYEAR AND RUBBER

THE AUTOMOBILE AND RUBBER. The automobile as we know it today would be impossible without rubber tires. Even the finest motor car would be a terrible thing to ride in if it had to jolt along on steel tires. That is why rubber is of first importance to the automobile industry. Rubber is also used in thousands of other useful and necessary things. The man who learned how to prepare rubber was Charles Goodyear.

CHARLES GOODYEAR. Charles Goodyear was born in New Haven, Connecticut. So he was another Yankee inventor. He had some schooling before he went to work on his father's farm. His father also had a small factory. Young Charles Goodyear spent much of his time in the factory. He liked to make things. He became interested in the study of rubber. This he made his life work.

INDIA RUBBER. India rubber was the name given to rubber in Goodyear's day. As a matter of fact it came not from India but from Brazil. Rubber is a milky liquid which comes from the rubber tree. This milky liquid flows just inside the bark of the tree. It is not the sap which carries plant food to the tree. The rubber liquid is called latex. It becomes somewhat hard when dried or heated. India rubber in the early days was considered as a toy. It could be bought in small chunks. It would bounce, and it was useful for "rubbing" out pencil marks. Water could not soak through rubber.

There was a Scotch clothing maker named Mackintosh. He wanted to make rain-proof overcoats. So he tried to put thin sheets of rubber between two layers of cloth. His raincoats were called mackintoshes. Rubber was not really very useful because it would often soften or melt.

GOODYEAR'S EXPERIMENTS. Goodyear set out to learn about rubber. He saw how useful it could be if it could be made to stand heat without melting. Other men were working at the same idea. Goodyear knew one of these men and even helped him in his experiments. The discovery of how to prepare rubber was Goodyear's own. The secret came to him by accident.

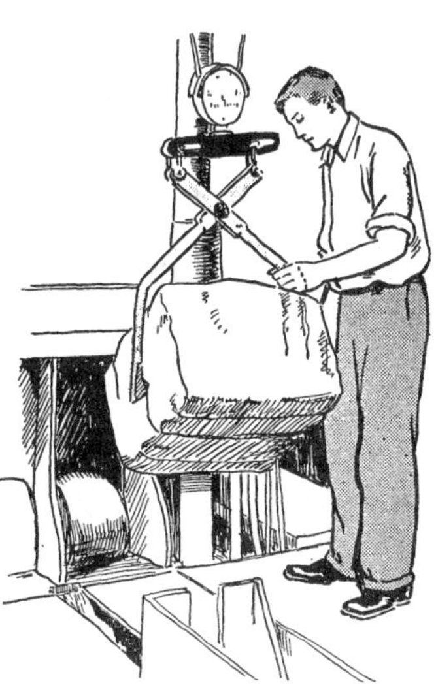

VULCANIZING RUBBER. One cold day in the winter of 1839, Goodyear was staying in Woburn, Massachusetts. He was trying to discover the effects of heat on a mixture of rubber and sulphur. Goodyear carelessly dropped some of the mixture on a hot stove and was surprised to discover that the rubber became hard. In that instant a great secret was discovered. Further experiments proved to him that rubber which is treated with sulphur before it is placed over heat will always harden. This is called vulcanizing rubber. The discovery made by Charles Goodyear resulted in a rubber product that had two fine qualities:

1. It would wear well.
2. It was not greatly affected by temperature.

GOODYEAR'S FORTUNES. Goodyear had no money when he made his great discovery. While he carried on his experiments friends gave him money to keep him from starving. Before he died Goodyear had taken out several patents and had discovered over five hundred ways of using rubber. It was not until many years after Goodyear's death that rubber came to be in very heavy demand.

The great growth of the automobile industry caused a great change in rubber production. The supply of wild rubber was uncertain and not large. Plantations for growing rubber were started.

THE BIRDMEN

FIRST FLYING MACHINE. The railroad train and the automobile gave quick transportation by land. The air was to become the next highway of rapid travel. Men had watched birds fly and had often dreamed about flying themselves. The dream that someday men would be able to fly was realized early in the twentieth century.

Several inventors of flying machines reached a certain amount of success at about the same time. However, we think of the Wright Brothers as the successful inventors of the airplane.

THE WRIGHT BROTHERS

A STRANGE GIFT. Two brothers, Wilbur and Orville Wright, lived in Dayton, Ohio. Wilbur was four years older than his brother but the two lads played together and liked the same sort of amusements. One day their father came home with a present. He did not hand his gift to his boys, he hurled it into the air. It flew. The boys were amazed.

THE "BAT." The boys watched the little machine as it fluttered about the room. "It's a bat!" they cried. The thrill of that flying toy never left them. The boys studied the machine carefully. They began to build one nearly like it. It was not very hard to make a "bat." It was merely a light frame covered with paper. It had a propeller which was spun by twisted rubber bands. The brothers made little flying machines. All sorts of light materials were used and many shapes were tried.

EARLY EXPERIMENTS. Toy flying machines had to be put aside while the brothers attended high school. After high school the Wrights opened a bicycle shop in Dayton. Any time that could be spared from the shop was used in experimenting with flying machines. The Wright Brothers were hoping to build a machine that would carry men. Experiments were made to discover what shape the machine should have. The form of the machine had a great deal to do with its lifting power. Nearly one thousand experiments were made to find out the best sort of a frame to use for the flying machine.

Photo by Brown Bros.

The Wrights finally built a machine that looked like a box kite. It could be balanced under all conditions. It could be righted even when the wind shifted suddenly or when the balance of the machine was upset.

THE FIRST FLIGHT. The next problem was to fit this frame with an engine which would spin propellers and thus make the machine fly. A light but powerful engine was built for this purpose. At last it seemed that their hopes would be realized. The brothers made their first long flight in September, 1905. They traveled six miles from the starting point. This was indeed a wonderful six-mile trip. They flew at a height of one hundred feet. This flight was a turning point in transportation. The flight of the Wright Brothers proved the possibility of aircraft as a carrier of people. These lads had really conquered the powerful force called gravity. This is the natural force that tends to attract all things to the earth. Soon others started to experiment with airplanes. Amazing progress began to be made in aviation.

Photo from Ewing Galloway

PROGRESS IN AVIATION. When the Great War broke out airplanes were used by both armies. Since the War some extraordinary flights have been made. Daring birdmen have crossed the ocean. Commander Richard Byrd succeeded in flying to the North Pole and later to the South Pole. Perhaps the most thrilling flight was that made by the air mail pilot, Charles A. Lindbergh. He crossed the Atlantic Ocean alone in an airplane.

The air mail is proving of great help to the merchant and the banker who need to have their mail delivered quickly. Many travelers today journey by airways where once they depended upon stage, railway, or steamboat. Europe, far China, South America, in fact, the whole world, is now connected by airplane routes.

The airplane has one great advantage over land routes. There is no right of way in the air. However, there are established routes between definite airports. The United States is bound by a network of airways which carry passengers, mail, and express packages.

The *China Clipper* now makes regular trips across the Pacific Ocean. The *American Clipper* and the *Yankee Clipper* carry passengers across the Atlantic Ocean.

STUDY SUMMARY

1. Terms to know. Be able to explain the meaning of each term listed.

macadam	asphalt	vulcanizing
birdmen	latex	transcontinental
gravity		quantity production

2. People to know. Be able to tell some important fact about each person named.

Richard Byrd	Charles A. Lindbergh
Wilbur Wright	Orville Wright
Henry Ford	Charles Goodyear

3. Places to know. Be able to locate on a wall map each place named. Give one fact about the place as it is located.

Washington, D.C.	Pacific Ocean	Detroit
Atlantic Ocean	Baltimore	Omaha

4. Dates to remember. Give one interesting fact related to transportation about each date listed.

1893	1905	1937	1939

ACTIVITIES

1. Posters. Make a set of at least three posters to show progress in railroads. Study pictures to get ideas.
2. Make a table.

PROGRESS IN ROADS	
Kind of Road	How Made
1.	1.
2.	2.
3.	3.
4.	4.

3. Make a list of at least three ways in which the United States government helped railroad building.
4. Write a paragraph telling—HOW RAILROADS HAVE HELPED OUR COUNTRY.
5. Posters or Brush and Ink Sketches. Show PROGRESS IN AVIATION.
   a. Wright Brothers' boxlike kite
   b. Lindbergh's monoplane, *The Spirit of St. Louis*
   c. Commander Byrd's flight over the North Pole
   d. Howard Hughes' circling of the globe
   e. The modern clippers

   Note: This study may be enlarged if time permits. Study pictures to get ideas for the illustrations.

STUDY TEST 51—Score 20

SELECTING ENDINGS. Underscore the term or date which gives the correct ending.

1. The speed of the earliest trains was
   15 miles per hour   60 miles per hour
2. The early railroads were
   crude   good   excellent
3. Early rails used by railroads were made of
   iron   steel   wood
4. The first transcontinental railroad was completed in
   1763   1869   1830
5. The greatest rival of the railroads is the
   canal   auto   airplane
6. Olden iron rails were replaced by rails of
   wood   steel   copper

7. Horses were brought to America by the
   English Spaniards French

8. The first of the modern automobiles was built in
   1890 1900 1906

9. Low priced cars were made possible by
   quantity production mechanics

10. The hard road building tar material is
    macadam concrete asphalt

11. Rubber is made from a milky liquid called
    latex sulphur sap

12. Rain-proof cloth was first made by a man named
    Goodyear Mackintosh Ford

13. How to vulcanize rubber was discovered by
    Charles Goodyear Henry Ford

14. The Wright Brothers made a successful flight in
    1905 1926 1834 1867

15. The process of vulcanizing rubber was discovered in
    1839 1863 1912

16. The Wright Brothers conquered the force called
    gravity vulcanizing mass production

17. Regular trips are now made across the Pacific Ocean by
    The Spirit of St. Louis *China Clipper*

18. The air routes or airways are
    definite routes irregular routes

19. The first airplane looked like a
    seaplane monoplane box kite

20. The most modern means of transportation for mail, passengers, express is by
    railroad canal airplane

UNIT XII: GREAT LEADERS OF MODERN TIMES

GROVER CLEVELAND
A COMMON-SENSE LEADER

Read to learn

1. How Grover Cleveland became a lawyer.
2. About the successful steps Cleveland climbed.
3. The fearless attitude of Cleveland.

SOME GREAT PRESIDENTS. The United States has had Presidents who did splendid things for our country. George Washington served the nation so well that he is called the "Father of His Country." Thomas Jefferson is remembered as the author of the Declaration of Independence. Abraham Lincoln was called the "Savior of the Union." Since the Civil War this country has had several leaders who in their own way have imitated Washington, Jefferson, and Lincoln.

GROVER CLEVELAND

AN AMBITIOUS LAD. Grover Cleveland was born in Caldwell, New Jersey. His father, a minister, was called to a church in Buffalo, New York, and took his family with him. Grover was only a lad when his father died. Young Grover went to work to help the family. His first job was in a grocery store. It was a case of hard work and poor pay. Fifty dollars a year was all he earned the first year. This was less than one dollar a week.

Young Grover Cleveland was tired at night. A day of waiting on customers, lifting barrels and boxes, and cleaning out the store, left aching muscles. Tired or not he knew there was only one way to get ahead and that was by educating himself. Grover Cleveland was no weakling. He often read and studied far into the night. He got along so well that he was given a position as a teacher in an asylum for the blind. Cleveland kept on studying and before long he was a practicing lawyer.

CLEVELAND IN POLITICS. As many lawyers do, Cleveland entered politics. He advanced step by step. First he was elected Sheriff of Erie County, New York. A few years later Cleveland was elected Mayor of Buffalo. The third step was reached when he was elected Governor of New York.

Cleveland after he was elected Governor of New York wrote to his brother, "I am honest and sincere in my desire to do well,—if mother were alive, I should feel much safer. I have always thought that her prayers had much to do with my success." Later Grover Cleveland was elected President of the United States.

PRESIDENT GROVER CLEVELAND. Grover Cleveland was a Democrat. Until his election all the Presidents elected after the Civil War had been Republicans. It has been said that Cleveland before his election as President had never been in Washington. He did not even know where the White House was located. He found it, however, and for the two terms he served, the people knew that they had an honest man in the White House.

Cleveland found that conditions were not very good in the government offices in Washington. Some of the presidents before Cleveland sometimes gave jobs to political friends. These friends were not capable in the jobs in which they were serving. Cleveland was not the type of man to put people in offices if they were not capable, even though they were his friends.

The story is told of how on one occasion there was a vacant government position. This position paid a very fine salary. The President could appoint any man he chose to fill this position. Cleveland believed that the man in Washington best fitted for that post was a Negro. Grover Cleveland dared to appoint the Negro. That was a brave thing to do in those days so soon after the Civil War.

THE PROBLEM OF HAWAII. Another incident will show the honesty and fairness of Grover Cleveland. Far out in the Pacific Ocean is a group of islands called the Hawaiian Islands. Many years ago these islands were called the Sandwich Islands. Hawaii was a small kingdom. A kingdom is ruled by a king or a queen.

Hawaii is a lovely spot and large numbers of Americans enjoyed going there. They invested much money, especially in sugar cane plantations. A number of Americans made up their minds to take control of the government of Hawaii. A revolution overthrew the queen of Hawaii and

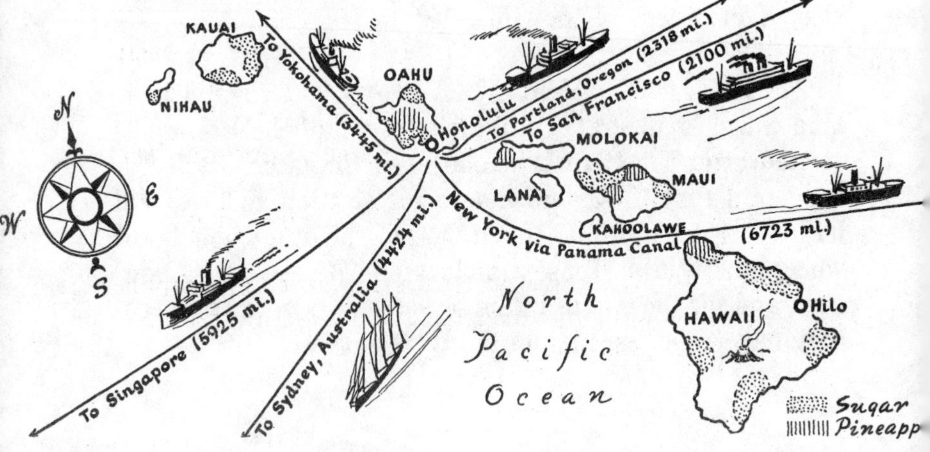

Photo by Ewing Galloway

set up a new government. Then the new government asked for union with the United States. Just then Grover Cleveland became President. He would not allow Hawaii to be annexed to the United States. When land is annexed it is brought under the rule of another country. Cleveland said Americans had no right to seize a country because its people were weak and could not protect themselves.

Five years later, in 1898, when William McKinley was President, the Hawaiian Islands were annexed to the United States. There had been much bitter feeling on the islands. Annexation seemed the best way to settle matters.

STUDY SUMMARY

1. Terms to know. Be able to tell the meaning of each term listed.

   asylum   annexation

2. People to know. Be able to give one important fact about each person named.

   George Washington   Grover Cleveland

   Abraham Lincoln

3. Places to know. Be able to locate the Hawaiian Islands on a wall map. As the Hawaiian Islands are located give an important fact about them.

4. Date to remember. Give an important event in American History that took place in 1898.
5. Word study. Be able to use each of the following words correctly.

   annex annexed annexation

ACTIVITIES

1. Make a diagram to show the steps by which Grover Cleveland rose to success.
2. Character study. Give an example to prove that Grover Cleveland possessed each of the following character traits.

   a. honesty
   b. fearless
   c. pleasant mannered
   d. determined

STUDY TEST 52—Score 10

YES—NO. Answer each question with YES or NO.

1. Did Grover Cleveland belong to a wealthy family? ____
2. Was young Grover Cleveland a lazy lad? ____
3. Did Grover Cleveland work hard to educate himself? ____
4. Was Grover Cleveland ambitious? ____
5. Did Grover Cleveland become a lawyer? ____
6. Was Cleveland an honest man? ____
7. Had Cleveland been to Washington often before he became President? ____
8. Was Grover Cleveland a Democrat? ____
9. Was the annexation of Hawaii approved by Cleveland? ____
10. Did Cleveland have the courage to always do what he thought was right? ____

UNIT XII: GREAT LEADERS OF MODERN TIMES

THEODORE ROOSEVELT
A FORCEFUL LEADER

Read to learn

1. How young Theodore Roosevelt gained his physical strength.
2. How Roosevelt won the respect of the ranchers.
3. The reasons for the Spanish-American War.
4. Theodore Roosevelt and the Rough Riders.
5. Why the Panama Canal was needed.

AN ACTIVE YOUNG MAN. Another great leader of recent times was Theodore Roosevelt, who came from an old and a rich New York family. As a boy young Teddy was not very strong. His father therefore built him a gymnasium and young Roosevelt exercised day after day. His strength increased and he entered Harvard University. By the time he had finished his first year at college he was able to take part in many forms of athletics. Young Teddy became a clever lightweight boxer and a powerful wrestler. Although his sight was poor, he became a fairly good shot with a rifle or a shotgun.

Theodore Roosevelt was graduated from Harvard in 1880. That same fall he joined a Republican political club in New York. His mind naturally turned to politics. He was interested in government. Illness, however, interfered with his plan. Roosevelt decided to leave New York for a time and go to the West, in search of health and adventure.

CHIMNEY BUTTE RANCH. The place Roosevelt selected was a town in North Dakota. This town, according to a cowboy visitor, had a population of "eleven—counting the chickens—when they're all in town." Roosevelt at first was not a favorite with his new neighbors. He came from the city and so was promptly called, "a tenderfoot." A tenderfoot meant a person who had just come into the West. Roosevelt soon won the respect of the ranchers. His bravery on a buffalo hunt, his ability to withstand the hardships of camping out, soon won the admiration of the cowboys. One of his guides said that Roosevelt was, "as handy as a pocket in a vest."

THE RETURN TO PUBLIC LIFE. Theodore Roosevelt returned to the East thoroughly strengthened in body. His mind had been made keener. His sympathies had been broadened by his western experience. He entered public life again and held a number of offices in New York and in Washington. While Roosevelt was in Washington the United States went to war with Spain.

THE SPANISH-AMERICAN WAR

THE REASONS FOR THE WAR. Notice on the map on page 468 that the island of Cuba is only a short distance from our own state of Florida. Since the time of Columbus, Cuba had belonged to Spain. The Cubans now wanted to be independent. Several times they had tried to break away from Spanish rule.

William McKinley was President of the United States when a new revolution broke out in Cuba. Some of the American newspapers became very much excited. They demanded that America help the Cubans. They demanded also that we protect Americans living in Cuba. These papers claimed that American lives were in danger by the revolution and that Americans who had property in Cuba would lose it.

THE *MAINE* DISASTER. The United States battleship *Maine* was sent to Havana Harbor. The visit of the battleship was made in a friendly spirit. Unfortunately, on the night of February 15, 1898, an explosion took place either inside or outside the warship. It sent the *Maine* to the bottom of the sea. The lives of two hundred and sixty men were lost. The Spaniards were blamed for this disaster. It never has been proven that they were actually guilty. The American newspapers printed exciting stories. The Americans were aroused to a fighting mood. "Remember the *Maine!*" became a war cry. Within a short time the United States was at war with Spain.

DEWEY AT MANILA. Our first victory took place in the Philippine Islands in the Pacific Ocean. These islands as is shown on the map are far across the Pacific Ocean. Admiral George Dewey, the gallant American commander, sailed his fleet into Manila Bay. He destroyed the

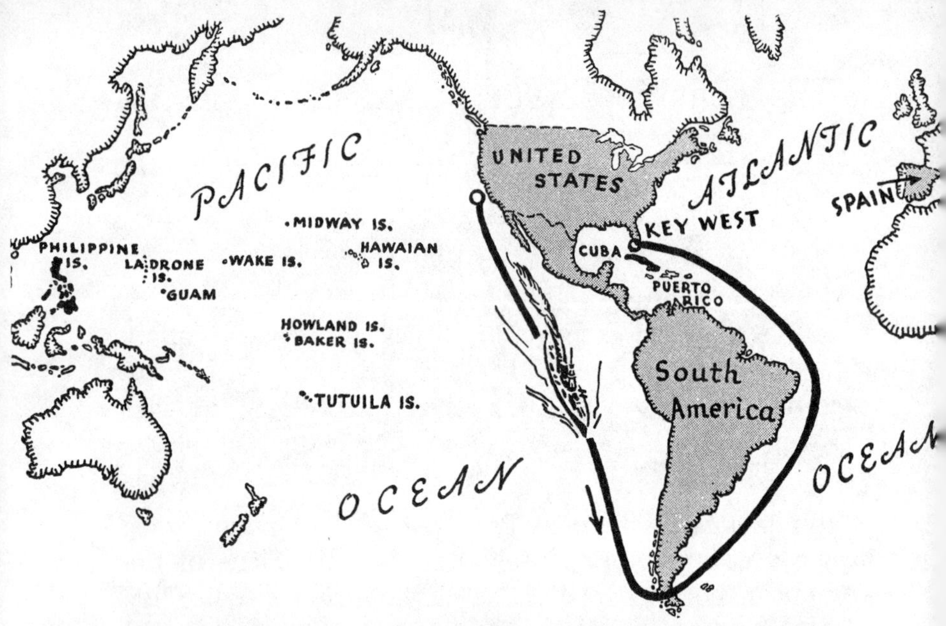

Spanish fleet and captured the city of Manila. The power of Spain in the Philippines was broken forever by this victory. These islands with their millions of Catholic natives were taken over by the United States.

Our government made an agreement with the Philippines in 1934. Under this agreement the island would become completely free in ten years.

THE CUBAN CAMPAIGN. Meanwhile American troops were active in Cuba. The newspapers reported everything they did. Their greatest favorites were the Rough Riders and Colonel Theodore Roosevelt. These men were volunteers. The volunteers are the men who enter the army by their own free will. The volunteers in this troop were miners, cowboys, Indians, and some young fellows from the East.

The Rough Riders took part in the fight at San Juan Hill, in Cuba. The American navy destroyed Spain's best ships off the coast of Santiago. The war was soon over. Cuba was free. The once great power of Spain in the New World was no more. At one time Spain had owned the greater part of the New World. Now she had not a single colony left in the Western Hemisphere.

PRESIDENT THEODORE ROOSEVELT

AFTER THE WAR. Theodore Roosevelt was very popular after the war was over. His "Rough Riders" had caught the public fancy. Some of the high Republican politicians did not like Roosevelt. He was too independent. So they thought they would give him an office where the people would lose track of him. They had him elected Vice-President on the Republican ticket when William McKinley ran a second time for the office of President. President McKinley was murdered by an assassin shortly after his re-election. Theodore Roosevelt succeeded to the office of President. The politicians and others soon learned that Theodore Roosevelt was determined to change some of the things in American life that he thought needed to be changed.

THEODORE ROOSEVELT'S PROGRAM. One of the lessons taught by the Spanish-American War was the need of a canal across the Isthmus of Panama. This isthmus is the narrow strip of land which connects North and South America as shown on the map on page 468. When war seemed certain our battleship *Oregon* was on the Pacific Coast. She was ordered to Florida. Sailing around South America the trip took two months. This was a journey of 14,000 miles. Had there been a canal through the Isthmus of Panama distance and time would have been saved. A canal would have great value not only in time of war but also in time of peace. Goods could be transported at a great saving. President Roosevelt was determined that there must be an American-owned canal across the Isthmus of Panama. The building of a canal across the Isthmus of Panama was a tremendous undertaking. A famous French engineer had already tried and failed.

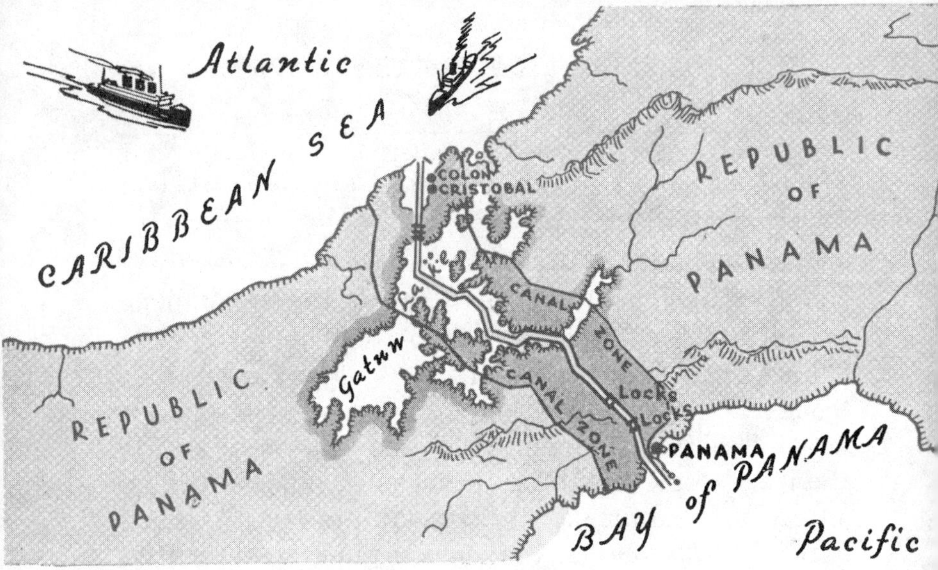

Atlantic

CARIBBEAN SEA

COLON

CRISTOBAL

REPUBLIC OF PANAMA

CANAL ZONE

Gatun

Locks

Locks

PANAMA

REPUBLIC OF PANAMA

BAY of PANAMA

Pacific

THE CANAL ZONE. The French attempt to build a canal had failed partly because of sickness. The Canal Zone was then one of the most unhealthful places in the world. The canal could not be built under such bad conditions. A United States army doctor, Major William C. Gorgas, was sent to Panama. His job was to make the place safe for the workmen and for the people who would have to live there. The swamps were drained, mosquitoes, and other pests were destroyed, and a supply of good water was provided. Gorgas did a very fine job. The actual digging began in 1904. Ten years later the Panama Canal was

Photo by Ewing Galloway

completed. The Atlantic and Pacific Oceans were united. The water route between the eastern and western coasts of the United States was greatly shortened.

ROOSEVELT AND CONSERVATION. Our country is rich in natural resources. Forests, minerals, plant and animal life, and waterways are called natural resources. They are the wealth of the land as they are the gifts of Nature. Unfortunately, Americans had been wasteful of these gifts of Nature. Whole forests had been cut down and nothing done to replace them. Forest fires had wiped out large areas of timber. These fires in many cases could have been prevented. The terrible damage could have been lessened had there been a proper forestry service. President Theodore Roosevelt set about to remedy this condition. He said the natural resources must be used wisely. The wise use of natural resources is conservation. Theodore Roosevelt was a good planner because he looked ahead and planned to have the natural resources wisely used. He set aside forest reserves and provided a force of men to take care of these forests. He demanded that large tracts of forest be saved from the timberman's ax. Roosevelt also ordered that new trees be planted.

ROOSEVELT AND IRRIGATION. Another problem which interested Theodore Roosevelt was irrigation. Irrigation means bringing water to lands that are dry and rainless. There were thousands of square miles of dry and useless land in the West. All this could be made productive with proper watering. Roosevelt strongly favored irrigation. The people agreed with him. Congress gave the necessary money. Dams were built across rivers, and ditches dug to carry the much needed water. Vast tracts of land that before had produced nothing but cactus were now made fertile. One of the greatest of all irrigation projects is well named the Roosevelt Dam.

STUDY SUMMARY

1. Terms to know. Be able to give the meaning of each term listed.

   conservation trusts natural resources
   irrigation politics irrigation
   tenderfoot

2. People to know. Be able to tell some interesting facts about each person named.

   Theodore Roosevelt Major William C. Gorgas
   William McKinley Admiral George Dewey

3. Places to know. Be able to locate on a wall map each place listed. Tell one interesting fact about each place as it is located.

   Colombia Isthmus of Panama
   Manila Philippine Islands
   Cuba North Dakota
   Santiago San Juan

4. Dates to remember. Be able to give an important event which took place on each of the following dates.

   1898 1904 1914

ACTIVITIES

1. Make a table and fill in the facts.

THE SPANISH-AMERICAN WAR			
Date	Causes	Events	Results

2. Make a list of the five most important groups of natural resources. Write one sentence about each group

3. Character study. Be able to give an example of how each of the following terms might apply to Theodore Roosevelt.

	active	fighting spirit
determined	brave	independent
good leader	good planner	

STUDY TEST 53—Score 15

MATCHING. After each term in Group I put the letter of the matching term selected from Group II.

Group I

1. Led the Rough Riders ____
2. Theodore Roosevelt's political party ____
3. Island people desiring independence ____
4. President during Spanish-American War ____
5. Americans chiefly interested in Cuba ____
6. Hero of Manila ____
7. American warship sent to Havana ____
8. Where Dewey defeated Spanish fleet ____
9. Where best Spanish ships were destroyed ____
10. Where Roosevelt determined to have canal ____
11. Gave the United States right to build canal ____
12. The wise use of natural resources is ____
13. Worked to make Panama a healthful place ____
14. Bringing water to dry land is ____
15. The United States has agreed to make them free in 1944 ____

Group II

A. Cubans
B. Santiago
C. Theodore Roosevelt
D. Conservation
E. Manila Bay
F. Republican
G. Across Isthmus of Panama
H. William McKinley
I. Major William C. Gorgas
J. Republic of Panama
K. Admiral George Dewey
L. Philippine Islands
M. The *Maine*
N. Irrigation
O. Sugar plantation owners

WOODROW WILSON, A FEARLESS LEADER

Read to learn

1. About the break in the Republican Party.
2. Wilson's ability as a leader.
3. How Germany forced the United States into the World War.
4. Our nation's response to President Wilson.
5. How the Americans turned the tide of the War.
6. What a depression is.

A BREAK IN THE REPUBLICAN PARTY. When Theodore Roosevelt's term of office expired one of his close friends, William Howard Taft, became President. Roosevelt's friend was also a Republican. Later, Taft and Roosevelt disagreed and they became enemies. This quarrel had far-reaching results. It caused a break in the Republican Party.

William Howard Taft became a candidate for President for a second term in 1912. Theodore Roosevelt became so angry that he left the Republican Party. Roosevelt organized a new party called the Progressive Republicans. There were three important candidates for the office of President in 1912:

William Howard Taft—Republican
Theodore Roosevelt—Progressive Republican
Woodrow Wilson—Democrat

It was a bitter campaign but Wilson was victorious. There had been no Democratic President since the time of Grover Cleveland. The years of Wilson's term of office were very important ones for the nation. During Wilson's first term several very good laws were passed. During his second term the United States took part in the World War.

UNIVERSITY PRESIDENT. Woodrow Wilson was a gifted young man whose wise parents believed in education. They saw to it that their son went to college. After finishing college Wilson became a lawyer. He left law to become a college teacher. He taught in various colleges, including Princeton University. Professor Woodrow Wilson spent much time studying while he was a teacher at Princeton. History and the science of government were his special studies. He wrote many books on these subjects. Some of his best work was done during these years. Wilson's talents marked him as a leader. He became president of Princeton University. His management of the University, his forceful speeches, his splendid writings, and his knowledge of government, made him known throughout the nation.

GOVERNOR OF NEW JERSEY. Wilson's friends urged him to become a candidate for Governor of New Jersey. Wilson succeeded in getting the nomination and won the election as a Democrat. Woodrow Wilson was a success as a governor. Many had wondered how the "schoolmaster in politics" would act. They did not have to wait long to learn. Woodrow Wilson carried on his duties so ably that his reputation reached all parts of the country. When the Democratic Party was looking for a candidate for President, in 1912, Wilson was selected.

PRESIDENT OF THE UNITED STATES. The election that followed was an exciting one. Woodrow Wilson's opponents were President Taft, the Republican, and Theodore Roosevelt who was candidate of the new Progressive Republican Party. Wilson won the election. The schoolmaster who had been a successful governor now became President of the United States.

THE WORLD WAR. President Wilson had not been long in office when a terrible war broke out in Europe. This happened in 1914. The war was called the World War. The Allies, England, France, and Russia, were fighting on one side. The Allies refer to a group of nations bound together to fight a common enemy. The Central Powers, Germany, Austria, and Turkey, were fighting on the other side. This group were called the Central Powers because of their central location in Europe. As the war went on each side brought in its friends among the nations. Within a short time Germany, Austria, Turkey, and Bulgaria were fighting Russia, France, Belgium, England, Italy, and Japan. The United States was the seventh nation to join the Allies in the war against the Central Powers.

THE UNITED STATES AND THE WAR. From the outbreak of the war in August, 1914, President Wilson tried hard to keep America neutral. A neutral party takes neither side in a fight. President Wilson issued a proclamation calling upon his countrymen not to take sides in any form whatever. At the beginning most Americans wanted peace but as time went on it was seen that peace was hardly possible for the United States.

AMERICA IN THE WORLD WAR

GERMANY FORCES AMERICA TO WAR. Germany had the finest army in Europe when the war began. England had the finest navy, so the Allies were able to force all German ships from the sea. Thus the Allies were able to throw a blockade around Germany. They could keep her from getting food or other supplies by water routes. Germany built a great number of submarines. These vessels are so built that they can travel under the water. Submarine boats attacked the ships of the Allies. They attacked merchant and passenger ships, as well as warships. They destroyed the lives of American citizens sailing on passenger ships. President Woodrow Wilson protested again and again. Germany paid little or no attention. Finally, the Central Powers told the United States that we could send only one ship a week to England. This act exhausted the patience of the United States.

THE UNITED STATES IN THE WAR. The United States on April 6, 1917, declared war on Germany. The United States was not at all ready for war. Our enemy Germany, was then the strongest military power in the world. Things were going badly with the Allies. The Germans were gaining ground. The Allies were in desperate need of help.

Eighteen months later the war was over. America had turned the tide against Germany.

OUR WAR ACTIVITIES. The whole nation backed up President Wilson. First of all, ships were needed to transport men and supplies. Immediately, our shipbuilders set to work. New shipbuilding yards were opened. As soon as one ship was launched the keel of the next was laid. Factories to make war supplies, such as guns and ammunition, sprang up all over the country. Before the war was over four million men were wearing the uniform of the United States. They were splendidly led by General John J. Pershing. Pershing's men had to be fed and clothed. Money was raised by the various Liberty Loans. "Do your bit to win the war," was the slogan.

MARSHAL FOCH. When America entered the war the French, English, and Italian armies each had their own commander. President Wilson urged that one man be placed in charge of all Allied and American armies. This would insure united action. Finally, when the Germans seemed about to win, the Allies acted upon Wilson's suggestion. The man selected was Marshal Ferdinand Foch of the French army. This great soldier was a splendid

Catholic. He declared that he would consecrate his armies to the Sacred Heart. Foch then gave the army of each of the Allies a definite task to perform. The American army had its own special work.

THE GERMANS AND THE AMERICANS. The Americans met the Germans at Belleau Wood and again at Château-Thierry. Our men fought with great bravery. The Germans, who had been winning, now began to lose.

Marshal Foch soon came to know that he could depend upon the American soldiers. They were well trained and they were good fighters. The Americans turned the tide from defeat to victory. Marshal Foch started a very determined offensive which was to be a movement forward against the German lines. It was to be a vigorous fight. One victory of the Allies followed another. Finally the Germans realized that they could not win against so strong an enemy, and agreed to sign an armistice on November 11, 1918. An armistice is an agreement to stop fighting for a time. It is a temporary kind of peace. Marshal Foch imposed severe terms which the Germans had to accept. The World War was over. The German Kaiser was forced to give up his throne. He sought refuge in Holland. The American Army had turned the tide of this fearful war.

THE PEACE CONFERENCE. A peace treaty was signed at Versailles, near Paris. America had not gone into the war to win territory or anything else. Our aim was to defend our rights. President Wilson went to Europe for the Peace Conference. He hoped that something might be done to guard against future wars and to insure universal peace. This ideal of universal peace means peace among nations for all times. He proposed to set up a League of Nations to hold nations to an ideal of peace. Wilson thought that a League of Nations would bind the nations together. War could never again cause so much sorrow and suffering if the nations were bound one to another in a friendly

League. President Wilson believed that many difficulties between nations could be solved through the League of Nations. The League was formed but the United States did not become a member of it. This was a bitter disappointment to Woodrow Wilson. Above is a picture of the palace of the League of Nations.

CHANGE OF PRESIDENTS. Before President Wilson's second term was over he became seriously ill. Worn out by worry and anxiety he did not live long after leaving office. President Wilson's party, the Democratic Party, was defeated in the election of 1920. Warren G. Harding and Calvin Coolidge were elected President and Vice-President on the Republican ticket. President Harding died before completing his term of office. Calvin Coolidge succeeded Harding as President.

THE CAMPAIGN OF 1928. The presidential election of 1928 was most interesting. Herbert Hoover was nominated by the Republicans and Alfred E. Smith was nominated by the Democrats. Smith was governor of New York and a well-known Catholic. The campaign was an exciting one. People listened eagerly to the speeches of the candidates. The radio, which was then a new invention, made it possible for very large numbers of people to hear each candidate's speech. The radio had never before been used for this purpose. Election Day came and Herbert Hoover was elected the thirty-first President of the United States.

THE GREAT DEPRESSION

HAPPY AMERICA. Throughout most of the history of the United States the American people have been well off. Some few have become very rich. There were others who were very poor. Most Americans, however, were neither very rich nor were they very poor. The father had a job that paid him enough to keep his family in a comfortable home. All the members of the family usually had good clothing and shoes and enough to eat. There have been times when this was not the case. Jobs became hard to get, and people then had no money. These are called times of depression.

WHAT IS A DEPRESSION? The word depression means to press down. Depression means a low place or a low condition. This word, depression, is used to describe conditions when times are bad. The greatest of all depressions began in the United States in 1929 when Herbert C. Hoover was President. Some of the sad things that happened during that time will explain why the word depression is used.

Throughout the United States many banks failed. That meant that the people who had put their money into these banks, expecting it to be safe, lost their money. People stopped buying things and therefore factories closed. When the factories closed down thousands of men and women were unable to get work. People could not pay their rent and they could not even buy food. Almost everybody was discouraged.

A CHANGE IN PRESIDENTS. Conditions in the United States were very bad by 1932. There were bread lines in certain cities. Here in these bread lines people patiently waited long hours for the food the relief agency had to distribute. Farmers were losing their farms because they could not pay their debts. What could be done? The Republicans said, "The worst is over. Elect President Hoover for a second term. He is an engineer and therefore knows how to plan. He can help the country get back in the days when everyone seemed to have a job and no one was really in danger of starving." The Democrats said that the country needed a change. They nominated Franklin Delano Roosevelt of New York as their candidate. Franklin D. Roosevelt promised the people of the United States a "New Deal." He meant that when he was elected the government would help the people to enjoy better times. The voters believed Franklin D. Roosevelt. He was elected President in 1932 and was re-elected in 1936.

STUDY SUMMARY

1. Terms to know. Be able to give the meaning of each term listed.

Central Powers	offensive
depression	Allies
neutral	League of Nations
bread line	Peace Conference
submarine	proclamation
armistice	universal peace

2. People to know. Be able to give some important facts about each person whose name is listed.

Herbert Hoover	Marshal Ferdinand Foch
Calvin Coolidge	General John J. Pershing
Woodrow Wilson	William Howard Taft

3. Places to know. Be able to locate on a wall map of the world each of the following countries.

Austria	France	Germany
Belgium	Turkey	Italy
Bulgaria	United States	Japan
England		Russia

4. Dates to remember. Be able to tell an important event in American history which took place on each of the following dates.

   August 1914 April 1917 November 1918

5. Character study. Give an example to prove each of the following statements.

   Woodrow Wilson desired universal peace.
   Wilson was a man of great ability.
   President Wilson was a good planner.

ACTIVITIES

1. Make a list of the positions held by Woodrow Wilson. Arrange the list in the order of success upward from college graduation to the Presidency of the United States.

2. Make a table showing:

ARMIES IN THE WORLD WAR	
Allies	Central Powers
1. Meaning of name	1. Meaning of name
Nations belonging	Nations belonging
1.	1.
2.	2.
3.	3.
4.	4.
5.	
6.	
7.	

3. Write a paragraph explaining Wilson's idea of a League of Nations.

STUDY TEST 54—Score 50

A COMPLETION OUTLINE. Fill in all missing letters to complete the outline.

A. Woodrow Wilson

- a. He became a
  1. l — — — — — —.
  2. t — — — — — — —.
  3. a c — — — — — — — teacher.
  4. p — — — — — — — — — of Princeton.
- b. He entered politics and was elected
  1. G — — — — — — — — of New Jersey.
  2. P — — — — — — — — — of the United States.
- c. He tried to keep America n — — — — — — —.
- d. He protested when G — — — — — — — sank passenger ships.
- e. He proved himself to be a good planner:
  1. New s — — — building yards were opened.
  2. Ships were built to transport m — — and s — — — — — — — —.
  3. F — — — — — — — — — to make guns and ammunition were opened.
  4. M — — — — — was raised by Liberty Loans.
  5. He advised that the Allied Armies be placed under one c — — — — — — — — — —.
- f. He attended the Peace Conference
  1. He hoped for universal p — — — —.
  2. He made it clear that the United States did not want t — — — — — — — — — —.
  3. He proposed a L — — — — — — of N — — — — — — —.

B. America in the World War

1. The President issued a proclamation calling on citizens to be n — — — — — — —.
2. President Wilson protested to Germany
   - a. when submarines attacked ships belonging to the A — — — — — —.

   - b. when m--------- and p---------- ships were sunk.
   - c. when lives of Americans were l---.
   - d. when Germany limited America to one ship a week to E-------.
3. The United States declared war against G-------.
   - a. The A------ needed our help.
   - b. S----- were built.
   - c. G--- and ammunition were made.
   - d. M----- was raised by L-------- L-----.
   - e. S--------- were sent to F------.
   - f. John J. Pershing was given c-------- of the American Army.
4. The fighting
   - a. American soldiers were good f--------
   - b. Marshal Foch knew he could d------ on the Americans.
   - c. The Americans won many v----------.
   - d. The Germans admitted d------.
5. The end of the World War
   - a. An a---------- was agreed upon.
   - b. The German Kaiser fled to H-------.
6. Peace Conference
   - a. T------ signed at Versailles, near P-----.
   - b. Attended by President W------- W------.
   - c. Wilson pleaded for p----- so that there could be no more w---.

C. The Depression
1. Means l-- conditions because times were bad.
2. Many b----- failed.
3. People stopped b------.
4. F---------- were closed.
5. Thousands of men and women were unable to get w---.
6. Many f------- lost their land.

Wide World Photo.

UNIT XII: GREAT LEADERS OF MODERN TIMES

FRANKLIN D. ROOSEVELT
A NEW DEAL LEADER

Read to learn

1. About the courage of Franklin Delano Roosevelt in overcoming his physical handicap.
2. The meaning of the New Deal.
3. How jobs were created under the W.P.A.
4. Something about the work of the Civilian Conservation Corps.
5. How the National Youth Administration attempts to help boys and girls to complete their schooling.

THE NEW DEAL. Franklin D. Roosevelt was a distant cousin of President Theodore Roosevelt. Both these men began life with many advantages. Franklin D. Roosevelt was born on a fine estate on the banks of the Hudson River, New York. His family had been in this country from the days of the Dutch settlers in New Amsterdam. As a boy, Franklin D. Roosevelt attended excellent schools. He attended, and graduated from Harvard University.

FRANKLIN D. ROOSEVELT IN POLITICS. After studying law Franklin D. Roosevelt entered politics. During the World War he served under President Woodrow Wilson as Assistant Secretary of the Navy. He was a candidate for the office of Vice-President on the Democratic ticket in 1920. Franklin Roosevelt was badly beaten. Shortly after this Franklin Delano Roosevelt became very ill. He was stricken with infantile paralysis. This dreadful disease often leaves its victims crippled. Franklin D. Roosevelt had splendid courage; he fought to win back his health. Little by little he improved. At last, with assistance, he could get about. He is an excellent example of how a person can overcome a physical handicap.

Roosevelt re-entered politics. He became a candidate for governor of New York and was elected. His victory on Election Day was so splendid that at once many thought he would make a good President. He became a candidate for the office of President. He was elected the thirty-second President of the United States in 1932.

THE MEANING OF THE NEW DEAL. Franklin Delano Roosevelt had promised the American people a New Deal. What did he mean by that? Roosevelt and his advisers believed the government of the United States ought to help all the people, especially when people could not help themselves. Franklin D. Roosevelt honestly believed that the government had a duty to help business, workers, farmers, as well as to help the youth, the aged, and the unfortunate, who needed assistance.

HELP FOR FARMERS. President Roosevelt thought that when farmers worked hard, yet could not make a living the government ought to help them. The President asked Congress to help the farmers to get better prices for their farm products. Congress tried to do this by passing the Agricultural Adjustment Act. This came to be referred to as the A.A.A. Under this act the acreage of certain crops was reduced and farmers were given government help to pay their farm mortgages.

The Supreme Court of the United States in 1936 declared that Congress had no right to pass a law of this sort. Congress later passed another law to help the farmers that the Supreme Court would not set aside.

HELP FOR CITY WORKERS. Most of the people of the United States live in cities. Many of the city people worked in factories. The President thought that the city people ought to be helped. The President asked Congress to pass a law which would help to get better pay and shorter hours for workers.

Therefore, the government undertook many large and small jobs under the direction of the Works Progress Administration. This is commonly called the W.P.A.[1] Workers under the W.P.A. have built roads, paved streets, built bridges, and erected public buildings.

HELP FOR YOUNG PEOPLE. There was another important problem the government hoped to solve. Many young people were idle. Before the depression when a boy left high school or college he was almost certain to find work. Depression times are difficult times for even grown men to find a job. There was very little chance that a young man could get work. Some say that in 1938 there were 5,000,000 young people in the United States who could not find work to support themselves. The Civilian Conservation Corps was organized to help some of these unemployed young men. The Civilian Conservation Corps is spoken of as the C.C.C.

[1] Later the letters W.P.A. stood for Works Projects Administration.

Photo by Ewing Galloway.

THE CIVILIAN CONSERVATION CORPS. The young men of the C.C.C. were trained to do many useful things. They planted millions of young trees. Many years from now these trees will have become fine forests. Forests protect soil and preserve the water supply. The forests of New York State, for example, preserve the water supply of New York City. Many bridges and miles of roads have been built by the C.C.C. As well as doing such useful work, the young men have a chance to improve themselves by attending special classes. The picture at the top of the page shows an instructor helping the boys in one of these classes.

THE NATIONAL YOUTH ADMINISTRATION. President Roosevelt had a plan to help boys and girls in high school and college. This plan was in charge of the National Youth Administration. Boys and girls who benefit by this plan do certain tasks for which they are paid a small sum of money. This money helps pay for carfare, lunches, and other school expenses. This work of helping boys and girls to continue their education has come to be called the N.Y.A.

HELP FOR THE UNEMPLOYED AND THE AGED. President Roosevelt aimed also to help people who lost

their jobs. He planned to collect a large sum of money, year by year. Then if a man lost his job there would be some money to pay him while he was out of work. This plan Congress made into a law by passing the Social Security Act in 1935. Under the Social Security Act the Federal Government assumes a responsibility to help the states with certain problems like:

1. Old age pensions
2. Pensions for widows left with children to support
3. A fixed amount of money for working men who are injured while at work
4. Help for persons who are disabled

ROOSEVELT AND PEACE. Before Roosevelt had completed his second term a serious war broke out in Europe. President Roosevelt had done his best to prevent the war from starting. Once it began he did his best to keep the United States out of the war.

An Arms Embargo Act was put into effect. Roosevelt feared that this Act might draw us into war. Under his leadership the Embargo was withdrawn.

At Christmas time, 1939, our Holy Father made an eloquent appeal for peace. President Roosevelt was happy to join in this effort with Pope Pius XII to reestablish peace in Europe. A minister was sent by President

Roosevelt to Vatican City. Thus, President Roosevelt felt that he could cooperate more closely with the Pope in the cause of peace. Vatican City is where the Pope resides. It is a small independent state near Rome, Italy.

ROOSEVELT AND LABOR

AMERICAN LABOR. One of the reasons our country is great is because our working men are much better off than the working men in most parts of the world. They are better off because they have been free to join together into unions and uphold their rights. The laboring men who have joined together or organized into unions are known as organized labor.

When laboring men first organized unions in this country they had a difficult time. Many people felt that unions were secret societies and should be broken up. Fortunately the laboring man had a great friend in Cardinal Gibbons, who was the Archbishop of Baltimore. He was always interested in the working man and felt that unions would greatly help labor. He even wrote a letter to Pope Leo XIII. In it he told what kind of men were in the unions and what they were trying to do for labor. Pope Leo was very much interested. Later Pope Leo XIII wrote a very important letter to all the Catholics of the world. He told them that the rights of the working people must be upheld.

AFL AND CIO. At the time Roosevelt became president organized labor was again having a difficult time. Strikes were frequent and dissatisfaction with laboring conditions was very great. Up to that time there was only one great union organization, the American Federation of Labor (AFL). It was mostly made up of unions of skilled laborers like the carpenters and bricklayers. But men began to think that all working men, skilled or unskilled, should be organized into unions. They started up another union organization called the Congress of Industrial Organizations (CIO). Because there were now two great union organizations new difficulties began to come up. President Roosevelt realized that if this country is to be prosperous there must be peace between the workingmen and their employers. Under his guidance the National Labor Relations Board (NLRB) was set up. Its duty is to see that the laboring man has the right to organize and to belong to the union he wishes and that the rights of the working man be protected.

OUR COUNTRY ADVANCES. You have read how far our country has advanced and about some of the people who helped it to advance. What a splendid record it is! Brave men and women from the time of the Norsemen to the present day have made many sacrifices to make America the land of opportunity. Let us also do what we can to make America even greater.

STUDY SUMMARY

1. A person to know. Be able to give a good oral biography of Franklin Delano Roosevelt.
2. Terms to know. Be able to give the meaning of each term listed.

New Deal	Works Progress Administration
depression	Agricultural Adjustment Act
corps	Civilian Conservation Corps
conservation	National Youth Administration
Supreme Court	Social Security Act

ACTIVITIES

1. Make a table. Fill in all missing facts.

THE NEW DEAL	
Name	Activity
Works Progress Administration	
Agricultural Adjustment Act before ruling by Supreme Court	
Civilian Conservation Corps	
National Youth Adminstration	
Social Security Act	

2. Discuss in class the powerful example of Franklin Roosevelt's courage in overcoming a physical handicap.
3. Explain the meaning of the New Deal.
4. Make a list of at least four groups of people who are helped by the Social Security Act.
5. Character study. Prove that each of the following statements truly may be applied to Franklin D. Roosevelt.
   a. He has great courage.
   b. He is a great planner.
   c. He is fearless in attempting new ways of doing things.

STUDY TEST 55—Score 15

ENDINGS. Underscore the term which gives the correct ending. Put a period after the term selected as the end.

1. The Franklin Delano Roosevelt family was
   poor rich
2. During the World War Franklin Roosevelt served as
   Assistant Secretary of the Navy Secretary of State
3. Franklin D. Roosevelt's plan was called the
   Square Deal New Deal
4. The Agricultural Adjustment Act was passed by
   New York State Congress President Roosevelt
5. A.A.A. was declared unconstitutional by the
   Congress Supreme Court President
6. Franklin D. Roosevelt is a
   Democrat Progressive Republican
7. The Civilian Conservation Corps was organized to help
   young men young girls old men
8. The Civilian Conservation Corps planted many
   trees vegetables flowers
9. Soil is protected and water supply is preserved by
   irrigation forests drouth
10. The National Youth Administration was planned to help boys and girls to continue their
    education recreation
11. The Social Security Act was passed by
    the President the Senate Congress
12. Old age pensions are now granted under the
    Works Progress Administration Social Security Act
13. Disabled persons who are dependent are helped by the
    Works Progress Administration Social Security Act
14. Widows left with children to support are helped under the
    Social Security Act Civilian Conservation Corps
15. The nation doing the most today for the welfare of its people is
    Russia England United States

INDEX AND PRONOUNCING LIST

This list of key words will help you to pronounce the words which are marked in this index.

plāy	tär	ĕlm	ĭt	nŏt	bûrn
tăp	câre	hẽrself	ôr	ūse	fōōd
tȧsk	mē	fīre	blōw	ŭs	good